D-Day on the Western Pacific

A Railroad's Decision to Dieselize

Special 81

by **Virgil Staff**

Interurban Press • Glendale, California

© 1982 Interurbans Publications

All Rights Reserved

No part of this book may be used or reproduced without written permission from the Publisher, except in the case of brief quotations used in reviews.

Library of Congress Cataloguing in Publication Data

Staff, Virgil, 1925-
   D-Day on the Western Pacific

(Interurbans special: 81)
Includes index.
   1. Diesel locomotives. 2. Western Pacific Railroad. I. Title.
II. Series.
TJ619.S7   625.2'66   82-1051
ISBN 0-916374-51-3   AACR2

FIRST PRINTING: 1982

DUST JACKET PAINTING

Flying white flags, a freight train headed by newly rebuilt and painted F-7 913A eases over the Altamont Summit. The Southern Pacific track curves underneath Bridge 56.96, the hills are green and this part of Northern California sparkles on a warm day in April 1978. These EMD covered wagons played a big part in the Western Pacific's entry into the Diesel Age. Painting by **Larry Fisher** from a photo by **Tom Moungovan.**

BACK COVER PHOTO

Two generations of Western Pacific diesel power meet up at the west switch of Carbona siding with covered wagon 919-D holding the main. There is a high-speed curve just east of this location, and this hurtling railroad activity momentarily ruffles the calm of this secluded retreat. **Joseph Ward**

FRONT ENDSHEET PHOTO

There is crew change activity here on the Keddie Wye on this wintry January 20, 1967. In a few minutes the six units of F-7 power will pull this consist off Bridge 0.02 for coupling in of helpers, seen idling at the entrance to Tunnel 1. **Joseph Ward**

REAR ENDSHEET PHOTO

An eastbound time freight heads north up the 1.50 percent grade out of Keddie with 9,000 horses of F-7 power astride Bridge 1.24. The snow only partially muffles the roar and growl of bigtime railroading on the Western Pacific this January 20, 1967.
Joseph Ward

To the men and women
of the Western Pacific
who've kept the trains rolling

This classic system cartogram of the Western Pacific dates from sometime just prior to 1931, at which date the 111.81 mile Inside Gateway was completed between Keddie and Nubieber, and prior to the Oroville line change in the 1960s.

Louis Stein Collection

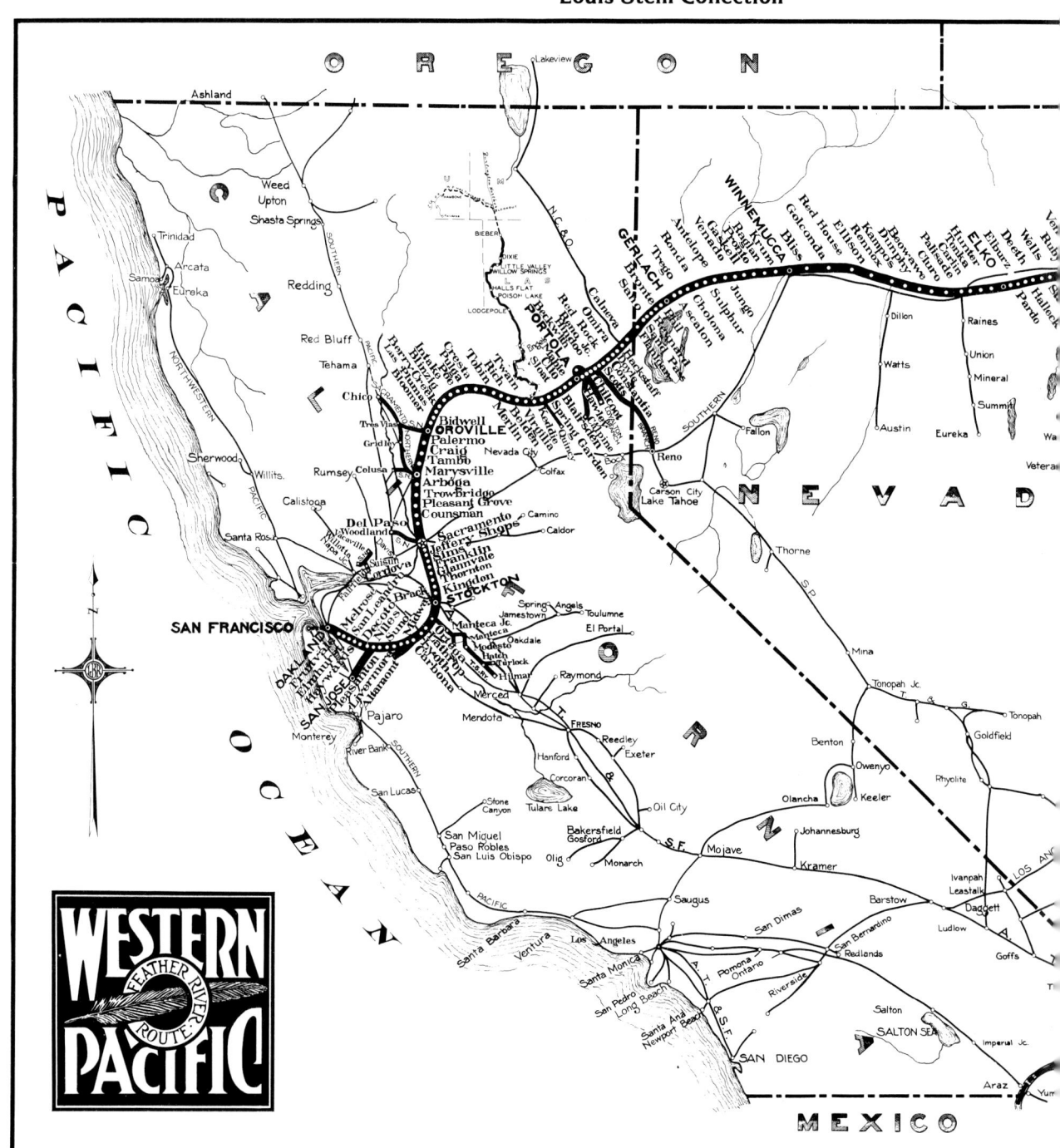

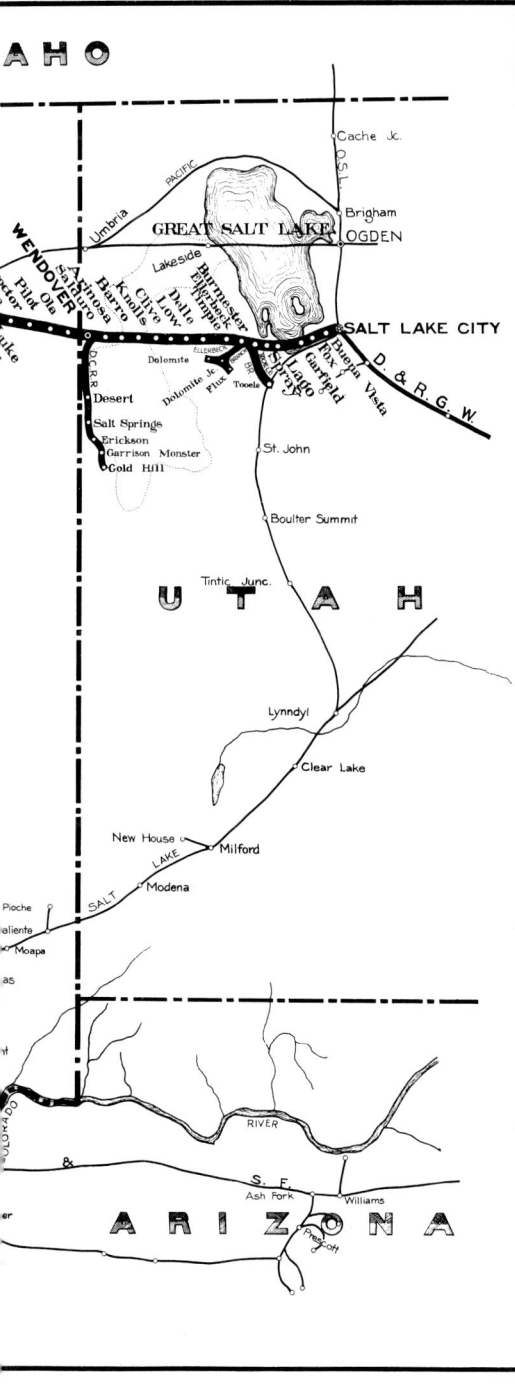

Table of Contents

	Preface	*7*
1	Enter the Diesel	10
2	Was the GM-103 Really That Great?	13
3	Knuckle Busters or Big Boys!	20
4	Eight Alcos or Ten Steamers	23
5	Power Shortages and World War II	25
	CZ—That Legendary Streamliner	*31*
6	CZ In; Steam Out	37
7	The Diesel Makes Its Impact	55
	Grooming the WP's Iron Horses	*65*
8	Dynamic Brakes on the FT	73
9	The Decline of Availability	75
10	How Much Can a Loco Lug?	77
11	Water and Other Problems	83
12	The Faster Handling of Trains	96
13	Maintenance and Fuel Ratings	104
14	A Matter of Oil	106
15	The Death of Steam	109
16	The RDC Experiment	115
	People Make a Railroad	*119*
17	The Navy Grows Old	122
18	How Much Power is Required?	127
	WP Weathers the Winter	*133*
19	The Search for Replacement Power	138
20	Getting a Move On	149
21	TOFC and How to Drag	154
22	The Krauss-Maffei	158
23	Oroville, Sacramento or Stockton?	162
24	Higher and Higher Horsepower	169
	The Canyon	*181*
25	Some Comparisons	186
26	The Perlman-Flannery Years	191
	Illustrated Rosters	200

Joseph Ward

Preface

AMONG THE STRICTLY private pleasures of consummating a research project is the assurance that, while some readers may find insufficient technical detail, others will have hoped for less. Moreover, a prevailing misfortune of the trade seems to be that the most knowledgeable commonly do not write, thus leaving the production of some secondary monographs to those whose special competency may lie elsewhere.

This chronicle of Western Pacific diesel history had its research beginnings in the early 1960s. Since that time, the three-by-five card files have grown in magnitude, but not always the anticipated solutions. It is hoped that the available facts have here been wielded into an account of aid in comprehending the process of dieselization as it occurred on the Western Pacific. A second object, although not necessarily secondary to the first, will be a consideration of means by which the modern diesel fleet came to its present posture. Certainly, any fundamental study of the Western Pacific should be most instructive, since the railroad's competitive position over the years was too tenuous to allow for incompetency or waste.

The reader will find nothing definitive about this review, since the writer, even at this time, frequently possesses more clues than solutions. Most of the men who maintained the early power are no longer with us, and the majority of written documentation has been retired and destroyed. Much minutiae were explored over extended periods only to terminate in the category of "insufficient information." These cul-de-sacs have been numerous, but not always unrewarding, and it is hoped that this inquiry will bring understanding of the process by which one American railroad faced the problems of developing and maintaining a modern diesel fleet.

This study is more descriptive than evaluative. It is a collection of facts leading in various directions, but most of all it should lead to an unstated assessment of company expertise. Although I have tried to pare this study to the bone, it has always been with the recognition that what is not published will ultimately be lost. Most of all it will be noted that I have attempted to relate motive power to the general activities of the railroad.

My respect and appreciation are here reaffirmed to all those people on the Western Pacific who over the years have shown personal and attentive interest in what otherwise would have been unachievable. Since there are no relevant monographs of value from which to draw, this study is primarily built on a foundation of tape-recorded interviews, company files, and years of personal contacts and observations. Hopefully, the number of errors is minimal. Certainly all are solely my own responsibility.

No such project would have been likely without the cooperation and continued interest of scores of individuals, and it is with gratitude that I express my thanks to a host of those who selflessly gave their time in order that I might come to some comprehensive view of what dieselization on the Western Pacific was all about. Embodied in the following acknowledgments are the names of those most responsible for the remainder of this monograph. A future volume, incident to Western Pacific's early history, will pay my respects to sundry other members of the Western Pacific family.

Of inestimable import have been John K. Kelly, Hyrum A. O'Rullian, Robert Redus, and the late William F. Stevens. Without them, this study would literally have been a cipher—a snap of the fingers—a flash in the pan. Included appreciatively are Myron Christy, Robert G. Flannery, Alfred E. Perlman, and the late Frederick B. Whitman.

Always available for statistical assistance were R.J. Cleland, J.G. Etchebehere, R.A. Failing, John L. Hicks, L. Byron Larson, Clyde A. Moll, and W.A. Thorpe.

I wish to express my deep appreciation to John B. Morgan who made himself available for statistical data, and whose noteworthy expertise cleared obscurities on numerous occasions.

Access to materials was appreciably eased by E.T. Cuyler and R.W. Mustard. In this search through documents, I could consistently depend for direction upon Robert W. Cunha, Norma French, Joseph R. LaMalfa, and Jean Smith. Stan Heaney was never too occupied to be of assistance, and when in need, without exception, I knew upon whom to depend.

One of the best informed and loyal employees of the Western Pacific is William B. Wolverton whose expertise was a ready source of psychic comfort. Also of outstanding utility in various ways were G.J. Benedict, R.J. Bradley, Marshall W. Brown, Richard F. Carter, Joe Dyer, Burnell Green, Steve Medlock, R.L. Millhiser, Pete Del Moro, J.E. Perry, Irma Piver, Wayne Pracht, and Mae Toomey.

Richard Shideler, with his incisive mind and wide experience, made himself available whenever, as it were, I gave him the signal.

Ray E. Schriefer and Earl Roider never smiled at my ignorance but patiently provided guidance through the labyrinth of recent diesel modifications. To these two extremely competent individuals I owe more than would be easy to state.

Norman E. Anderson's suggestions and encyclopedic knowledge were always available, and his very significant assistance was essential to coverage of the GP20s through the GP40s.

The late Lester H. Clapham was a routine source of information in the early years of this study, and his passing, as with that of William F. Stevens, created gaps that can never be filled.

Mickey T. Pantalone provided opportunities for perusal of axles and bearings, and Clifton J. Conley, R.L. Thomas, and Robert Valencia furnished hundreds of occasions to see the diesels as an electrician and a machinist would view them.

Nino Poncioni and Henry Casarez were my chief source for information on various paint schemes, and Richard Hurst never failed to make himself available when my interests strayed to problems of lubrication.

In various respects relating to dieseldom I have depended on individuals who attempted to ease the difficulties of familiarizing myself with various aspects not easily noted here. Among these are Douglas Brown, R.W. Crumpacker, Donald A. Davis, J.F. Flynn, William B. Gray, William Gault, George H. Heintz, Charley Humphreys, H.J. Kelly, C.B. Kirkpatrick, Jay Kump, G.J. Morgan, C.L. Myers, Frank Rogers, Orson Shephard, Edward Steuben, and A.J. Stout.

Various enginemen afforded insights into the world of diesel operation. Among these were Herb Berg, James Boynton, Joe Burt, Boyd Davis, Norman Holmes, W.A. (Bill) Pennington, N.L. Pilatti, and Graham Snyder. William R. DuBois, John Haeberle, O.E. Lyles, W.F. (Billie) Metzger, Leonard J. Tadson, and Robert W. Turner were generous in providing published operating materials otherwise difficult to acquire. General operating information of great historic value was gleaned from Douglas S. Brown of Portola, Abbe Coleburg, Charlie Ellis, Clifford F. Fields, Tim Hanlon, Tom Hunter, George Lorenz, Seth Manca, John J. McNally, Raymond Moore, Glen Morton, J. Clinton Rice, George T. Rutherford, Al Sanford, Henry Stapp, William D. Taber, and W.E. (Abe) Tout. Gordon Addis, Rodger Collins, Louis John Fischer, Jack McClure, W.C. (Boomer) Philbeck, Cecil Spoon, and John Taylor aided me in innumerable ways, as did Vern Brain, William Eyre, Guy Hardy, Robert C. Lemon, Frank H. Long, Jack Merkley, Eddie Newman, Harold Parks, Norman Roberts, Mario Ragusa, and W.L. (Woody) Spillman.

The hospitality and generosity of my good friends Robert and Ruth Grubbs, Sam and Sue Heath, Frankie and Ruth Lemon, Robert and Edna Turner, Bruno Selmi and family of Gerlach, and Kenyon, Elaine, Treece and Trudy Riddle of Knolls, will always be a high point in my life, as will the little courtesies, so important in such a study, extended by G.L. Boates, W.F. Brown, Val Catanho, Leroy Clark, Charlie Gonzales, Gordon Ingle, Charlie Jewell, Clarence Mitchell, George Moody, George Pollock, Mike Quinn, V.J. Vallarino, A.A. Van Meter, and Ted Woods. Of aid, beyond what they might suspect, were Ron Helmich, Bernard Long, Maxine Naisbitt, Logan Paine, Barney Peterson, W.J. Powell, Jerry Ross, Manuel Silva, Paul Silva, John Streck, and F.A. Tegeler.

My good friend, the late John J. Duggan, provided encyclopedic data on the 1940s, and George Naylor's memory seemed never to be lacking. Clayton L. Foss, Edward J. Hillier, J.R. Summers, Jim Taylor, and J.P. Wirick were useful in various ways, and E.L. Nielson and Carl Rowe provided dispatching insights essential to this study.

Glen Curtis, John C. Lusar, Jim Lynch, L.D. Michelson, and C.G. Yund attempted to be helpful, as did Edwin B. Allison, H.E. Baldwin, Jim Brennan, W.J. Caroni, James A. Forst, Robert F. Golden, E.W. Goodrum, Mason P. Gordon, Pete Norgaard, John Rossi, Paul E. Scott, Victor Seastrom, K.J. Tinker, and Walter Treanor.

Asa Arnall, W.F. Damaske, Grant Evans, W.L. Fisher, R.L. McQuarrie, Jim Murray, P.F. Prentiss, Curtis Risk, and H. Van Fleet never lacked information of historical import, and I owe thanks to Kenny Crouse, Tim Kelly, Andy Stene, Frank D. Webb, K.P. Wood, and Jack Work for numerous courtesies in the yards.

Of considerable assistance in studying line data were Myron K. Anderson, Alice Angiulo, Dwight Bellows, Gene Carlock, A.W. Carlson, M.J. Crespo, Jim Dunn, C.A. Gerstner, John G. Howard, Frank Hyatt, Wm. Houdyshell, Augustus Kramm, Jim Larson, Erich Thomsen, B.L. McNeill, Jr., John C. Miller,

Crawling the hill through Paxton, California, just west of MP 278, is the 3547 East with three units on the agreeable morning of July 25, 1979. The GP-40-2 wears the latest paint scheme on the Western Pacific and, unlike the 3051 class of U30Bs, locomotives of the 3545 class do not have oscillating hood lights. **Virgil Staff**

R.H. Rauschmeier, Paul Reinking, and A.E. (Curley) Thompson.

The quest for information was simplified in sundry ways by Ella and Henry Gerdes of Oakland, Roy Harrison of Spring Garden, J.E. Hightower, Ernst von Ibsch III, John Kirkland, Henry Ozga, L.C. Sherwood, Ray Smalley, and Ted Wurm. Tom Irion provided occasional technical assistance, and James Arthur Easton of Berkeley was a ready source of expertise concerning the fundamentals of practical electronics. My thanks also to Guy L. Dunscomb of Modesto whose knowledge of the Western Pacific makes him one of the better informed individuals of our day.

Something of the dynamics of train operations became shared information thanks to Grant Allen, W.S. Cope, and M.C. McManus. Larry Contri and R.L. Meyer have been of cordial encouragement, and Andrew Kinicki and Glenn Metzdorf assisted in ways that must have been very time-consuming.

My thanks to the Library Photographic Service of the University of California at Berkeley, and more especially to Dino Bevilaqua, Bob Kahle, and Dan Johnston, for vitalizing many of my negatives on photographic paper. Also a debt of gratitude to Carl Bridenbaugh, John D. Hicks, and Kenneth M. Stampp whose graduate seminars at the University of California in the 1950s installed an appreciation for the techniques and methods of historical scholarship.

Readers will note that little has been included concerning rolling stock, blocking of trains, inspections, reduced points of crew change, receivership, or the control case. Space, and considerations of my present lack of knowledgeableness, have precluded consideration of these but such will hopefully come under consideration in a future volume.

In general, the discussion of locomotive changes is carried into 1979, with only cursory mention of the rebuilding program at Morrison–Knudsen where 33 units went through their shops in 1980.

Finally, it is clear to me that the constant encouragement of my wife, LaVada, was a necessary concomitant to the completion of this study. Together we have tromped the ballast over most of the railroad, met the same friendly reptiles, fought the same gnats and mosquitos, and together enjoyed the thrill of flanged wheels on steel rails.

Virgil Staff
July 21, 1981

1

Enter the Diesel

THE WESTERN PACIFIC is a Class I line-haul railroad with general offices at 526 Mission Street in San Francisco. Prior to November 1978, car ferry connections across San Francisco Bay into Oakland provided the western terminal of a main line reaching to the Salt Lake gateway. Most tonnage is destined for points in the middle western and eastern United States, or to and from points in the Northwest via the famed Inside Gateway between Keddie and Bieber.

The two-division, single-track, east-west main has a ruling grade of one percent compensated with maximum 10°15′ curvature; that between Keddie and Bieber possesses a maximum gradient of 2.2 percent compensated with maximum curvature of 10°12′.

There are double-track portions in Oakland between Chestnut Junction and Clinton, and on the paired trackage with the Southern Pacific between Weso and Alazon, both in Nevada. On this latter trackage, all eastbound trains move on the Western Pacific, and all westbound on the Southern Pacific.

Traffic density, which is slightly greater westbound than eastbound, consists largely of military and civilian transportation equipment, manufactured goods, steel and steel scrap, barytes, plasterboard, lumber, wood chips, canned goods, beer, feed grains, fresh fruits and vegetables, sugar, paper, and chemical and allied products. During the period of 1974 through 1978, approximately 31 percent of Western Pacific traffic originated on-line for points off-line, 32 percent neither originated nor terminated on-line, 32 percent was received from off-line and terminated on the system, and about 5 percent was local traffic.

The WP is highly dependent on the traffic bridged across the system and to and from other rail carriers, and is highly sensitive to depressed conditions along the roads of these carriers. Competition with other carriers depends significantly on the railroad's ability to provide specialized equipment to shippers, and on the need to remain sensitive to shipper needs.

The small-but-strategic WP is, then, a railroad with a simple route structure—a single east-west main line and a single north-south feeder. Mother Nature, however, added a rugged profile and threw extremes of weather at the railroad, so that the motive power requirements of the Western Pacific became far from simple.

•

The year 1938 had been a trying one for the Western Pacific, with loaded freight car miles down to 79,616,841. This study begins early in 1939 when Edward M. Smith, of Electro-Motive, by then the diesel locomotive-building division of mighty General Motors, called upon WP President Charles Elsey and General Manager E.W. Mason. Smith thought the EMC SW-1 diesel-electric switching locomotive would be a good addition to Western Pacific's power, then all-steam. As of January 1, 1939, the WP stable included 167 locomotives, of which 28 were coal and 139 were oil. Sixteen of these oil burners were 0-6-0 fantail switch engines, and additional switching power was available in the form of Consolidations with footboards.

Despite the disappointing results of 1938, Mason expected a steadily improved economic trend in 1939 and he and Elsey were willing to consider purchase of three new diesel-electrics. William J. O'Neill, superintendent of motive power, suggested these three goats be numbered 167-169 so as to numerically follow the highest numbered fantail. But E.W. Englebright, assistant to the president, assured O'Neill that management

Charles Elsey
He was willing to consider the diesel.

E. W. Mason
1939 would be better, he thought.

intended to purchase additional diesels and such numbers would shortly conflict with the numbering of 171 Class Mountains. It was J.P. Quigley, superintendent of transportation, who suggested numbers 501-503 might be less troublesome. The management shortly decided to buy the new switchers, which would be built by Electro-Motive, in spite of a steam roster primarily purchased from American Locomotive Co. As with most future diesel orders for a long time, the engines would be shipped F.O.B. Shafter, Nevada, and would be cut out at Elko for service tests.

The first of the SW-1s to arrive was initially known by its builder's number, 906, and worked 30 hours at Elko starting on September 26, 1939. This 906, later to be numbered as WP-501, is said to have handled four cars of coal up the incline with as much ease as did the steam power. The 906 then worked six shifts around the clock at San Francisco starting October 3, followed by about two weeks at Stockton and two weeks at Portola. Every yard possessed its own peculiar problems and the intent was to give the 906 every opportunity to indicate its capabilities. At each terminal, a steam fantail was placed on a comparable job, and statistics were collected for comparison. Fuel consumption figures especially impressed the mechanical department. For the 78 hours that the 906 switched Elko and San Francisco, fuel consumption had been 459 gallons, or 5.885 gallons per hour.

At Portola it seems to have been first officially recognized that the fireman had comparatively nothing to do. All gauges, including the bell control, were on the right side of the cab, and the most that a fireman could be expected to do was to watch the switches and the signals. The first engineers received about 20 minutes of instruction from the Electro-Motive instructors, and while the handling of cuts was considered a little rough, it was anticipated this would remedy itself when the men became accustomed to using "ground speed" in place of "exhaust speed." Certainly some of the men were impressed when the 906 pulled 3,500 tons up the east lead, most of which is 4/10% grade, and got it moving without any trouble and without any slack, and perhaps as easily as a Consolidation would have done.

Western Pacific performance records on the 906 were undoubtedly a factor in management's decision to purchase this locomotive and to order the construction of two additional

A part of the Western Pacific's very first order of diesels, SW-1 unit 502 is working the Sacramento yards on April 20, 1963. It wears essentially the second switch engine color scheme and was in Duco Orange 254-6273, Aluminum 254-9614, and Black 246-2048. Sister 504, of the second order, was the first switcher in the new livery, and came out of the paint shop on March 17, 1951.
Don Hansen

SW-1s contracted for on November 30, 1939. The three new 100-ton type 600-hp diesel switchers bore seller's numbers 906, 988 and 989, and buyer's road numbers 501-503. No changes in the 502 or 503 were recommended by Trainmaster J.P. McSweeney or Road Foreman of Engines Karl Muhl, both of whom had ridden Southern Pacific diesel switcher SP1000, other than the crossing over of a branch pipe to enable the fireman to start the bell ringer if he chose. In the meantime, engine 906 went back to work at Elko for further tests from November 18-23, after which it was taken dead-in-train to Oakland for service in San Francisco where it was intended to remain.

The 906 initially lacked identification stenciling and medallions, but received both, including its road number, on December 16, 1939. The 502 and 503 arrived in Elko on December 24, with first mileage being made on December 29, and December 27 respectively. Each worked two days in the Elko yard after which the two were moved dead-in-train to Oakland where they were given electrical inspections by C.W. Odermatt prior to their beginning to work continuously on January 4, 1940. Electro-Motive service engineers, and Road Foreman of Engines Muhl were on the scene to qualify sufficient engineers. Accurate statistics were maintained of the 501 Class performance, the comparison being with the 151, 152, 155 and 157 steam fantails working the two terminals. In San Francisco a fantail would take 20 empties, or equivalent of five cars of rock, from 25th Street to the scales. The 501 could do the same or better, and sometimes would drag as much as one-third more tonnage. SW-1 statistics for the period of July through December 1940 show cost of repairs for this 501 Class to be about .4816, with average fuel oil burned per hour at about 4.727 gallons. Low fuel oil consumption, absence of urgency for regular water stops, ability to safely leave a locomotive unattended, and ease of starting or shutting it down, reduced delays, cut the number of trips to the roundhouse, and enabled almost continuous service around the clock.

The SW-1s were painted black wtih a minimum of white striping, but did not possess the white diagonal stripes later applied. These possessed 6-567, Vee-type, two-stroke cycle engines operating at 800 rpm with 8½x10″ bore and stroke, thus comparing favorably with the old 201A engine with its 750 rpm, and bore and stroke of 8x10″. The 567 engine had a greatly simplified and more rugged crankcase than the EMC 201A engine, and its pistons, heads, liners, connecting rods and bearings possessed a greatly extended life. Camshaft was overhead to eliminate push rods and to simplify maintenance, and there was never a doubt that this was a significantly superior engine to the earlier 201A. Scavenging blowers, governor, and pumps were easily accessible for removal, and inspection of pistons and liners could be done with ease.

The three locomotives were delivered with D-4A or D-4 generators, D-7A traction motors, and like all later Electro-Motive freight power delivered new to the railroad, possessed a 62:15 gear ratio. Two cooling fans were located directly behind the manually controlled shutters, and their speed was proportional to the speed of the engine. There were no traction motor blowers, and traction motors were operated in series at all times.

2

Was the GM-103 Really That Great?

IN LATE 1939 and early 1940, Electro-Motive exhibited its line-haul demonstrator No. 103, by circulating this four-unit, 5,400-hp locomotive in a series of tests on several American railroads. EMC's Smith had spoken to President Elsey about the possibility of trial runs on the Western Pacific, and Chief Engineer J.W. Williams informed Mason on March 1, 1940, that he had no objections to the proposed operation since there would be no clearance restrictions, and axle loadings were about the same as with the M-80, 201 Class of Little Mallets. The locomotive would be too long for a standard 110- to 120-foot turntable, but could be broken up into two-unit, 2,700-hp components should there be need for turning.

In the series of tests that followed, the Western Pacific sought to learn just how well the GM-103 would perform—especially over helper districts, and in comparison with the M-100, 401 Class of single expansion articulated 4-6-6-4's over Wendover Hill, and with the 251 Class of single expansion articulated 2-8-8-2's then working the one percent of the Feather River Canyon between Oroville and Portola. On the morning of May 6, 1940, the Rio Grande delivered the big streamlined diesel-elecric freight locomotive to the WP at Roper Yard. O'Neill personally signed the joint inspection form. What he saw was a distinctive four-unit 5,400-hp experimental design in dark green with yellow stripes, and extending back 193 feet over the coupler faces. The four covered-wagon type units were in an A-B-B-A arrangement with drawbars between cab and booster units of the first and second sections. Total loaded weight was approximately 911,800 lbs., and initial tractive effort was reputed to be 228,000 lbs. at 25 percent adhesion.

The GM-103 was known as a drawbar-buster since it had broken drawbars on the Santa Fe, Great Northern, and Northern Pacific. This was precisely the kind of bruiser the Western Pacific management wanted. Tank cars 1105 and 1167 were sandblasted, and loaded with diesel oil at the Richmond refinery—the former being sent to Salt Lake and the latter to

D-Day on the Western Pacific: this is the test train, headed by General Motors locomotive 103 in A-B-B-A configuration. It is May 1940. **D.F. Davis, Author's Collection**

Portola. There would be a dozen or so men with the GM-103, a Burlington man on the dynamometer car, and an array of superintendents, trainmasters, road foremen, and mechanical department personnel. Makeup of the train out of Roper Yard would include the CB&Q dynamometer car No. 30 on the head end, followed by Pennsylvania tourist car No. 2207, a WP diner, and WP material cars 1105 with fuel oil, and 17733 with tools. Approximately 20 to 25 men had to be housed and fed, and Western Pacific provided a dining-car crew that served meals at no charge around the clock. Regular tonnage would be confined to cars normally in No. 61's consist, with the addition of a business car on the rear.

Train No. 61, with 76 cars, 3,744 actual trailing tons, departed Roper Yard at 7:12 A.M. on the morning of May 7, 1940. The mechanical department had hoped for a heavier train to determine what the GM-103 would do over Low and Wendover Hills, but neither the continuous rating of 15 mph in the 8th notch, nor the one-hour rating of 12.7 mph, allowed the kind of tonnage they had hoped to operate in this first test between Roper Yard and Oakland Yard. Moreover, such heavy tonnage would not have allowed No. 61 to maintain its schedule.

The operation was generally held to the lowest maximum timetable speed. The GM-103 passed Delle Station at 26 mph, and thereafter its lowest speed on the 8/10ths percent grade was 21 mph on the 5° curve at MP 872, at which point the drawbar pull (DBP) registered 75,500 lbs. Ascending, the one percent on Wendover Hill brought the DBP to as high as

General Motors demonstrator No. 103 with 76 cars and 3,550 actual gross tons pauses for its portrait east of Garfield Pit, Utah, on May 13, 1940. **D.F. Davis, Author's Collection**

14 D-DAY ON THE WESTERN PACIFIC

The ten 2-8-8-2s of the Third Subdivision each possessed a tractive power with booster of 150,900 pounds, or 137,000 pounds without booster. These bruisers would lug 4,000 tons up the Canyon, or 1,900 tons up the 2.2 percent out of Greenville; just short of an ability to equal four units of FT diesel, or three units of F-7. Here's the 258 at Keddie on May 28, 1938. **Wilbur C. Whittaker**

94,000 lbs. with the speed slowing to between 17.5 and 18.5 mph. At Elko, O'Neill dispatched a telegram to Mason in San Francisco: MY A-50 AND A-51. MINIMUM SPEEDS ON ONE PERCENT EIGHTEEN MILES PER HOUR. FUEL USED ROPER–WENDOVER FIVE TWENTY FIVE GALLONS. WENDOVER SUMMIT SIX HUNDRED GALLONS. TOTAL DELAYS INCLUDING FIFTEEN MINUTE WENDOVER INSPECTION: THIRTY MINUTES. EXCELLENT PERFORMANCE THROUGHOUT.

In order to understand O'Neill's elation, it is necessary to consider the capabilities of the M-100, 401 Class coal-burning 4-6-6-4's then operating over Wendover Hill between Elko and Wendover or Salt Lake. Locomotive and tender weighed approximately 991,500 lbs. with 339,000 lbs. on the 70" drivers. Cylinders were 22"x32", and boiler pressure ran 265 lbs. per square inch. Maximum tractive force was rated at 99,600 lbs., with penciled worksheet calculations indicating what was termed as cylinder tractive force (CTF) of about 96,000 lbs. up to about 10 mph after which the CTF began to fall off. Additional mechanical department calculations and graphs showed that boiler tractive force (BTF) was initially greater than CTF, but rather rapidly fell off, so that on reaching 21 mph the CTF exceeded the BTF, and continued to do so at higher speeds. The mechanical department had initially figured that the M-100 Class should be capable of pulling 3,730 tons on the one percent, with an adjustment factor of 5.5

Eastbound coal burner 403 descends the one percent at MP 774 between Silver Zone and Arnolds Loop. It was the GM-103's performance against this class of steamer which pleased the superintendent of motive power; the M-100 (401) class was considered to be better than two FT diesel units, but never the equivalent of four.
Wilbur C. Whittaker

WAS THE GM-103 REALLY THAT GREAT? 15

The famed 401 class of seven coal burners roamed the Eastern Division between Elko and Salt Lake City. Rated at 99,600 pounds of tractive power, these challengers maintained a fast freight schedule eastbound over Wendover Hill with 3,500 tons, or westbound with 2,850 tons. Here is the 403 at Wendover, Utah, in 1939. **Ted Wurm**

tons per car. This was a drag rating and too slow to make symbol schedules. They then established a rating of 3,450 tons, or 49.4 cars of 70 tons each. But since the westbound one-percent grade out of Wendover has some 44 curves, they set the rating at 2,850 tons, thus allowing tonnage over the hill at a bit over 20 mph, or where the CTF most closely matched that of the BTF, with maximum DBP at that speed of about 72,278 lbs. So that when the GM-103 pulled its 76 cars over the hill at between 17.5 and 18.5 mph—a train that would have been drag tonnage for the 401 Class—and exerted as high as 94,500 lbs. of DBP at 18 mph, the mechanical department took notice.

The afternoon of May 8 arrived with train No. 61 moving out of Stockton Yard with 55 cars and 2,758 actual trailing tons. The GM-103 maintained a speed on the Altamont one-percent grade of 24 mph with the dynamometer car registering 65,000 lbs. of DBP. No. 61 arrived in Oakland Yard at 7:20 P.M., the total running time from Salt Lake City being almost 32 hours. Total amount of fuel oil used was 4,295 gallons.

In test No. 2 on May 9-10, the GM-103 handled train No. 62 from Oakland Yard to Portola in a total running time of 14 hours and 56 minutes. Consist out of Niles Junction included 93 cars with 3252 actual trailing tons. From Livermore to Altamont, approximately nine miles, and mostly .80% grade, the GM-103 spread the distance over a period of 19 minutes. This tonnage was roughly 500 tons more than would be given an MK-60-71 Mikado, and slightly over twice the tonnage that would be given a C-43 Consolidation. Out of Oroville Yard the GM-103 handled 75 cars or 3213 actual trailing tons up the canyon. Total running time between Oroville Yard and Keddie was four hours and fifteen minutes, followed by an eight-minute inspection at Keddie and two hours and eighteen-minute total running time between Keddie and Portola. This was the Feather River Canyon's one percent—251 Class Country, as some called it, after the ten great articulateds that worked the hill.

The M-137-151 Class of single expansion articulated locomotives possessed a 26-inch bore and 32-inch stroke, 63-inch drivers, and boiler pressure of 235 lbs. Their total weight was 1,066,450 lbs., with 549,656 lbs. resting on the eight driving axles. These big bruisers purportedly possessed a maximum tractive effort of 150,900 lbs. with booster, and could drag 4000 tons up the roughly 117 miles of one-percent grade out of Oroville. No one, except possibly the machinists, said anything bad about the 251 Class. They had made helper service relatively rare in the canyon, and could easily move 3,400 and 3,500 tons up the hill with only two water stops. But while they had a reputation for being capable of moving about anything that was movable, they possessed inherent characteristics not easily remedied. One of these was the relatively low starting tractive power as compared to the diesel.

When the GM-103 departed Keddie for Portola at 2:14 A.M. on the morning of May 9, the dynamometer car registered 208,000 lbs. of drawbar pull. According to mechanical department figures, the 251 Class could be expected to produce 145,928 lbs. of tractive power up to about seven miles an hour after which it would begin to drop off. By 10.5 mph the TE had dropped to 144,211 and by 21 mph to 115,025. The GM-103 possessed an even greater loss as the speed increased, but its initial starting TE (at 25 percent adhesion) of 228,000 lbs. was so great that up to approximately 11½ mph, it could be expected to exceed the roughly 139,000 lbs. of TE provided by the 251 Class based on 25 percent adhesion.

An additional factor that related to the first was the presence of a BTE that exceeded CTE only up to 15½ or 16 mph. Up to about 10 mph the 251 Class could show a BTE of approximately 198,500 lbs. By 15 mph the BTE had dropped to 132,000 lbs. At greater speeds, the CTE, without booster,

Brute force vs. the mountains. On September 4, 1939, 2-8-8-2 articulated 254 assaults the hill through Paxton, California. This class boasted a tractive power, with booster, of 150,900 pounds and a 4.08 factor of adhesion.
Wilbur C. Whittaker

WAS THE GM-103 REALLY THAT GREAT? 17

While not the biggest, possibly the most respected power on the Western Pacific in steam days were the "Little Mallets," one of which is seen spotted at Westwood, California, on August 28, 1947. The two classes were rated at 80,000 pounds tractive power, and would lug 2,200 tons up the one percent of the Third Subdivision, or 1,170 tons on the 2.2 percent out of Greenville. The railroad figured these goliaths equal to about two units of diesel FT, and they could get down to a crawl.
Ted Wurm

exceeded the BTE. The likelihood of running at much higher speeds with a late cutoff seemed remote due to back pressure that developed when excessive quantities of steam could not be exhausted from the cylinders, and due to the existence of a CTE that had exceeded the BTE. Attaining higher speeds required a shortening of the cutoff which meant a diminishing of steam pressure at these higher speeds.

Since it seemed clear that neither steam nor diesel, with big tonnage, would perform with any considerable speed on a one-percent grade, the chief items of interest seemed to be those in which one or the other excelled. Average speed between Oroville Yard and Keddie had been 18.35 mph, or comparable to 251 Class performance. The GM-103 possessed the best starting performance which was of utility in getting moving on the one percent. Its great advantage rested in the large number of driving axles controllable by one crew, and in its ability to employ full power output for quick acceleration. The GM-103 employed maximum use of its weight. All locomotive weight rested on the driving axles, whereas in the steam locomotives, a considerable portion of the weight could never be turned into tractive effort. Fueling records for the 251 Class are not presently available, but the 1,380 gallons of fuel oil used by the GM-103 between Oroville Yard and Keddie, a distance of 78 miles, is known to have been impressive to the mechanical department. This 1,380 gallons comes to 17.69 gallons per train mile, or 4.84 gallons per 1,000 gross ton miles.

Steam vs. diesel. This was not the kind of contest the railroad had in mind when the 253, running light, and diesel 901X (first diesel road power on the WP) met on the 1.50 percent grade on the Inside Gateway east of Robbers Creek, California, on September 10, 1947.
Al Sanford Collection

The Western Pacific's first FT diesel test train stretches nearly to infinity west of Salt Lake City in May of 1940. A long line of diesels would follow.   **D.F. Davis, Author's Collection**

When test No. 2 terminated at Portola, the GM-103 cut off from train No. 62 and ran light to Keddie for test No. 3. At 3:19 on the afternoon of May 10, the GM-103 departed Keddie on No. 182 with 64 cars or 2,409 actual trailing tons. An 80,000 TE Little Mallet, the 205, helped No. 182 up the 2.2% grade into Almanor, after which it was cut off. Total running time was 1 hour and 21 minutes, with average running speed of 18.81 mph. Total running time between Almanor and Bieber was 3 hours and 38 minutes, with average running speed of 23.80 mph for the 86.4 miles—almost 22 of which were 1.50% grade.

Test No. 4 took place on May 11 with GM-103 on the point of 65 cars or 3,267 actual trailing tons. Train No. 181 departed Bieber at 2:00 A.M., with the GM-103 taking its consist up the 1.50% grade out of Pit River. At Dixie, the M-80 Class engine No. 201 was cut in for helper service over the 18¾ miles of 1.80% grade into Halls Flat. No. 181 averaged 17.02 mph with total running time over these 35.4 miles, between Bieber and Halls Flat, of 2 hours and 5 minutes. The 76.4-mile run into Keddie was then made at an average speed of 25.30 mph in a total running time of 3 hours and 1 minute.

Both tests on the Inside Gateway—or North Line as it was sometimes called—were somewhat inconclusive since the tonnages were considered too heavy for the GM-103, but somewhat light for the GM-103 and an M-80 Class helper. M-80 Class steam power could be expected to move 1,170 tons up the 2.2% grade into Almanor, and 1,427 tons up the 1.80% grade into Halls Flat. Retainers were turned up at Halls Flat on the eastbound trip, and at Almanor on return. The GM-103 did not possess dynamic braking, and the Electro-Motive people shortly felt that an electric holding brake would be of considerable usefulness, not only over the descending grades, but over the rolling profile between Norvell and Halls Flat.

The final test of the series, test No. 5, took place on May 12-13 aboard First 62 between Portola and Roper Yard. First 62 departed Portola at 8:04 A.M. with 79 cars or 3,504 actual trailing tons, and arrived at Roper Yard at 8:03 A.M. of May 13, in a total running time of 17 hours and 16 minutes. The GM-103, with the same tonnage allowed an M-100 Class Challenger, moved its train up Wendover Hill from Shafter to Silver Zone in 20 minutes, followed by a delay at MP 773.3 because of a pulled drawbar on business car No. 104 at the rear of the train.

An acceleration test was conducted out of Wendover, with the entire train undoubtedly being on the −0.80% grade beginning just east of MP 807. In 9/11th of one minute, DBP reached 162,000 lbs. at 11 mph. In one minute the DBP had dropped away to 124,000 lbs. although the speed had only increased to 14 mph. Two minutes indicated 24½ mph with 66,000 lbs. DBP; three minutes—30 mph with 51,000 lbs. DBP; and four minutes—34½ mph with 48,000 lbs. When graphed, the first 2.759 miles, covered in 6 minutes, show a fantastic DBP up to 11 mph after which the DBP gradually fell away as the speed increased. East of Lago, First 62 stopped for its portrait. The front-end cars involved in the test were cut off and pulled to Garfield, and the GM-103 ran back light to its train where photographs were taken between MP 910.1 and 913.6.

In summary, the GM-103 demonstrator while on the Western Pacific had traveled a total of 2,077.9 miles in an actual running time of 73 hours and 6 minutes. Average speed was 28.42 mph with gross ton miles hauled of 8,037.5. Total fuel oil used was 12,340 gallons, which averaged 5.94 gallons per mile or 1.54 gallons per thousand gross ton miles. Total amount of lubricating oil used was 90 gallons which averaged out to 0.0896 pints per thousand gross ton miles. These figures are somewhat affected by the use of helpers on tests 3 and 4, but provided excellent statistics for a future occasion when Western Pacific would be in the market for additional power.

3

Knuckle Busters or Big Boys!

THE YEAR 1940 showed considerable economic improvement over the United States, and loaded freight car miles on the Western Pacific reached 97,718,228, compared to 87,946,604 for 1939. The year 1941 would ultimately produce a loaded freight car mileage of 123,981,529 with gross ton miles of cars and contents at 7,579,948,000. The Western Pacific was in the market for power, and what was envisaged was something big that would replace the M-100 Class steam locomotives, and eliminate helper services between Elko and Wendover.

On February 7, 1941, a conference was held between Mason and O'Neill to discuss purchase of 10 4-8-8-4 steam locomotives for service over Wendover Hill. In this conversation, it was suggested that the M-100 Class could then be converted to oil and operated between Winnemucca and Portola. Contacts were immediately made with the Union Pacific, and WP considered having its own order attached to that of the UP power then under construction.

By March 21, 1941, the management had second thoughts, and Mason wrote O'Neill that "in view of the probable high cost of this type of engine and the fact that it will take 10 of them to handle the peak business . . . it occurs to me that we should give serious consideration to the purchase of four or five 5,400-hp diesel-electric locomotives, which we can probably obtain in much less time than would be the case with the steam locomotives and which can be used anywhere on the line whereas the 4-8-8-4 cannot. Furthermore, we are faced with a large expenditure at Winnemucca and Elko roundhouses to take care of the 4-8-8-4's at Elko and the 4-6-6-4's at Winnemucca."

O'Neill then evaluated test results from Santa Fe diesels 101 and 103, in addition to digging out statistics earlier collected on the GM-103. There were those whose analysis differed from that of the management, in that, over a period of time, they felt steam would compare favorably with diesel when allowing for the higher horsepower available in the steam locomotive at speeds exceeding about 18 to 20 miles per hour. But management, for its own reasons, had decided to purchase diesels, which placed Western Pacific among the early users of the newly developed FT design.

On June 5, 1941, the company contracted with Electro-Motive for the construction of three 5,400-hp FT, dry-sump locomotives of four units each in an A-B-B-A configuration.

The 903 steps eastbound out of Wendover, Utah, in March 1942, with the salt flats ahead and Wendover Hill in the background. This was the original paint scheme for FT power, and consisted chiefly of Woodfield Green Duco, Diamond Yellow, Omaha Orange (for the narrow striping), Black Duco for the pilot and Black Dulex on underframe and trucks.
Wilbur C. Whittaker

Each unit possessed a 16-567 engine, one D-8 main generator and four D7K traction motors. Brake schedule was 8-EL, and each cab and booster unit was connected by a drawbar.

The fateful day of December 8, 1941 (one day after the Japanese attack on Pearl Harbor), brought delivery of the first of the new diesel freight locomotives to Elko where it was set up for immediate movement westbound and down the canyon to Oroville. Trainmaster Henry Stapp took her down the hill that night—the ominous shadows of war already making their presence known in the form of United States Army troops strategically placed at tunnels and bridges throughout the Feather River Canyon. In the cab of the 901 was a brilliant, young ex-service engineer from Electro-Motive by the name of E.T. Cuyler. Ed Cuyler is said to have studied mechanical engineering at the University of Iowa from which he entered the service of the Rock Island as special apprentice in 1929. On September 9, 1932, he completed his apprenticeship, at which time he became a machinist and motor car maintainer until 1937. During this time he also worked on steam locomotives, served as temporary foreman, and instructed engineers on the operation of motor cars. In 1937, Cuyler joined Electro-Motive as service engineer on diesel locomotives. This position brought him to a number of railroads, as one of his chief functions was to train railroad personnel in the maintenance of this new type of power.

It seems clear that Western Pacific management did not believe the diesel to be of only transitory significance, and Electro-Motive was asked for one of their best men to take over control of the newly developing Western Pacific diesel fleet. Cuyler was the recommendation, and in late 1941 he departed the Electro-Motive Division of GM for his new position as "Assistant to the Superintendent of Motive Power in Charge of Operation and Maintenance of Diesels"—a position becoming effective on December 1, 1941. This proved to be one of the most unique events in the railroad's history, and time would show the immense influence of Cuyler over the motive power destinies of the Western Pacific.

The 901 had been placed in immediate service, as were the 902 and 903 when delivered on-line December 29, 1941, and January 16, 1942, respectively. The plan was to run the 901 in Canyon service between Oroville and Portola, or on the High Line between Keddie and Bieber, until such time as the crews became familiar with the handling of these locomotives. On account of Keddie not being equipped to do much work on these diesel engines, it was the preference to run them between Oroville and Bieber for two or three round trips before running back to Oroville for necessary servicing and inspection.

Engines 902 and 903 would run between Oroville and Salt Lake, or between Oroville and Wendover, whichever would lead in a given instance to the smallest turnaround time and delay in acquiring sufficient tonnage for a return trip. Superintendent of the Eastern Division, John J. Duggan, was concerned that the new power receive maximum utilization during the short stay of the factory men who accompanied each locomotive and would be training engineers. On January 15, 1942, he wrote to O'Neill: "We believe that in order to give enginemen a chance on all districts to familiarize themselves with the operation of these diesels that the two should operate between Oroville and Salt Lake City on first through tonnage train ready for them at either end after they are available. Believe that we should endeavor to secure 74 loads for them at each end. This would not, of course, permit them to run regular schedule of 61 and 62, but it would insure their handling maximum tonnage and would enable all the men to become familiar with their operation." Of great importance was the necessity to provide the longest wait at Oroville since this would be the center for diesel maintenance. All power was to be fueled from tank cars at Oroville, with refueling of eastbound runs from tank cars at Elko so as to avoid refueling at Salt Lake except in emergency.

In these early weeks following delivery, no one knew precisely what the maintenance schedule should be on this new power, but should the chief dispatcher wish to turn the engines at Elko, or at Wendover, this was acceptable to Cuyler in order to "get all the miles and pull all the tonnage we can with these engines. However, we do not want to keep turning them too many times at one point because Oroville is the place set up to take care of the repairs and servicing of the motors, etc." Roundhouse foremen kept a book record of each engineer and fireman dispatched on this diesel power in order to be informed of when given individuals had sufficient experience to be called for this service. The number of road foremen of engines was increased and these men made determined efforts to ride as often as possible and to get qualified so as to be in a position to qualify the men following departure of the instructors.

Before the close of December, complaints were heard that the crews were unable to hear the horns on the 901 Class. These horns were Leslie Tyfon A-200-LPYA which produced something of a deep-resounding, booming effect. Steam whistles had never been a problem in the canyon, but with several curvatures between the power and the caboose, and with the flagman back another three-quarters of a mile, the calling in of the flagman had sometimes not been heard.

According to Engineer Herb Berg, the normal procedure in steam days was to whistle in the flagman and then give him time to protect his return with fuses and torpedos. When it was estimated that he had been given sufficient time to make a fast walk back to the rear of the train, the engineer whistled off. Should the flagman not yet be in, the conductor would pull the air. However, when the 901 Class called in the flag, the fact might be unbeknown to the man three-quarters of a mile behind his train. The engineer tried to give him sufficient time to get back to his train and then proceeded to whistle off, but if the conductor failed to pull the air until the slack ran in, the result was frequently a broken knuckle. On one occasion, the train whistled off with the flagman never knowing that he was now alone in the canyon.

A number of reports indicated the ease of breaking-in-two should the engineer wait insufficient time for the brakes to release on the rear of the train. On some occasions this interval is said to have been as long as 10 minutes, and with the tremendous starting tractive effort of an FT locomotive, considerable patience had to be shown if the train was not to be broken-in-two. On January 5, 1942, Extra 901 East, just east of Keddie on the NCE, had just pulled out to the 74 carboard and had stopped to load passengers on the caboose. In starting from that point, and after attaining a speed of from six to eight miles per hour, the engineer widened on the throttle a little too soon which stretched the slack with such a severe jerk as to pull the drawbar on the east end of the head end car in the train. Road Foreman of Engines John McNally, and a factory representative were aboard that trip, and Superintendent of the Western Division G.W. Curtis wanted to know where they were at that time, and why they had not prevented the engineer from making such a mistake.

Many break-in-two's were caused by defective knuckles, but Road Foreman of Engines Tom Hunter believed that most occurrences in the canyon were caused by the conductor pulling the air from the rear after the train had started or while running. Enginemen needed time to familiarize themselves with the fine points of operation, and it took them some time to recognize that the brake pipe pressure did not show on the gauge of the diesels unless the air had been put into emergency from the rear end. With experience, the engineers came to watch the transition meter when starting. If the indicator moved to the right after coming over to the left, it was a sign that the air was being pulled and that the load was being built up on the traction motors faster than it could be used. One means of circumventing this problem where signals could not readily be seen or passed between the head and rear end, was for the engineer to apply the air and signal for a plug test. When he received the plug, he knew the flagman was in.

A fourth cause of break-in-two's appeared on the Eastern Division where an engineer might misjudge his distance when coming to a stop and find that it was necessary to draw off additional air. This tended to throw the train into emergency and sometimes broke the train in two. Diesel-powered trains were frequently somewhat heavier than those with steam and Cuyler suggested that engineers "start braking far enough back so that if the stop were made too far from the objective, the train can always be moved up after the stop has been made. . . ."

H. A. O'Rullian

E. T. Cuyler
The WP asked for the best man.

Its company herald worn away by time and work, the 903-DC and companion F-3 pass through Marysville, California, on the westward journey to Stockton. Such power consists were usually cut in at Oroville and taken off at Stockton. Catenary belonged to WP subsidiary Sacramento Northern. The date is August 12, 1959. **Don Hansen**

4

Eight Alcos or Ten Steamers

WITH BUSINESS on the increase, management in late 1941 again considered acquisition of switching power to release Consolidations for road service. Western Pacific's Glen W. Curtis had watched the progress of Rio Grande's 1,000-hp switchers 101 and 102 working the Bingham & Garfield Railway, and Curtis, Duggan, and O'Neill preferred 1,000-hp units to anything of lower horsepower capacity. General Manager Mason then reported on October 22, 1941, that he was placing an order with American Locomotive Co. for eight 660-hp diesel switching locomotives, and Quigley recommended they receive numbers 504 through 511. Agreement was signed on October 17, 1941, with court authority being given on November 10.

Mason proposed the concentration of these engines at a minimum number of points to save expense of providing an excessive number of diesel oil facilities. Choice of terminals would be based on the likelihood of around-the-clock operation, and the presence of fantail switch engines to be released for replacement of Consolidations for road service. Both San Francisco and Oroville possessed diesel fueling facilities. In November 1941, a facility was under construction at Oakland, and only one additional facility would be immediately required at Stockton.

In the concentration of diesel switching power, one could expect certain economies connected with the relative ease of breaking in suitable mechanics to properly care for these units, with supervision being concentrated and fewer spare parts required than if the engines were scattered over the two divisions. Eastern Division Master Mechanic William Parry was in agreement with this plan, and presumed that Portola might be wisely avoided since the 660-hp diesels would probably be too light for the heavy cuts being handled by steam power in the Portola hump yard.

In January 1942, President Elsey heard from J.J. Pelley, president of the Association of American Railroads, that the

Steam fantail 166—old No. 88 of the United Verdi Copper Co.—is working here at Stockton and represented one of two classes of steam switchers owned by the Western Pacific. These gutty little fellows possessed a tractive power of 34,400 pounds, compared with the 31,200 pounds of the earlier 151 class. As World War II intensified, the WP needed more switchers. The question was, would they be steam or diesel?
Dudley Westler

The new switching power turned out to be Alco S-1s, of which the 505 was the second placed on the roster. It is seen here at Oakland on February 23, 1946. Delivery was in black and white striping as shown here. Their Blunt trucks nosed badly, and a speed limit was set at 35 mph. Starting tractive effort at 25% was 49,750 pounds, similar to the original SW-1s.
Guy Dunscomb

Western Pacific might not receive this order of eight Alco switch engines, and he sought to know what steam power could be repaired for service. Elsey replied that he had no steam locomotives set aside and that the entire roster was in active use including three new freight diesels. Moreover, the eight diesel switch engines were necessary if 10 Consolidations were to be released for road service.

Carloadings for January were up 56 percent, and trailing gross ton miles in December and January, both abnormally slack months, were higher than any October ever recorded except for 1941. The WP had no facilities for construction of locomotives, and should the eight Alco switch engines not be forthcoming, an order should immediately be established for at least 10 large capacity steam locomotives to carry the anticipated load for which military authorities had informed the Western Pacific that it should make preparation.

Western Pacific received its new switch engines between May 16 and June 16, 1942. All worked at least one shift in Elko Yard, after which they were double-headed with trains onto the Western Division. The paint scheme was in black with white trim, black and white tiger stripes over the battery box cover, and all carried black and white diagonal striping for better visibility in blackouts, and as protection against accidents when operating on city streets. After delivery, all received blackout shields to headlights, both front and rear, as did all other power operating in or between San Francisco and Oroville. Final assignments placed one in Oroville, five in Oakland and two in San Francisco. Four Consolidations working Oakland Yard were thus released for road service, and three Electro-Motive SW-1s from Oakland and San Francisco were moved to Stockton where they released one Consolidation for road service and two superheated 163 Class fantails for replacement of two Consolidations then working Portola. One small 151 Class fantail was also released from San Francisco and held at Oakland for relief yard service, and to take the place of diesels tied up for the monthly inspection.

The 504 Class of S-1s possessed a four-cycle, six-cylinder vertical 539 engine with 12½x13" bore and stroke, and developed full rated horsepower at 740 rpm. The main generator was a GE552-A series with its shunt field excited by a GE GMG139-A1 exciter, one component of which was self-exciting from its own armature, and another component of which received excitation from either the battery or the auxiliary generator. Generator output was delivered to four GE 731-traction motors with continuous ratings per motor of 740 amps, and there was a single 45-inch-diameter fan to deliver air for radiator cooling. As with all later Alco switch engines purchased new, this power possessed 14-EL brake schedule, and a gear ratio of 75:16.

The new 504 Class, as it was called, almost immediately developed an engineering defect requiring remedial action. This defect was in the lubrication oil pump drive shaft. The key in this shaft tended to shear off thus leaving the engine without lubrication. American Locomotive Co. was already aware of this problem and had developed a larger drive shaft to be applied to eight of the 504 Class between June and September 1942.

Another very serious problem that appeared late in 1942 was the presence of shelling out and loss of babbitt in the connecting rod bearings, which if not caught in time would result in scoring of the crankshaft. Cuyler noted that some changes had been made in these bearings due to the government taking away metals formerly used so that it was necessary to develop a new type bearing. The old bearing had a shell, or back, which was twice as thick as the presently used bearing shell, and was kept from turning in the rod by bearing cap bolts whereas the later bearing had only a 7/16" dowel pin, which was acceptable as long as the bearing did not turn in the rod.

Cuyler replaced the 7/16" dowel pins with larger dowels so as to more nearly fit the hole in the shell. Such problems did not improve availability even though the builder admitted the bearing failures resulted from improper fitting when the engines were assembled.

5

Power Shortages and World War II

WORLD WAR II brought a dramatic quickening of the tempo on the WP, and the year 1942 produced loaded freight car miles of 153,493,735 with gross ton miles of cars and contents attaining 9,715,608,000. Yard switching in 1942 reached 1,210,038 switching miles as compared with 857,880 miles in 1941, and 662,694 miles in 1940. All power was fully occupied and the latter half of 1942 brought the leasing of 10 steam locomotives from the C&NW, DMIR and D&RGW. The year 1943 would be even tighter for power, and the WP went scouting for locomotives—steam or diesel. Seven of the Consolidations taken out of yard duty by the 504 Class had to be returned to yard duty because of increases in traffic, and the yards at all mainline terminals were jammed with tonnage for movement.

What the WP wanted was additional diesels, but War Production Board allocations were not easy to acquire, and the intent was to buy six additional simple articulated 2-8-8-2 locomotives from Baldwin, and six heavy 4-8-4s of the C&O Class from Lima. However, these 4-8-4s possessed driving axle loads of 71,650 lbs. and could not have been operated over the paired trackage in Nevada since the Southern Pacific had imposed a limit of 70,000 lbs. per axle. Ultimately, the WPB allocated six 4-8-4s from a Southern Pacific order of GS-6s, and an order was placed with Electro-Motive on July 16, 1942, for three additional 5,400-hp locomotives. Engines 904 and 905 were delivered on July 5 and 18, 1943, and there was little assurance that the third would be received until its actual arrival on property during October.

This 904 Class possessed 567A wet sump engines, and included gear train modifications from that of the 567 engine. Maximum width of the 567A engine was reduced by moving the blowers inward, although the camshaft centers remained the same. The number of idler gears between the crankshaft and camshaft was reduced from four to two. Straight spur gears were used which incorporated floating bushings rather than pressed-in bushings—thus eliminating the thrust problem present with the older helical gear. The new gear train gave

Western Pacific's last new steam power arrived in 1944. The six Northern GS64-77s, of which 486 (shown moving off the table at the Oakland roundhouse) was an example, were diverted from a Southern Pacific order of "Daylight" locomotives. WP was only tolerably satisfied with this class, but they would handle 1,900 tons up the Canyon and keep passenger schedules with 15 heavyweight coaches.
John H. Kahler from L. T. Clark Collection

about a 4 to 1 improvement in wear due in part to better lubrication of the gear bushings. At the same time, the 567A crankcase was simplified over that of the 567. The transition lever now had a neutral position besides the four previous positions. Moving lever to the left operated the transition; moving it to the right operated the new type rheostatic dynamic brake. This transition lever was moved from the top of the controller to the side, and included a new locking device which prevented the engineer from slipping by his proper transition position.

Finally, the PCS switch was given an additional function. Whereas formerly this switch when opened would take control of the engines away from the engineer, causing them to stay in idling position, there was added another feature that shut off the fuel pump to each engine. If the engineer did not close the switch in time, all of his engines would die due to fuel pumps being shut off and engines not getting fuel. As with all FT power, the main carbody was painted with Woodfield Green Duco, and horizontal bands of Diamond Yellow Duco, and Omaha Orange Duco. The pilot was in Black Duco, and underframe and trucks were in Black Dulex.

The defense effort had the WP packed tight with traffic, and on November 10, 1942, an order was placed with American Locomotive Co. for eight 1,000-hp S-2 diesel-electric switch engines to be known as the 551 Class. These weighed 230,000 lbs. and had a maximum TE of 57,500 lbs. Each was very similar to the 504 Class except that this new 551 Class possessed a DC generator type GT 553-A, with a GMG139-A2 GE exciter, and like later classes of Alcos, each possessed a Buchi turbocharger. The 660-hp S-1s had been too light for some of the heavier jobs, so that these 1,000-hp S-2s were shortly scattered between Oakland and Elko. For example, the 660-hp engine 511 had been working Oroville Yard which possesses an ascending grade on each end of the yard. The 557 replaced the 511 at Oroville and released it for somewhat lighter duties at Stockton. A diesel fueling facility was under construction at Sacramento and by the middle of 1944 all three 600-hp SW-1s were working at that point. This allowed the stocking of spare parts at one point and released steam power in yard service for road service.

Gross ton miles of cars and contents in 1943 mounted to 10,263,127,000 and would increase to 10,506,478,000 in 1944, and 10,888,236,000 in 1945. Gross tons per train, excluding locomotive and tender, were up to 2,620 tons in 1944 with average speed of trains being about 17.1 mph. Available records indicate that motive power, both steam and diesel, was resolutely maintained in a manner that minimized delays and not infrequently drew praise from government inspectors.

But in 1943 and 1944, Western Pacific continued to remain desperately short of power, and on September 29, 1943, an order was placed for six additional 5,400-hp locomotives to be essentially similar to the 904 Class delivered in July and October. October 29, 1943, was the date of contract with Electro-Motive, and engines 907-909 were accepted at Shafter in July, with 910-911 arriving in August, and the 912 in November 1944. As with the 904 Class, this new power went into immediate service between Oroville and Salt Lake City, and provided brief respite for steam power at terminal turn-around.

Yard switching locomotive miles climbed to 1,393,356 in 1944, and would increase to 1,410,420 in 1945, and 1,175,364 in 1946. Additional switching power remained in demand at several terminals, so that on June 28, 1945, an order was placed for five Baldwin VO-1000s (Baldwin Order No. 44511-C: Specification No. 44-DE-7, dated June 30, 1945). These four-cycle engines, to be known as the 581 Class, weighed between 242,970 and 248,650 lbs. with maximum TE figured at 60,000 lbs. The eight 12¾x15½" cylinders were of vertical type; Westinghouse DC generators were of type 480-B, and traction motors were Westinghouse DC type 362-D. Brake equipment was 6-DS and gear ratio was 68:14.

This was the last power to be ordered during the war years,

26 D-DAY ON THE WESTERN PACIFIC

with delivery of two taking place in October, and three in November 1945; and it was to be the final power purchased essentially for purposes of maintaining Western Pacific's ability to carry its share of the wartime burden. Future power requirements would be based on the movement towards dieselization rather than on need, and from this point onward, one could expect to see fewer Class 1 and 2 locomotive repairs, and longer lines of steam power shoved into dead lines awaiting the scrapper's torch. In 1946 the roster stood at 169 steam locomotives compared to 72 diesel units. Steam was no longer king, especially among the yard goats, but there would continue to be steam in service, especially during peak periods.

Eastbound Train 2, with TP-29 4-6-0 No. 81 on the point, hastens through Hayward, California, on the bygone afternoon of September 23, 1943. Thirty-six of these ten-wheelers were purchased new, and they were highly respected as a miniscule powerhouse that would get up and move. Tractive power rating was 29,100 pounds or 812 tons up the one percent of the Feather River Canyon.
Wilbur C. Whittaker

FT 906-D was one of the 1943 order which helped rescue WP from a World War II power chaos. In the photo above 906-D and train prowl the rails at Berry Creek on the old line later inundated by the Oroville Dam project. Below, the 906-D heads up 8,700 horses to swing downgrade through Keddie on October 10, 1964. The Keddie local is spotted to the left.

Both: Don Hansen

Switchers 551-558 arrived during World War II to help the hard-pressed Western Pacific. Unit 553 pulls a cut of cars eastbound down Third St. in Oakland (above) on April 10, 1968, while passengers wait for the *California Zephyr*. **Virgil C. Staff** At right, S-2 No. 556 handles a rake of reefers being iced at Stockton. This paint scheme employed Dulux Black 254-2234 and Dulux White 58-488. A new scheme of Duco aluminum 7025 and Orange 254-6273 with black stripes became standard on July 21, 1952. **Haas & Associates from Western Pacific Collection**

CZ

That Most Legendary of Streamliners...

It was born March 20, 1949, and lived only two decades. But in that short time Western Pacific trains 17 and 18 —the *California Zephyr*— established a special following among passenger train aficionados as America's premier streamliner. One could hardly call the Western Pacific a passenger railroad. It was built for freight, and lots of it. But the WP ran a fine CZ, in partnership with the Rio Grande and the Burlington, and ran it with pride and professionalism. The CZ had a slow schedule, mountains to climb, meandering rivers to follow. So it converted mountain railroading into its greatest asset: scenery. Such a beautiful train, combined with such wonderful countryside, made for photographs beyond counting, words beyond totaling, praise beyond measuring. If any train became a legend in its own time, it was the CZ. Here is our photographic salute.

Opposite Page: FP-7 805D heads train 17 near Paxton in March of 1970.
Tom Moungovan

Right: The eastbound CZ climbs the Altamont on April 30, 1967.
Joe Ward

Train 18 comes booming out of Tunnel 1 in Niles Canyon on December 13, 1966, on a short stretch of one percent grade. Perhaps that police car parked on the Niles Canyon Road, above the train, is waiting for a speeder! **Joseph Ward**

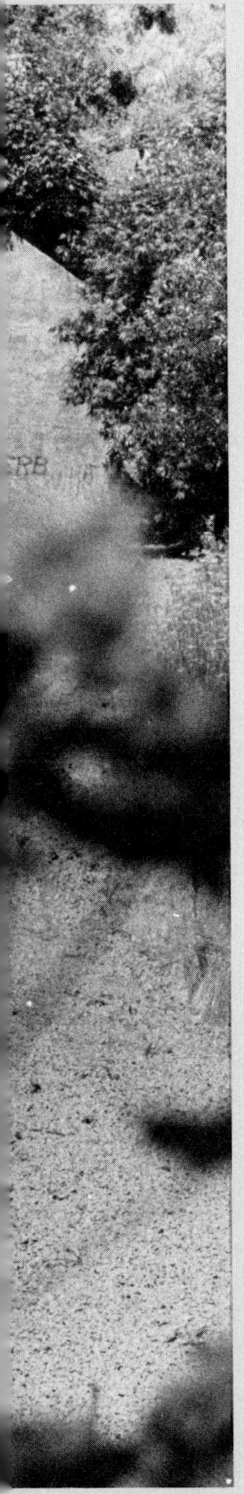

Before going into revenue service, the Western Pacific displayed its new streamliner to admiring crowds along the system. On March 14, 1949, the *Zephyr* exhibition train is spotted at the 19th and J streets station in Sacramento.
Both: H. A. O'Rullian

With its time on earth nearing an end, the eastbound *California Zephyr*, above, hastens past a cemetery at Marysville, California, on its final run on March 21, 1970. **LaVada Staff** Happier times, below, brought crowds to see the CZ off on its long journeys. In this scene eastbound 18 gets its highball from Conductor Jim Murray at Oakland on a spring morning in 1966. At right a "Zephyrette" (train stewardess) walks to the depot office in Oakland while No. 18 waits in background. **Two: Virgil Staff**

It is 11:13 a.m. on December 30, 1967, and Train 18 climbs the Altamont up the .80 percent grade 20 poles east of MP 52. Startled passengers peer at the earthling out here in "nowhere" and the hogger has blasted two shorts in greeting to the photographer who visited with the crew prior to leaving the No. 5 Adeline Street roundhouse. **Virgil Staff**

The two *Zephyrs* meet east of Oroville in December 1966 with No. 18 holding the main and No. 17 some four hours off the published. This is the new line west of Intake built to enable Oroville Dam waters to inundate a portion of the old line between MP 209.51 and MP 232.4 **Joseph Ward**

6

CZ In; Steam Out

TOWARDS THE LATTER part of the war, the Western Pacific, D&RGW, and Burlington again considered their earlier plans for a diesel-powered, streamlined train to be operated daily between San Francisco and Chicago. The exciting new train would capitalize not on speed but on scenery. Plans were formalized in early 1945, and on October 16, an order for passenger equipment was placed with the Budd Manufacturing Co. of Philadelphia. Six trains would be required, and consists would include 10 or more cars each.

Western Pacific's management made the decision to power the new train with F-3s using an A-B-B power consist of one F-3A and two F-3B units in each train. The original order for nine units of F-3 was dated August 20, 1945, with authority covering revised prices dated May 22, 1946. Freight power was receiving various experimental paint schemes at this time, and the new F-3s would be attractively finished with carbody in orange, and stainless steel lower side panels, and fuel tank, trucks and slips below the side sill in aluminum. The "bulldog" nose would be orange, as along the carbody ports, with a medallion placed between the two "flying wings" painted red and bordered in white. This would be by far the best paint scheme ever seen on the Western Pacific, and would continue on most Zephyr power until retirement.

On December 16-19, 1946, an Electro-Motive F-3 demonstrator, No. 754, roamed the Western Pacific in an A-B-A configuration. The test train consisted of the No. 754, CB&Q dynamometer car No. 30, and 10 other cars. Total weight of train—locomotive and cars—was 1,232.16 tons, and was intended to be approximately the same weight as the streamliner

The Train of Tomorrow was displayed at Sacramento on November 18, 1947. This General Motors display convinced WP officials that the new Zephyr trains must have domes.
H. A. O'Rullian

equipment. President Harry Mitchell was greatly interested in this test, and was responsible for it being a four-day daylight round trip between Oakland and Salt Lake. Motive Power Chief O'Neill, Mechanical Engineer E.E. Gleason, and Cuyler were aboard and found the power and riding qualities very satisfactory. The one serious defect lay in the three 1600-type 4516 steam-generating plants, which together proved unable to heat an 11-car train. Had this power been pulling a regular passenger train, the locomotive would have had to be replaced.

W. J. O'Neill
A promise from EMD on steam generators.

Boiler coils became covered with soot, and constant efforts were required to keep the steam generators operating. In spite of the presence of visiting experts and maintenance crews on board, the boilers had shut down on the westbound run between Elko and Winnemucca, and between Gerlach and Portola. Within 50 miles of leaving Salt Lake City, the generators were smoking so badly that the entire train was beginning to fill with fumes. Cuyler concluded that the most that could be expected was approximately 10 hours of service after which the generators would fail due to soot on the coils. To return the generator to operation, it would be necessary to partially dismantle it and scrape and blow out the soot with compressed air. Such a generator clearly could not be used on the Western Pacific since it must run continuously for 40 hours before arriving at a maintenance point.

Another characteristic of Demonstrator No. 754 which perplexed Cuyler was the nature of the transition on these units. Cuyler approved of the new type electro-hydraulic governor as a marked improvement over that of the FT, but he felt this governor was too slow in response to the throttle, and that it would not allow the kind of acceleration that Western Pacific wanted for its new streamliner. He also noted that the automatic transition was slower at acceleration than the manual transition; that in automatic, especially on grades, all units did not make transition at the same time. This caused the fuel consumption to be unequal as the units remained in different positions of transition for many miles, especially when the speed did not increase on grades.

This slower acceleration, in automatic transition, concerned the mechanical department considerably since the railroad had numerous curvatures, and a train on occasion might have a considerable number of slow orders. Manual transition, when tested on the 754, demonstrated that when all units made transition at the same time, there was no jerk to the train, and acceleration in speed was much faster. The builders disputed these views, but Cuyler was so impressed that at a later time, for these and other reasons, he ordered the blocking off of automatic transition on all passenger units, in which state they remained until the day of the scrapper's torch.

Cuyler continued to insist that the three F-3 locomotives, when delivered, should have suitable steam generators with soot blowers, and he was surprised that no noticeable improvement had been accomplished toward eliminating this source of trouble over a period of five or six years. Should the new power arrive with these generators, there would be numerous failures which the mechanical department could not remedy through regular maintenance. On January 21, 1947, EMD admitted to O'Neill that the 754 did not possess the latest steam generator but he was promised that Western Pacific would receive a greatly improved one upon delivery of the F-3s. The builder's story was that the boilers had been revised; that they would now make a 2,500-mile trip without failure; that no one else was having trouble with them; and that much of the problem undoubtedly was based on faulty maintenance.

Western Pacific's three new F-3s were received from the Rio Grande at 4:10 P.M. on July 3, 1947, and departed on train NCE-3 for Elko about 7:00 P.M. The plan was to run the new power on the *Exposition Flyer* between Oakland and Salt Lake City. The power would be maintained at Oakland, and layover there was such as to allow approximately seven hours for maintenance. This use of the 801 Class on train Nos. 39 and 40 would allow Oakland Diesel Foreman William F. Stevens to build up his diesel maintenance forces at Oakland, so that when the streamlined equipment arrived for use on the *California Zephyr*, there would be a diesel maintenance crew immediately available. Since the new diesel shops at Oakland were still uncompleted, the new power would be delivered at the Oakland roundhouse where it could be broken up and turned for servicing and maintenance.

The new 801 Class of F-3s possessed 567B engines, D12 main generators, and D17 traction motors. The D12 was rated at 1,050 kw, or 100 kw higher than the 950-kw D8 generator of the FT. Gear ratio was 57:20, and unlike the earlier FT power with D7K motors, these D17s permitted additional tonnage until the speed was pulled down to approximately 21 mph. D17 traction motors, like the D7K of the FT, were rated at 700 amps, but possessed an additional kw capacity of 24. FT locomotives had been rated at 800 rpm and 80 BMEP, but on the F-3 the builder raised the BMEP to 92, or equivalent to 1,500 guaranteed horsepower to the generator available for the traction motors.

The new 567B engine incorporated a direct engine-driven auxiliary generator and main generator blower, and the pumps were increased in capacity by 20 percent. Unlike the FTs, these possessed one AC blower per traction motor, and actual CFM per motor was increased from 1,900 CFM on the FT to 2,100 CFM on the F-3. Gear train on the 567B engine was similar to that on the 567A engine except that the stub shaft for the two idlers was in one piece rather than composed of two separate stub shafts. Oil was then fed to the gears through cored passages instead of through oil lines externally mounted. This new design had been found necessary because of troubles that had developed in the 567A gear train oil lines due to high-frequency, low-amplitude vibrations.

The 567B gear train also incorporated a wider upper idler to drive the auxiliary generator drive gear, so that the upper idler drove both a camshaft gear and an auxiliary generator drive gear. As in all 567 Series engines, main bearing lubrication was from the top through the unloaded upper bearings instead of

Sometime prior to the inauguration of the *California Zephyr* engine 801 poses for a photo with an eastbound special somewhere west of intake on the old main line.
Barry Evans; Louis Stein Collection

Author's Collection

William F. (Bill) Stevens
A chance to build.

through the lower main bearings as in the 201A engine.

The F-3 got away from the electro-pneumatic governor of the FT by being the first to employ an electro-hydraulic governor. On the FT, the engine speed increased almost as fast as the throttle handle, and engine loading was controlled only by the load regulator. The new type governor better synchronized the loading and speed of the engine so that on the F-3 model, engine speed is said to have increased only at a rate that could be utilized for engine loading. Engine speed actually increased at a slower rate although this did not affect the increase in horsepower output. The F-3 also possessed automatic transition to be installed at the Oakland diesel shop and then blocked off by Western Pacific forces. Automatic transition was intended to be superior to manual transition since the individual units would go through transition independently of each other and create less shock to the train. But the mechanical department said that this transition tended to "hunt" on the grades of the Western Pacific, and all passenger power therefore operated with manual transition where all units were controlled simultaneously. Transition operation differed from the FT in that on the F-3 the transition lever could be moved from 2 to 3 position or 3 to 2 position with throttle in any of the eight running positions.

The maiden run of the 801 in passenger service occurred out of Elko on July 9, 1947, and arrived at Oakland on the following morning. Passenger trains were too important to leave to chance, and the three locomotives of the 801 Class received considerable mileage in freight service before sufficient adjustments enabled them to see service on trains 39 and 40. So, it

Engineer Louis Fischer brings the westbound CZ into Stockton station for a short stop and a highball for Altamont Pass, Livermore, Pleasanton, Fremont and Oakland. It is the afternoon of April 2, 1967. **Virgil Staff**

was not until July 18 that the F-3s began running through regularly from Oakland Pier to Salt Lake and return. Three F-3s were necessary to pull the same passenger train, while a 481 Class 4-8-4 could easily handle 16 heavyweight cars up the canyon and on schedule. The 4,500-hp diesels accelerated somewhat faster in the lower range of speeds than did the 481 Class, and showed marked advantages as the grade increased.

During the first 30 days, not a single successful trip was made with the 1,600-lb. 4516 boiler. And without the instructors constantly working on these generators, there would have been no possibility of operating them on regular passenger runs. No two boilers worked alike and none responded similarly. Electro-Motive maintainers were unable to keep them operating, nor was the Vapor Heating Co.'s maintainer. Western Pacific had been assured that the 801 Class would receive the latest 4516 boilers, rather than the obsolete 4516s said to have been installed on Demonstrator No. 754. But when the maintainers ordered new replacement parts, they ordered new and revised appliances which led O'Neill to conclude that the 801 Class had been delivered with a boiler similar to that on No. 754. Moreover, numerous parts removed for replacement had "U.S. Navy" stamped on them.

It was clear that these boilers could not be counted upon in the winter, even with attendants aboard. The Oakland–Salt

The *California Zephyr,* with Engineer Woody Spillman in charge, highballs eastward out of Tunnel 2 in Niles Canyon on the overcast morning of April 23, 1967. **Virgil Staff**

The new *California Zephyr* diesel and passenger facilities at Oakland on September 21, 1947. Passenger consists were pulled off the balloon track to the right and pushed through the washer prior to the spotting of cuts on the background coach tracks. Passenger power was spotted to the front of the two-stall diesel facility until early 1950, after which this became home base for the two RDC cars.   **John H. Kaler; H. A. O'Rullian Collection**

Lake round trip was approximately 1,846 miles and Cuyler needed a boiler that would provide approximately 40 hours of service without interruption. Winter would be arriving in a few months and drastic changes were required if the 801 Class was to be a dependable source of passenger power through subzero temperatures. Mechanical department forces in Oakland began revisions on these boilers which contained orifices as small as one-eighth inch in size, and which, if a fleck of scale came through, placed the boiler out of commission until cleaned out. The Vapor Co. sent one of its experts to Oakland and mechanical department forces began revisions including changes in piping bypass water to water tanks, changing out fuel nozzles, heat exchangers, bypass regulating valves and servo fuel controls for newly designed and revised units.

This work was so successful that the changes made on the fuel nozzles and servo fuel controls tended to develop such a hot fire in the firing area that all the parts such as domes, air deflectors and coil pads began deteriorating to the extent that they had to be renewed constantly. Excessive heat in the combustion area was burning out the air rings and the cement in the fire pots. This occurred when steam demand was such that when the generators went on full load the fire was too hot, thus causing these parts to deteriorate. The high temperature switch tubes were becoming warped and had to be renewed at regular intervals. The outside of the coils was becoming white from heat and the Durex brick cracked under the terrific heat.

Additional modifications were required, and by mid-December 1947, Western Pacific forces had sufficiently revised the 4516 boilers to make them dependable for one round trip. But it now became clear that these boilers possessed insufficient steam capacity and could involve the company in considerable embarrassment during subzero weather. Cuyler had always believed them to be inadequate and the winter of 1947-1948 proved it. Probably the closest test of 801 capability to heat the train was with 14 cars at five below zero, and employing all three steam generators. The mechanical department had the generators sufficiently operative to depend on heating a 12-car train at zero temperatures. But should the temperature fall to 20 below zero, it was clear that the last few cars might not be so warm.

There would, however, be no danger of freezing the train if all generators were operating properly. But this was unacceptable since the Western Pacific wanted a steam capacity to heat a train up to 16 cars in any subzero weather, and regardless of the condition of the train. In fact, what the mechanical department demanded was an ability to heat any consist the power was capable of pulling.

Almost from the beginning, Cuyler had desired a larger steam capacity output. Ultimately he concluded that the standard figure of 250 lbs. per car as used in computing requirements of latest equipment, could not be used in determining the requirements per car of antiquated equipment that had been in service for any extended period of time. The requirements of such equipment might rise as high as 400 lbs. per car in subzero weather.

"A 12-car train of such equipment would require 4,800 pounds which was the maximum output of the three generators and would not leave much to depend on," he wrote. There appears, then, to have been two phases to this problem: the first when the generators operated improperly; the second when it was clear that they provided insufficient steam capacity output. A 12- to 14-car train on the *Exposition Flyer* would be on the "ragged edge," as would a future *California Zephyr* if additional equipment should be added to the consist. "Should one of the generators fail, or go off the line, the other two generators could not then adequately heat the train and dire conditions could result," Cuyler said.

On March 20, 1949, the Western Pacific's new premier train, No. 18, the *California Zephyr,* moved out of Oakland Pier on its inaugural run. The three 4,500-hp F-3 locomotives provided the power for this new streamliner, and would run to Salt Lake and return with insufficient layover for any point other than Oakland. A two-stall diesel shop in Oakland was in the process of construction, and all maintenance would initially take place at the old 10-stall, No. 5 Adeline Street roundhouse.

The mechanical department was never very pleased with this arrangement, and Cuyler, at least as early as February 1946 was positively convinced that dependable diesel-electric operation of the new *California Zephyr* would require a minimum of four locomotives with servicing and maintenance at Oroville. In the past four years, the railroad had built up a sizable diesel force at Oroville, and with passenger locomotive repair work mainly accomplished on day shifts, the required augmentation of day and afternoon shifts would be minimal. Average labor costs per locomotive mile at Oroville would be at about 13.7 cents a mile, whereas with three units maintained at the Oakland facility, the costs would rise to as high as 20.8 cents a mile.

Little assistance could be expected from second and third shifts because, exclusive of roundhouse foremen, only four men were employed on the second shift, and three men on the third, and these had to be retained full time on steam locomotive repairs. Thus, a considerable work force would be required at Oakland to assure dependability of diesel locomotive service on the streamlined train. The smaller the force employed, the more likely an occasion would arise when it would be humanly impossible to complete the work necessary before a locomotive could be dispatched. There would be a very close margin of safety in the availability of power, and steam power should be on standby to give full protection to runs.

In early October 1948, Cuyler had a conversation with President Mitchell in which he stressed the advantages that might be gained by possession of a fourth 4,500-hp passenger locomotive. Cuyler remarked that since the chief maintenance shops were in Oroville, the acquisition of a fourth passenger locomotive would allow maintenance of passenger power at that point with consequent reduction of the maintenance forces at Oakland. The Oakland diesel forces came to 33 men. This roster included Diesel Foreman Stevens, later to become the second general diesel supervisor of the railroad; R.J. Dowe, electrician inspector; two electricians, three electrician helpers, one machinist inspector, seven machinists, six machinist helpers, one cellar packer, two sheet metal workers, one sheet metal worker helper, and eight laborers. The Oroville diesel shop force at that time totaled 67 employees, and Cuyler suggested that this force would require 10 additional men. The Oakland force could then be reduced at a net saving per year of approximately $99,000.

Mitchell was apparently impressed. Moreover, the Electro-Motive people had done studies dated August 1947 and November 1948 concerning the possible dieselization of the property. Certainly the trend toward dieselization was manifest in that since 1939 the railroad had purchased six steam locomotives compared with 76 diesel units. Switching opera-

Pleasanton, California, was a flag stop for the CZ. Here we catch No. 18 bursting with energy as it accelerates through Bridge 41.72 toward the Altamont Hills on March 31, 1969. **Virgil Staff**

tions were essentially dieselized with steam normally on standby. Fifteen steam locomotives had been retired in 1947, and while only one steamer was retired in 1948, Mitchell noted to O'Neill that steam locomotive miles in road freight service during the first five months of 1948 had dropped to 72 percent of that operated in the corresponding period of the previous year, and passenger service steam locomotive miles had dropped some 33 percent of those operated in the first five months of 1947.

It is now known that by the close of 1948 management intended to dieselize the entire railroad, with the 607-mile Eastern Division being the first step. The *Exposition Flyer* had been dieselized in March 1948, and two additional 4,500-hp passenger locomotives would allow diesel passenger maintenance at Oroville, and make possible the dieselizing of the *Royal Gorge*—the railroad's only secondary passenger train. The close of 1948 would show freight service 58.63 percent dieselized compared with 51.55 percent in 1947, and 59.23 percent following the 1949 diesel locomotive deliveries. Yard service in 1948 was 88.01 percent dieselized as compared with 85.06 percent in 1947, and 84.39 percent in 1949.

By the end of 1949, 32 additional steam locomotives had been retired or sold, thus leaving 121 steam locomotives in service at the close of the year compared with a steam roster of 153 on January 1. The subsidiary Tidewater Southern had been dieselized since 1948, with the TS-132 steamer being used only during the peak perishable season each year. During 1948, the No. 132 was operated 42 days, or a total of 4,780 miles, while in 1949 it was used only 21 days, or a total of 2,400 miles. No mileage is recorded for the year 1950, although the No. 132 built up 6,201 miles in 1951, and 1,744 miles between February 1952 and October 1953. Undoubtedly the TS-132 would have been sold to the Stockton Terminal & Eastern in 1952 but for the presence of one bridge on the Tidewater Southern which would require extensive repairs to accommodate a 100-ton diesel. Finally, the subsidiary Sacramento Northern continued to employ both diesels and electrics through April 10, 1965, after which time this subsidiary was completely dieselized.

The motive power stables were somewhat crowded in the period following the war. And while locomotive miles in 1948 continued to drop from their 1945 high mark, they began a gradual ascent in 1949 which intermittently have continued to this day. The grand total of car miles began a quick rise in 1950 and Western Pacific was ready with additional diesel power in the form of two 4,500-hp FP-7 locomotives in an A-B-A configuration, nine 6,000-hp F-7 locomotives in an A-B-B-A configuration, and four 1,000-hp Alco S-2 switching locomotives. All three classes had been purchased under a conditional sale agreement dated December 1, 1949, and amended by letter agreement of February 3, 1950.

The 913 Class was accepted at Elko between January 29 and February 6, 1950; the last power to be delivered being the S-2s accepted at Elko between February 26 and March 5. In the meantime, the 804 Class of FP-7s and their boosters had been accepted at Elko on January 29 and February 1, 1950, and was immediately placed in service—the 804 taking train No. 1 out of Elko on January 30, and the 805 handling No. 2 out of Oroville on February 2. Both Western Pacific passenger trains were now essentially dieselized.

Scrapping of steam power —Consolidations and switchers—at Sacramento in September of 1947. Diesel power was the new order on the Western Pacific.

H. A. O'Rullian

It is late afternoon on an overcast April 16, 1967. The westbound AP, 40 minutes behind No. 17, struggles upgrade just east of the East Portal of 415-foot Tunnel 3 on the Altamont. It is a tremendous show and a fine performance. It is railroading (and train watching) at its best. **Virgil Staff**

The FP-7 units and their boosters, like the F-7 freight units, possessed 567B engines, D12-D14 main generators, and D27B traction motors. Passenger units possessed the usual 57:20 gear ratio, while that of the freight units remained at 62:15. As in all covered wagons, subsequent to the FTs, booster units contained a hostler's control station, and automatic transition was blocked off. The paint scheme on the 804 Class was similar to that on the F-3s, and the 913 Class comprised the first new freight units to arrive in the recently accepted paint scheme for freight power intended to appear much like the passenger units but calculatedly downgraded in appearance.

Freight units received an orange essentially similar to that used on the passenger power, and lower side panels were in a metallic gray to simulate the stainless steel side panels on the F-3 and FP-7 power. Trucks and underframe were in black, as were the two horizontal stripes on either side of the vitreous medallion. Standard scheme for the pilot was in black and orange tiger stripes. President Whitman was not overly enthused with this freight unit paint design, and it was undoubtedly about this time that in some quarters the railroad came to be known as the "route of the rolling pumpkin."

Traction motors on the F-7s were higher rated than on the FT power since the D27B motors possessed silicon insulated armature coils. Kilowatt ratings remained similar to that of the D17 motors of the F-3s, but amperage capacity was increased to 825, and traction motor blower capacity increased by 300 CFM over that of the D17 motors of the F-3. By this time only FT units received D-17 motors, although the WP began a program of upgrading armatures with the original class "B" coil insulation. D-7 motors were converted to D-17 type through the application of oil lubrication to armature bearings and felt wick lubrication to motor suspension bearings. D-17 motors were converted to D-27 motors by application of silicon insulation to the motor coils and armatures. The idea was to upgrade motors and make them interchangeable, and ultimately even FT power received the D-27-B motors. Cuyler had hoped to build a traction motor shop at Sacramento in 1943 but management did not immediately agree to this, and Electro-Motive established a general store in Emeryville in the latter part of 1944 which, at least temporarily, put an end to discussions of such a facility on company property.

The four new road switchers of the 559 Class possessed a Type P single- and multiple-unit control, improved engine cooling arrangement, diagonal number boxes for road service, and a special step arrangement, requested by the Western Pacific, which initially became the cause of the first locomotive being held temporarily by the New York Central at Utica, N.Y., as it would not clear their trackage right-of-way all the way west. The WP intended to run these locomotives in road service, and the multiple-unit feature would allow the creation of a 2,000-hp locomotive which might be employed on the Reno Local without necessity of the Reno turntable.

A test was established to determine how well a brace of 559 Class power would function, and on November 17, 1950, the 561 and 562 took the First CFS from Oroville to Stockton with 70 loads and 4 empties, 3,668 actual tons. This train bucked a heavy wind all the way from Oroville to Stockton Yard, and encountered heavy rain over most of the district. Trainmaster John McNally and Road Foreman H.R. Allen concluded that "in our opinion these engines are not suitable for through freight service except in case of emergency as we are satisfied that they will not make maximum speed in level country with the tonnage trains that we are now handling." So died the likelihood that such power would be regularly employed on the Reno Local, or on SN trains over Santa Fe rails between Stockton Yard and Pittsburg.

Arrival of the 804, 913 and 559 classes enabled the complete dieselization of the railroad east of Portola under Dieselization Plan "A." Eastern Division steam power then faced storage in dead lines, or movement westward for operation on the Western Division. All diesel road power normally ran east out of Oroville or Portola and the 559 Class, which had MU control features, received road power assignments on the Eastern Division. Thirty-one steam locomotives were retired, sold or scrapped in 1950 leaving 90 locomotives on the steam roster at the close of the year. In September 1950, 88 diesel units handled 647,900 MGTM, with 60 steam locomotives taking the 230,590 MGTM overflow.

The peak season of August through October brought all 21 of the 5,400 and 6,000-hp diesels onto the Eastern Division, and business was so heavy on the Inside Gateway that it became necessary to revert to the use of 2-6-6-2 compound mallets in helper service with 2-8-8-2 simple articulateds. By

the close of 1950, freight service was 78.80 percent dieselized, and yard service up to 85.68 percent.

Mechanical department policy had been to maintain a number of steam switchers for standby service or peak business, and to retire as much of the smaller road power as was consistent with operations. Big power was generally retained for present or future use, although such decisions were based on the nature of repairs, outlaw dates, and upon expenses required to keep the power serviceable. O'Neill had retired as Superintendent of Motive Power on April 1, 1949, and was replaced by Mechanical Engineer E.E. Gleason who had worked with steam power almost from the beginning of the railroad. Ed Gleason regularly studied his Form 407—Condition of Engines—and in November 1950 he concluded that retirement of certain 2-6-6-2 compound mallets, and purchase of three additional 6,000-hp freight locomotives would provide attractive savings.

For a number of years these "Little Mallets," as they were called, had been employed almost exclusively on the Inside Gateway between Keddie and Bieber. Nine of the original 10 remained on the roster; three were in service, two were in the Sacramento Shops undergoing repairs, and the 204, 205, 207 and 209 were out of service requiring general Class 3F repairs at an estimated average cost of $35,000 each. Should three new 6,000-hp diesels not be obtained, it would be necessary to repair these four locomotives at a total estimated cost of $140,000. Furthermore, it would be necessary to put the forces at Keddie roundhouse back to the normal complement of 30 men.

Purchase of three 6,000-hp diesels would provide savings of $140,000 in general repairs, $114,000 in the reduction of maintenance forces at Keddie, $144,000 in engine crew wages, and $172,000 in fuel cost. This much saving would nearly pay for one locomotive, and the estimated continued savings after the first year would be approximately $400,000 per year. Diesels of 6,000-hp could alone handle normal tonnage trains, so that such purchase would, except for a very limited amount of helper service, completely dieselize the Inside Gateway.

Moreover, the acquisition of two more of the 559 Class of Alco switching engines would greatly reduce steam yard engine hours. Diesel locomotives worked 13,764 yard engine hours in September 1950, with steam locomotives working a total of 3,192. Based on this performance, Gleason explained to General Manager Harry Munson that the addition of two 1,000-hp Alco switching engines would increase the diesel locomotive yard engine hours to 15,188 and reduce that of

Early morning on June 3, 1967, finds Engineer Vern Brain and the GGM crossing the Southern Pacific and Bridge 53.40 through the lower reaches of the West Altamont. Meadowlarks and bawling cows compete for attention with the F-7 grinding and throbbing at 15 mph up the hill. **Virgil Staff**

Seven months after the demise of the *California Zephyr*, a westbound San Jose Turn with the ex-CZ power, swings down the one percent just east of Niles Junction near Fremont, California. **Virgil Staff**

steam to 1,768. The savings in fuel alone for one year of two diesel switchers as compared to two steam switchers working the same yard hours would amount to $32,220 since mechanical department statistics indicated that steam switchers used 13 gallons of fuel for every gallon used by a diesel switcher.

Fuel consumption figures for the first four months of 1949 indicate that in road freight service, the diesels consumed 1.8 gallons per 1,000 gross ton miles, or 16¢, as compared to that of steam in similar service with fuel consumption of 8.88 gallons of crude or black fuel, costing 44¢. OS-E reports for years 1938 through the first seven months of 1945 show average consumption of various types of fuel per 1,000 GTM as follows: coal, 118.6 lbs.; crude fuel oil, 7.93 gallons; diesel fuel oil, 2.05 gallons over a 55-month period. On the basis of equating against 2,000 lbs. of coal, an oil burner could be expected to burn 133.7 gallons of crude fuel oil, while a 5,400-hp diesel would use 34.6 gallons.

Munson and President Whitman were impressed. Three 6,000-hp F-7 locomotives, to be known as the 922 Class, were ordered from Electro-Motive on November 29, 1950. These were similar to the 913 Class except for minor features, one of the most important being the additional visibility made possible by the channel between the ventilator and the window proper being located so that the window was two inches wider. Other changes in carbody structure brought the window 2½ inches higher than the older style window on the F-7. An order was also placed with American Locomotive Co. for two 1,000-hp S-4 switching locomotives according to proposals to Whitman dated November 30, 1950. These were quite similar to the 559 Class in that they employed MU control equipment, two 45-degree number boxes on the front end, a modified step arrangement, and were turbocharged. Unlike the 559 Class, they had AAR trucks, and automatic shutter control.

By the close of 1950, all terminals, including Wendover and Winnemucca, boasted diesel switching power. Road steam locomotive miles decreased 43.7 percent, while road diesel locomotive miles increased 57.6 percent compared with 1949. Steam locomotives handled 21.2 percent of the gross ton miles while diesels handled 78.8 percent. All passenger trains had been dieselized since delivery of the 804 Class.

In late 1949, the sleepers and diners on secondary passenger trains Nos. 1 and 2 had been discontinued, and the railroad requested the public utilities commissions for authority to replace the then-current Nos. 1 and 2 with triweekly service using Budd-built RDC cars. Rail diesel cars 375 and 376 were accepted on May 26 and July 20, 1950, respectively; the 375 placed on order dated January 23, 1950, with specifications references for the 375 changing from Project #1604 of September 14, 1949, to Project #1804 revised February 24, 1950. The WP then proposed to purchase a second RDC-2 for which the board voted in the affirmative on June 1, 1950. The Budd cars were inaugurated in September, with the first eastbound run on September 15, and westbound on September 17, 1950. Now, Western Pacific owned two F-3 cab units in excess, and these were kept on passenger power standby on the Western Division, but were placed in regular freight service to be retained on the Western Division at all times.

The Korean War kept the power moving, and gross ton miles of cars and contents increased to 8,061,191 MGTM in 1950 after an almost continuous decline since the close of World War II. The Eastern Division was redundant with essentially unused steam facilities, and authorization was received to retire the old roundhouses and certain trackage and fueling facilities at Wendover and Winnemucca, and to install small diesel facilities there to allow for greatly reduced maintenance and operating costs. Portola Roundhouse continued later than Wendover and Winnemucca since some steam power remained in service east of Oroville. Mechanical forces at eastern points were drastically reduced, but Oroville forces were gradually expanded. Sacramento Shop forces remained about the same.

In 1951, 37 steam locomotives were sold or scrapped, leaving 53 such locomotives for possible further service. Average steam locomotive road miles per month equaled 41,730 while that for road diesels came to 950,276. Diesel locomotives handled 91.37 percent of all gross ton miles in freight service during 1951, with steam power handling 8.63 percent. By the end of June, essentially all steam had departed the canyon and the Inside Gateway, and steam power was used only between Oakland and Oroville.

The presence of the F-7s enabled dieselization of all through business between Oroville and Salt Lake, with sufficient power to spare to handle the Santa Fe–Great Northern connections between Oroville and Bieber. The running of the F-7s through from Oroville to Bieber made possible a change of crews without tying up the power in Keddie for long periods of time. Additional power made available thus dieselized the Inside Gateway and practically abolished the Keddie Terminal at the end of the shift on May 29, 1951.

During 1951, steam power requiring general repairs was shoved onto the dead line, and the first half of the year appears to have been the cutoff point for general steam repairs, although engine 334, which would be used in excursion service, came out of the backshops with a Class 3-F repair on July 3, 1951. Even less steam would have remained on the roster had the threat of complete war mobilization not presented the extreme difficulty of quickly augmenting the complement of diesel locomotives already on the roster. In such an event, steam power would have been returned to service to handle tonnage on the third and fourth subdivisions, with application of lighter class locomotives to local, work, yard and helper service.

Moreover, steam mechanics were becoming difficult to muster in any large force, and to protect itself in case of war emergency, the WP continued to temporarily maintain intact its steam locomotive facilities at Oakland, Stockton, Sacramento, Oroville, Keddie, and Portola. Steam operations were

E. E. Gleason
With steam since the start.

becoming a rarity, and would be found chiefly west of Oroville in local and branch line service, and to supplement diesels in through freight service.

Extensive elimination of steam locomotive servicing and fueling facilities was accomplished in 1951. In early 1949 the plan had been established to skeletonize the force at Elko, and decentralize diesel switcher maintenance from that point to points at which these would be operating. The roundhouses at Wendover and Winnemucca then came down, and small and compact diesel houses were completed. Each would be used to house the diesel switcher at that point and to provide a place in which monthly inspections could be made, if necessary, by forces from Elko. Plans called for a much larger diesel shop at Elko for 1952, and were in preparation for permanent diesel installations at Portola, Oroville, Stockton, and Oakland.

Considerable preparation had gone into decisions of the kind of power that should be purchased for the replacement of steam. As early as the spring of 1948, a 1,000-hp engine of the 551 Class had worked the Reno Local between Portola and Reno. The engine had sufficient power to handle the tonnage moved from Portola to Reno and return, but possessed a cooling system that was insufficient to maintain engine temperatures in proper range when under sustained load, especially on grades. This engine did very well from Portola to Chilcoot but after about eight miles on the one-percent grade going south, temperatures began to rise and could only be controlled by closing the throttle. It was Cuyler's recommendation that a 551 Class engine be traded for a 581 Class at Stockton, since the 581 Class possessed more radiation and was an eight-cylinder engine rather than a six, and therefore had more water capacity.

The daily-except-Sunday equivalent of the SJP, handling tonnage from the San Jose area to Stockton, growls eastbound between Sunol and Hearst on the morning of September 18, 1966. The orange nose of the 917-A makes comprehensible the occasional and not unfriendly epithet of "Route of the Rolling Pumpkin." **Virgil Staff**

But the VO-1000s were considered somewhat low in horsepower, and the opportunity arose to test the 1,500-hp 53,000 TE Baldwin Demonstrator No. 1501. The trials began September 11, 1948, on the Westwood–Halls Flat Logger and continued well into October over various portions of both divisions. On October 7, 1948, Engineer Kendall and Conductor Lucas departed Elko for Wendover on the 2-54 with 3-67-1673 tons. According to Road Foreman C.F. Fields, "This engine is equipped with one air pump and it took 30 minutes to charge the train line at Elko and make the air test. Between Elko and Wells, 28 mph was the highest speed that we were able to make. From Rockland to the top of the hill at Hogan and from Shafter to Silver Zone speed of 2½ to 3 mph was the best speed we were able to make with engine working to the maximum capacity and necessary to keep sand on the rail at all times. After starting over the top of Wendover Hill, it was necessary to work the engine at half throttle to keep air pressure as near maximum as possible. Engineer Kendall had very much trouble keeping his train line charged and rear cars of train brakes were not releasing as he did not have main reservoir capacity."

Runs were made on the Tooele Valley Local between October 11-13, and Road Foreman G.M. Lorenz generally commended the performance, although saying, "In through freight service with heavy tonnage, the operation would be entirely too slow." After test trips on the Reno Local out of Portola, Western Pacific's V.H. Edwards commented, "Baldwin locomotive 1501 is much faster for mainline service but on actual pull and lift WP 584 is as good or even better because it does not slip as bad and will hold on better at slow speed."

Undoubtedly the runs of September 14-15 were most effective in killing any likelihood that 1,500-hp Baldwins would be employed on the Western Pacific. On September 14, Baldwin 1501 departed Keddie on the Portola–Keddie Local, with tonnage between Keddie and Portola varying between 680 and

770 tons. At no point on the one-percent grade did the top speed become more than 20 mph. Maximum temperature was 152 degrees with 111 gallons of fuel oil consumed. The engine was then run light to Oroville on September 15. Maximum speed on the one percent between Bloomer and Grays Flat was 22 mph with 597 tons. Out of Grays Flat the 1501 made 21 mph with 656 tons. Total fuel consumed between Oroville and Keddie was 272 gallons, with the return trip down the descending grade on September 16 using 52 gallons.

Road Foremen John McNally and Tom Hunter immediately commented that while the engine was rated to handle 1,640 tons on a one-percent grade at a speed of 10.5 mph, the higher the speed the less tonnage it would handle. Since it would only make a maximum speed of 20 miles per hour with from 680 to 770 tons, it would not be as desirable an engine in local service on the third subdivision as would a Consolidation engine which could easily handle this amount of tonnage at a higher rate of speed. Fuel oil consumption was low, and the engine seemed economical to run, but could not keep the schedule where local runs had numerous stops to unload freight and pick up and set out.

Towards the early part of October the 1501 was making branch line runs east of Portola, but Cuyler's recommendations were that 1,500-hp locomotives were insufficient to handle the tonnage at practical speeds that would enable locals to clear other trains without delays. He therefore recommended the use of not less than 2,000 hp and preferably 3,000 hp for such an engine. In December 1948 an opportunity arose to test a Baldwin 2,000-hp demonstrator, but O'Neill insisted that 1,500 hp had been insufficient, and he and Cuyler preferred something between 2,500 and 3,000 hp.

In early April 1949, Gleason was consulted about testing a Fairbanks–Morse 1,500-hp, 37,000 TE locomotive. Gleason informed Munson that he wasn't interested since tests made some months before with the 1,500-hp Baldwin demonstrator had clearly indicated that 1,500 hp was not sufficient to handle any assignment other than yard work. However, he was willing to make a comparison with the Baldwin since manufacturers frequently claimed tractive effort and horsepower in excess of what actually could be developed in tests, and it might be interesting to learn what the FM would do on the various locals.

The FM, No. 1503, arrived about the middle of May 1949 and saw service over most of the system. It was an excellent demonstration up to the point its rated horsepower would permit. But 1,500 hp would not move the tonnage at speeds required for WP locals. At MP 256, the 1503 could not build up over 16 mph with full throttle and 1,154 tons. In some places the maximum speed was 14 mph which was considered too slow for mainline service. On the Reno Local, on account of not being able to attain maximum speed of 40 mph on level grade with 930 tons, the train had to lay in the siding to clear other trains, which caused delay in arriving at Reno. The highest speed attained between Portola and Reno Junction with 930 tons was 38 mph, and acceleration was so slow that the train gained only about two mph per mile.

Gleason and Cuyler considered the FM to be a superior machine to the Baldwin which had been tested on the WP, but the most serious operating complaint was that the cab filled with exhaust fumes when the locomotive was working hard.

City railroading. The staccato blasts of the Leslie Tyfon A-200-LPYA clear the way for the 922-A as Engineer Bob DuBois takes train GGM down Oakland Third Street on the foggy morning of September 11, 1971. **Virgil Staff**

An unattractive feature, from the maintenance standpoint, was the necessity for any maintenance point to be equipped with a five-ton crane to remove the top crankshaft in order to remove cylinder liners. Cuyler feared that a short service life of the integral parts would cause additional expense. In his opinion, neither the Baldwin nor the FM had sufficient horsepower to efficiently handle local train assignments, and as a matter of fact, they were superior only to the 1,000-hp engines by a few miles more in speed per hour, and would not handle any more tonnage.

On November 19, 1949, 1,500-hp Electro-Motive Demonstrator No. 100 was delivered to the Western Pacific at Oakland. The locomotive was placed in yard service that night to be followed by various road tests, the last of which was with the Tooele Valley Local on November 28. Shop Engineer R.E. Schriefer and General Electrical Supervisor R.F. Carter covered these tests with ultimate conclusions that power as high as 1,500 hp was not required for any present switching operations, and that, in fact, the No. 100 was too heavy and less maneuverable than the 1,000-hp switchers. Gleason suggested to Munson that such a locomotive would be satisfactory for certain local runs where mountain grades were not encountered. In fact, it had given a very good account of itself on No. 62 between Oakland and Stockton Yard. In this Test No. 2, the No. 100 had put out a total of 1,550 hp with average speed of 16.5 mph on a .8% grade with 1,980 tons. Also, on Train No. 2, Test No. 9 from Elko to Salt Lake with seven cars, it had made good performance.

From a design standpoint the most serious defect seemed to be the insufficient displacement capacity of the compressor. On Test No. 7 at Portola it required 24 minutes, while standing in the yard with throttle position ranging from four to eight, to charge the trainline. And on Tests 7 and 9 while drifting downgrade, it was necessary to "rev" the engine much faster than idling speed in order to charge the trainline fast enough. In several instances it was necessary to speed the engine to the sixth throttle position for this purpose.

On Test No. 9, steam generator fumes filled the cab, with cab ventilation unable to clear the fumes. The engine, however, had excellent riding qualities, and showed no tendency to overheat at any elevation. Average fuel consumed per 1,000 gross ton miles of road freight service was 1.8 gallons, while that consumed per passenger train mile was 0.19 gallons. Average speed on the main line was 22.1 mph in freight service and 51.6 mph in passenger service. Generally speaking, it was a fine locomotive.

Two Electro-Motive 1,200-hp locomotives belonging to Weyerhauser, engines 302 and 303, received tests on the WP between September 1-11, 1951. Between 15 and 17 demonstration trips were accomplished during these days with locomotives operating singly and in multiple. The locomotives were equipped with 12-tooth pinion gears which caused them to be about 10 miles per hour slower on level track than the speed that could have been attained with a 15-tooth pinion gear. Western Pacific personnel were favorably impressed, and it was noted that performance of a 1,200-hp unit operating singly equaled the performance of a 1,500-hp GP-7 on grades, and was only about five miles per hour slower on level track. In yard service there was considered to be no comparison between the 1,200-hp unit and the GP-7, and the former was far superior to the latter having been designed for yard service.

Trip No. 17 was made with two units in helper service between Keddie and Almanor, and it was concluded that these would be very effective in such service. These tests convinced Gleason and Cuyler that the 1,200-hp switch locomotive was much more versatile and economical for work in local, yard, work train and helper service than the 1,500-hp GP-7 locomotive.

Whitman and Munson had been the motive force behind many of these tests, and the conclusions pointed to the utility of purchasing 1,200-hp locomotives. In August 1951, Gleason was advised that the Santa Fe was operating 1,500-hp GP-7 locomotives out of Richmond, and there was interest in knowing if these new locomotives were similar to the GP-7 tested by the WP in 1949. WP representative R.C. Madsen rode Extra 2667 east out of Richmond, on October 8, 1951, on an eight-hour and five-minute, 68-mile trip between that point and Mormon. The X2667 started from the east switch at Richmond Yard on the one-percent grade with 1,087 tons and topped the grade at 16 mph in a distance of approximately one mile. In comparing the performance of the GP-7 on the one-percent grades, with that made by the two 1,200-hp Weyerhauser road switchers over the one percent from Omira to Chilcoot—a distance of 18 miles—with 71 cars and 2,403 tons, at not less than 15 mph, it seemed clear that the operating characteristics of the 1,200-hp road switcher and the 1,500-hp engine were almost identical at lower speeds.

On November 27, 1951, a meeting was held in the office of Superintendent G.W. Curtis in Sacramento. Present were Curtis, Gleason, Cuyler, Power Coordinator Larry Contri, and Chief Dispatcher E.T. Gallagher. The topic of discussion concerned the number of diesels that would be required to complete dieselization on the Western Division. In this discussion, it was contended that additional road power could be gained by replacing the 2,700-hp FT road engine on the Tooele Local, Wendover Helper, Portola–Gerlach Local, and Elko–Winnemucca Local, with two 1,200-hp road switchers on each of the three former jobs, and one 1,500-hp road switcher on the latter.

Moreover the purchase of additional 1,200-hp and 1,500-hp switchers would allow the release for other service of two 1,000-hp switchers on the Keddie–Westwood Local, and one each on the Reno Local, Portola–Keddie local, Oroville–Keddie Local, San Jose Local, and one at Portola Yard. A 1,500-hp switcher could replace one Consolidation on the Trevarno Local, and another on the River Rock Local. The two 1,200-hp switchers that replaced the Wendover Helper could also do the work of the 1,000-hp switcher working Wendover. The 1,500-hp GP-7s would be equipped with dual controls to enable operation from either side of the cab, thus avoiding the necessity of having to turn them at turnaround points, or of requiring a turntable at Reno. That property could then be released for industrial purposes, and would avoid the necessity of constructing a wye track at that point. The GP-7 at Portola Yard would provide sufficient horsepower to do the heavy switching on the east lead, and would provide an engine at that point to make reliefs of 1,500-hp engines assigned to locals working in or out of Portola, or could be used for emergency reliefs in other services.

Twenty of the 600, 660, and 1,000-hp engines were required on the Western Division for switching purposes during peak season, and four on the Eastern Division. Additional switching power could then be employed on Sacramento Northern, at least one would be in the shops at all times, and at least two could be used on work trains. One additional engine would be required for one year on the Port of Stockton job from May 1, 1952, to May 1, 1953. The tentative plan had been for six 1,200-hp units, then on order, plus 12 road units. The present recommendation was for 21 units, or three more than had been tentatively planned for 1952.

Thundering up the east slope of the Altamont with a crescendo that shakes the bystander, a brace of ex-*California Zephyr* units on a San Jose turn crawls over the hump west of MP 57. Temporarily the roar of the diesel silences the meadowlarks and red-winged blackbirds as the Turn sweeps past the lonely section house. It is after March of 1970 and a power-short Western Pacific has placed these ex-passenger units in continuous freight duty to finish out their final miles.   **Virgil Staff**

President Whitman and General Manager Munson were feeling their way slowly so as not to acquire power in excess of peak demand. On December 4, 1951, the Board of Directors authorized the purchase of six 1,200-hp road switchers, and in February 1952 it further authorized nine new 1,500-hp GP-7s. The SW-9s and GP-7s had 567B engines, with 12 and 16 cylinders respectively. Generators were D15C and D12-14 respectively, and traction motors were probably D-27Bs. Both classes possessed multiple-unit control.

GP-7s had dual controls and were the first units to possess dynamic brake regulators which measured the grid current and regulated the main generator if there was excess main generator excitation. Transition circuits included no shunting, and operation was in series-parallel or parallel. Initially, the GP-7 draft gear allowed greater side thrust than had been experienced with the M-380 draft gear in the F series locomotives, and upper and lower seals always leaked until improved seals were perfected. SW-9s were the first switching power to be delivered in the new paint scheme of orange, aluminum, and black essentially similar to styling on engine 504 approved by Munson on May 3, 1951. GP-7s were also in orange, aluminum, and black, with 7½-inch alternating orange and black stripes at a 38° angle both front and rear. Prior to this time, all switch engines had been painted in Duco black with striping of white.

Calculations indicated that there should be approximately 26 steam locomotives in condition to make mileage throughout 1952, and 17 more through a portion of 1952. The SW-9s began appearing in June 1952 with in-service dates between June 5 and July 31, and the GP-7s went into service between October 25 and November 4. Twenty-eight steam locomotives were retired in 1952, leaving 25 still owned by the company. Steam locomotive repairs decreased 52.57 percent from the previous year, and any steam operations were carefully controlled to "run out" the miles on serviceable locomotives. Those needing heavy repairs were set aside for retirement instead of repair, and the purchase of diesels had been carefully planned so as to replace the steam power set aside. The

Train GGM east of Midway on May 1, 1966, hurtles over Bridge 64.43 and downgrade over the minus one percent before exiting Altamont Pass. Additional tonnage will be cut in at Stockton Yards, and the Alco goat behind the road units will be cut out for repairs. **Virgil Staff**

small diesel facilities had been established at Wendover and Winnemucca early in 1952, and the diesel house at Elko was nearly completed by the end of the year. By the close of 1952, freight service was 94.60 percent dieselized and yard service 81.98 percent.

Steam was dead in 1953. The Portola engine house was under construction, and 16 steam locomotives were retired in that year, with only nine remaining, and these in storage. The cacophony of big steam was no longer heard along the Main, and there were those who sensed that the times were out of joint. But Munson saw an exciting turning point ahead, and he once suggested to Power Coordinator Contri the opportunities before them in obtaining better utilization through standardization of locomotives. It wasn't that Munson hated steam locomotives, but rather that he preferred to memorialize them in storage or in parks. Every steam locomotive trip over one subdivision cost the company needless sums of money, and every effort was made, short of losing business, to move the tonnage with diesels.

In 1953, steam locomotive repairs decreased by 91.83 percent from 1952, and few steam locomotives were used in regular service except for emergency cases in yard service. Diesel-electric repairs increased by 13.07 percent since steam locomotive use had been eliminated, and diesel power—some of it now 12-13 years old—was showing increased cost of maintenance. Power utilization was no longer what had been expected in the 1940s since the leftover runs could no longer be given to steam, nor the gravy to diesels.

When a railroad becomes fully dieselized the utilization and availability figures take a downward trend, as it is then necessary to protect work trains, locals and helper service with diesel locomotives which, when they are in service, do not make many miles per month and are waiting for trains about 50 percent of the time. This presents a different picture from when the diesel locomotives were protected by steam power and the diesels were operating on so-called "cream runs" or high-mileage runs in which they were able to make an exceptional record on utilization and mileage figures each month.

The completion of Dieselization Plan "B," with consequent absence of the possibility of any regular steam operation, came about when the Board of Directors, on January 6, 1953, authorized the purchase of four additional 1,500-hp GP-7s similar to those of the previous order. These were received at Elko between April 7-14, 1953, and except for unusual peaks or emergencies, the Western Pacific was now sufficiently dieselized to provide for its own needs and for those of its subsidiaries.

7

The Diesel Makes Its Impact

WHEN THE WESTERN PACIFIC inaugurated operations at the beginning of the century, crew-change points became established at locations considered to be one workday's journey apart. Steam locomotive servicing and maintenance seemed best suited to power changes at each terminal, and the presence of gradient disparities often demanded terminal power changes in order to make the best possible use of a particular wheel arrangement for a given amount of tonnage. Mainline roundhouses came to be established at Oakland, Stockton, Oroville, Keddie, Portola, Gerlach, Winnemucca, Elko and Wendover, with a modern erecting and longitudinal machine bay shop at Sacramento, and maintenance and servicing of power at Salt Lake accomplished by the Rio Grande at Roper Yard.

All of these roundhouses, with the exception of Gerlach which had twice burned, were still in operation at the time that the first diesels were delivered, but none could be considered adequate for maintenance and servicing of diesel-electric power. O'Neill and Chief Engineer Tom Phillips were responsible for essential track and interior roundhouse alterations at Oroville and Elko just prior to delivery of the 901 Class. No one had seen the new power and no one possessed any experience in what to order, so that expenditures for spare parts and tools were based on lists compiled by Electro-Motive. There were the usual friendly discussions between the purchasing agent and the superintendent of motive power, in which the former believed the latter was stacking away too much, whereas the latter speculated on management's probable displeasure, should lack of such parts necessitate holding power off the runs.

In the early years of dieselization, the railroad never expended any considerable funds on its diesel facilities. About 1943, Stockton and Oakland roundhouses each received the addition of one and two stalls respectively, with hoists to enable removal of cylinder heads. San Francisco received a one-stall engine house in 1944, and four stalls were built onto the roundhouse at Oroville, in addition to two small shops attached to the roundhouse where filters could be serviced, and finishing and grinding of parts could be expedited. Up to October 1949, when heavy diesel locomotive maintenance was moved from Oroville to Sacramento, any heavy repairs took place at Oroville. A wheel shop was being established in Sacramento in December 1949, and would make possible the "Magnaglo" inspection of all axles.

The Sacramento heavy repair shop was a magnificent facility dating from the early years of the railroad, and boasted excellent facilities enabling the completion of shop work on schedule. Movement of heavy repairs to Sacramento made possible the significant reduction of forces at Oroville with only a small increase at Sacramento. On at least two occasions, Cuyler indicated interest in developing an electric shop in Sacramento where WP could rebuild its own traction motors at attractive savings. But nothing came of this idea and traction motors were shipped east prior to 1944, and to EMD at Emeryville sometime following this date.

At Oakland and San Francisco, the Western Pacific in June 1942 was working seven Alco S-2s around the clock. Cuyler and O'Neill were anxious to keep this switching power away from the roundhouse where there would be numerous delays

and consequent lack of availability. This was accomplished by placing a man on monthly salary who would ride all these engines each day at Oakland, making whatever repairs were necessary, and then on the following day or two he would make whatever repairs were necessary on the other side of the bay. The diesels were refueled approximately every four days, and these normally were brought to the roundhouse only once every 30 days for their monthly inspection.

When the diesels first arrived, some manner of maintenance had to be established in order to operate them successfully. As this work was to be done progressively, it was necessary to keep records of any work accomplished so that the forces would have them available at all times to check back on and learn just what work was due. At Oroville, the system of maintaining the power provided for three lead men, one on each shift, to check maintenance charts and record books of a given locomotive prior to its arrival at the terminal. The lead men then informed the foreman in charge of how many machinists would be necessary to service the engine while at Oroville— the number of mechanics never exceeding three for any one locomotive.

When the diesels first arrived, there were no men at the terminal with experience in the maintenance of diesel power. The three lead men—one for each shift—were given thorough instructions, and these in turn assisted other mechanics when they came over to work on the diesels. If there was not too

Keddie roundhouse basks in the glory of a day long gone. Steam ruled the Western Pacific on September 3, 1939, when this photograph was taken, and Keddie was one of several such facilities necessary for the efficient functioning of the railroad.
Wilbur C. Whittaker

much work, the lead man performed the work alone. Should the amount of work be excessive, the lead man notified the foreman who provided the proper number of machinists to get the work done. When a machinist became experienced, it was not necessary for the lead man to check his work. Inexperienced men received assistance from the lead man, and by this means the Oroville diesel force was built to a point where in January 1945 it was composed of two foremen, 11 machinists, two apprentices, four electricians, 17 helpers and 16 cleaners.

In the event that all three of the 901 Class diesels came into Oroville at the same time, one locomotive would be held and worked, while the other two would be dispatched on a Portola turn to avoid layover in wait for the working force to prepare them for a trip. One of the functions of the chief dispatcher was to employ the 5,400-hp locomotives in such manner as to assure that no two would arrive at Oroville within a period of 12 hours. Cuyler argued that this increased availability and utilization, and cut the number of maintenance forces to a minimum.

From the beginning, the railroad also spread the annual and semiannual tests over the year so as to permit the use of a minimum force. In later years, when heavy maintenance became imperative, the work was scheduled so as not to take place during the peak season. This was not so difficult as might seem since from the beginning there had been main-

THE DIESEL MAKES ITS IMPACT 57

tained a running account of costs that helped provide information as to the condition of the equipment.

Some railroads, with nearly the same number of diesels as the Western Pacific, had constructed sophisticated facilities at considerable expense and staffed them with a large force of men who worked only on the diesels. In October 1943, one railroad is known to have hired 85 men to maintain 34 power plants, whereas the Western Pacific was maintaining 24 plants with 15 men, no regular groups of which would be found working the diesels alone.

In the very beginning, the Oroville diesel force consisted of three electricians, three lead machinists, six helpers and three or four laborers. These men were spread over three shifts so that on any one shift the maximum force used was three machinists, four helpers, one electrician, and four laborers. The biggest force, available on days, was 15 men. The afternoon shift consisted of two machinists and one electrician, with one machinist and one electrician on nights. These men worked diesels when they were in, with the remainder of their time spent with steam.

In this manner, Western Pacific achieved 90 percent availability or better, with four units per locomotive operating at all times, and unlike some railroads, did not attempt to increase availability by employing riding maintainers. Certain railroads frequently ran their trains with one unit shut down and a crew of men back working on a dead unit. Less time was therefore required at a maintenance terminal, and these railroads proudly reported increased availability. Tonnage, of course, had to be reduced although availability would show up favorably in the records. A glance at the gross ton mileage would quickly clarify who was getting the most value out of their locomotives.

Cuyler's attitude was that a dead unit in a train was not available for work, and the fact that it was moving in train did not

Portola—in steam days and a generation later. View at left was taken about 1939. **Charles Ellis Collection** Below we see the Portola diesel facility at the east end of the Feather River Canyon on September 23, 1973. **Author's Collection**

58 D-DAY ON THE WESTERN PACIFIC

Oroville roundhouse, the hub of the WP diesel fleet, on May 3, 1969. This was at the foot of the Feather River Canyon and served a similar function to Roseville on the Southern Pacific. **Virgil Staff**

make it available. Diesel-electric power was available after being released for service and not before. Clearly, availability statistics might be misleading should one not be aware of the method of computation.

In fact, Cuyler did not want anyone tinkering with the units after they left Oroville. When the power departed Oroville it was in top mechanical condition and he saw no reason why the units should not run all the way to Salt Lake and return, with a few additional runs between terminals, without any tinkering from anyone. Maintainers or riders were expensive and their accomplishments on board were considered detrimental to good operation. Cuyler often stated that Electro-Motive knew what it was doing; that riders would be tempted to experiment, and to try to make the units better than Electro-Motive had built. If anything went wrong on the road, the unit could always be shut down. If the diesel could not then handle the tonnage, the tonnage could be reduced. An "educated" electrician or machinist in Elko might be able to make repairs and cut the unit back in, but this was the only exception.

Firemen were instructed to go back through the units every 20 minutes or so to check over the engine, or should the alarm bells ring they should go back to locate the cause. This was frequently on account of the change in wind or adjustment of the shutters. Should the engine not cool down, or the problem be corrected, it could always be shut down. What was clear was that Cuyler did not want anyone tinkering with these machines, and for this reason the Western Pacific never employed riders.

In July 1944, John F. Flynn was placed in complete control of the diesel shop at Oroville, and R.T. Ronan took responsibility for the steam power, terminal facilities, and dispatching of the diesel engines as they were released for service. Delivery of the 12 units of 904 Class in 1943, and 24 units of 907 Class in 1944 added to the problems of assigning trains in such manner that only one 5,400-hp locomotive would be in Oroville at a given time. Each locomotive was given a thorough inspection, and in November 1945 it took four machinists, four machinist helpers, two electricians, and two electrician helpers working from eight to 12 hours in order to keep these locomotives in condition.

The tendency on numerous railroads seems to have been either to overmaintain or the reverse, and from the beginning some maintained their diesels in the same arbitrary manner that they had overhauled their steam power. This required the overhaul of a certain number of units each month based on a time or mileage basis. Cuyler insisted that this was wasted expense, and that it was detrimental to engine life to tear down a locomotive in the shop when the parts were nicely seated with no evidence of malfunction or necessity for renewal.

"It is detrimental to machinery to tear it apart when it is running properly, and all parts can be inspected without disassembly, because when the bearing parts are disturbed and

THE DIESEL MAKES ITS IMPACT 59

Every night was like Christmas Eve at the old No. 5 Adeline Street roundhouse in Oakland. The kittens received their usual delicacies, and the necessary inspection and repairs never slackened. The time is 9:15 p.m. of March 19, 1970, and the final eastbound *California Zephyr* will go out the morning of March 21. **Virgil Staff**

replaced they have to wear into a new bearing surface which shortens the life of such parts," he said. Cuyler believed it to be less expensive to overhaul on the inspection basis without reference to time schedules. In this system, there was no shopping interval, and the system permitted securement of maximum service life of parts to the extent that it permitted the mechanical department to run its engines as long as 15 years before they were totally disassembled.

This system of checking engine components seemed ultimately successful since, for instance, it enabled the railroad to run main generators up to 15 years. Heavy repairs in the early years were usually unnecessary since this was precluded by a system of maintenance that progressively replaced worn parts with the latest improvement, and took advantage of the long service life of parts. In the first 10 years, the Western Pacific never shopped a locomotive. All repairs were running repairs and were mainly performed at Oroville. No specialized mechanics were in the force as there was insufficient equipment to maintain such an arrangement. All mechanics were required to know how to work on every phase of diesel work, and this system permitted the railroad to operate with a minimum force.

Philosophically speaking, progressive maintenance procedures meant there was an attempt to keep the locomotives in service all the time. Locomotives were tied up somewhat more often, but for shorter intervals. If there was any flaw in the procedure, R.E. Schriefer, manager, planning and scheduling, noted that "to an extent at least, you couldn't control it; the

High above the town of Quincy, California, lie the steel rails linking Oakland with Salt Lake City. Here we see the 921-D at Quincy Junction eastbound for Portola on the morning of August 8, 1971. **Virgil Staff**

locomotive controlled you." But Cuyler always argued that careful inspection, accompanied by precise records of the service life of parts, would allow tremendous savings with a minimum of delays.

Diesel locomotives maintained consistent with this philosophy would never wear out, but would become uneconomical through obsolescence. Since the Oroville shops possessed only a minimum force, work was scheduled so as not to all come at the same time. Careful records over the years enabled the mechanical department to develop a good average of how long the various materials could be expected to last, and a regular program was planned so as to spread this work over a period of time and thereby keep the average cost per month evenly balanced during the period of a year.

There was always some debate about Cuyler's conclusion that maintenance costs would not rise perceptibly as the power became older—that with progressive maintenance procedures in effect, costs would level off after which they would continue to maintain themselves at about the same level. For example, 901 Class repairs were considerably less than might have been expected. Cost-per-mile figures for 1942 were at 6.317 cents, and rose to as high as 11.520 cents in 1948 during which year they tended to level off with fairly consistent figures only slightly on the rise following that time in spite of increases in material costs.

This was all the more remarkable when one notes that, unlike some railroads, the WP mechanical department never held materials in capital account as all material was in store accounts and when taken by the mechanical department, it then paid the full cost of these items. This included main generators, trucks, engines, traction motors, and other materials. Moreover, there was no classified repair charge as there was only one account, and that was running repairs. Some railroads had a classified repair account, and when a locomotive received heavy classified repairs, its running repair costs would be correspondingly low. Comparison of one railroad's statistics with that of another could be misleading, and one needed to be aware of the basis of comparison.

With the exception of the Nevada paired trackage, the Western Pacific was a single-track railroad with one percent to 2.2 percent grades. This cut down the mileage and reduced the MGTM per month. In fact, the Western Pacific locomotives always used more fuel per unit mile and per unit MGTM than did many railroads. But these larger fuel figures were necessary to produce more horsepower to accomplish the same work because of the mountain grades. Thus it would not appear that an MGTM or a mileage figure would be a reasonable comparison to make when considering costs unless the two railroads being compared tended to have the same characteristics. What is clear is that numerous mechanical departments found Western Pacific cost statistics so impressive that they sent observers to California in an attempt to learn how the railroad managed to maintain its motive power at such low cost.

When a locomotive was released for service, the engine crew that took it up the hill out of Oroville had been qualified by Electro-Motive instructors or by the road foreman of engines. In the beginning, 10 trips were usually assumed to be sufficient, although this tended to vary. No enginemen operated alone without considerable instruction, and unqualified firemen were not permitted to go with them up the hill although exceptions were allowed coming west out of Portola since there was little for them to do on the downgrade. Delays on the road were sometimes occasioned by engine crew failure to make the proper checks of battery-charging ammeters, starting contactors, ground relays, and overspeed trips before leaving the terminal.

Firemen sometimes started the locomotive without making the proper check of starting contactors and ground relays after they had started the engines. Considerable learning was necessary in a relatively short interval, and the crewmen sometimes forgot how to properly place an engine back on the line or to properly start the diesel engine. Such forgetfulness met with considerable patience since it was understood that some of these men might have been on weeks of steam runs in the interval since their last run on a diesel.

Road foremen accompanied the crews, whenever possible, and quizzed them as to their knowledge of safety switches, how to reset ground relays, and to restart an engine when it died. Terminal tests were made to learn if the crews were making the proper inspection, and this could be done by manually tripping out ground relays and then checking with the crew at the yard to determine if they had noted the ground relays were out. Road foremen kept a notebook record of the men whom they had qualified, and of the occasions on which they had reviewed these procedures. In 1954 Electro-Motive Instruction Car No. 100 had been on the railroad at least twice, and Gleason

When the Canyon shuts down, the yards fill up. A train on the ground below Keddie occasions this collection of rolling stock at Portola on the morning of July 24, 1979.
Virgil Staff

Twenty-seven hundred horses in dynamic roll downgrade through the Feather River Canyon at Virgilia on March 27, 1960. This was the standard paint scheme for all road freight locomotives after August 1949. Nose and center panels were in Duco Orange 254-6273 with upper and lower panels in Dulux Aluminum smudge-resistant enamel 166-23698 to simulate the stainless-steel panels on passenger units. Roofs, trucks, and the two front-end nose stripes were in black and pilot zebra stripes were in alternate black and orange. **Don Hansen**

observed to Munson that "Our engineers are among the best trained of the railroads."

By October 1942, the qualification of men was completely the responsibility of the road foremen, and no particular number of trips was required. A book record was maintained at the roundhouse of the men qualified by the road foremen, and when a crew was called, the roundhouse foreman consulted his record. If the crew was not qualified, the road foreman was notified to ride with these men. In the event that a road foreman was not available, the next crew out was called in which case the unqualified crew was paid runaround.

In October 1942, O'Neill was able to report that up to that date operational problems were minimal and no failures due to engine trouble had been reported. "What troubles we have had have been due to substitute material and engineering defects," he said. "We have not lost a cylinder liner, cylinder head or a piston and the locomotives are all nearing the 80,000-mile mark."

The mechanical department never ceased to display renewed confidence in these 5,400-hp machines, and Cuyler often stated his pride in the ease with which Western Pacific crews had become knowledgeable in their operation and maintenance. The number of road foremen had early been increased to nine in order to assure sufficient supervision. As late as 1945 the road foremen were making up to 10 trips a month with the diesels, and one heard comments that in addition to their steam power responsibilities there was not much time to maintain the records. Road foremen did not arrive home for days, and sometimes weeks, and the necessity of watching the handling of the air tended to keep these men on the power long after all crews had been qualified.

When the 901 Class first arrived in Oroville, it was apparently placed on turns between that terminal and Portola. On January 18, 1942, the first 5,400-hp diesel was dispatched east of Portola. In these early weeks the diesels were ordinarily placed on No. 62's connection. No. 62 had heavier tonnage

THE DIESEL MAKES ITS IMPACT 63

than No. 54, and with a noon arrival at Salt Lake, the power could be turned back on first 61 at 2:00 P.M. or second 61 at 6:00 P.M. The plan was to get the power on fast, heavy runs and to build up the greatest amount of mileage possible in the smallest amount of time. To reduce layover at Oroville, the power arriving on No. 61 would often turn back to Portola with No. 54, where it would be turned and returned to Oroville in time to cut in on No. 62 for the Eastern Division and Salt Lake. Three trips to Bieber were allowed after which the power must be returned to Oroville.

In early 1942 the aim was to complete an Oroville–Salt Lake–Elko–Salt Lake–Oroville run after which the units would receive six to eight hours of maintenance. No one was quite certain of what the maintenance schedule should be, and Cuyler was feeling his way carefully. July 1943 had Eastern Division Superintendent John J. Duggan and Chief Dispatcher H.M. Yoe concerned about the shortage of power and the difficulty of keeping on top of westbound business which had necessitated putting on a considerable number of oil burners in coal-burning territory.

Cuyler agreed to let the diesels coming from Oroville make two additional round trips between Elko and Salt Lake which would give them 2,500 miles between inspections. He momentarily considered this the very limit and diesels would be closely watched on the third trip out of Salt Lake to assure they had sufficient lubricating oil and water. Elko roundhouse would keep a record of how many times the power had turned, and the chief dispatchers and roundhouse foremen would confer to be sure that all westbound tonnage was moved out of Salt Lake with a minimum of delay.

By the end of February 1944, Cuyler was deleting the 2,500–3,000 mileage mark as the period between inspections, and authorizing any mileage as long as the power returned to Oroville every seven days. This would enable his forces to inspect each unit once each month, with four inspections or maintenance periods on any locomotive per month. This gave the chief dispatcher more leeway since he could now move the power about as he chose as long as it was returned to Oroville in seven days.

The westbound San Jose Turn out of Stockton proceeds through Altamont Pass at about MP 64. It is a slow crawl, or a fast walk, and the hills ring with the roar of F units straining mightily at the drawbars. This particular effort took place on May 1, 1966.
Virgil Staff

Grooming the WP's Iron Horses

The locomotive facilities scattered over the Western Pacific system underwent drastic change as steam gave way to diesel. The men and machines changed, gradually, as well but one element remained: a fundamental dedication to the task of keeping the trains moving. Here at the Sacramento shops, workmen are installing a pilot-type plow. As steam power was retired, an increasing number of diesels received this application.
H. A. O'Rullian

Oroville Serviced the Diesels...

Unit 921-D on the table at Oroville roundhouse in the middle 1950s, above. As of 1943, Oroville became an 18-stall facility, the home of the 251-class big articulateds. It became the chief point for diesel running repairs until construction of the Stockton Shops. Photo at right shows passenger power truck repairs at Oroville in the early 1950s.
Both: H. A. O'Rullian

Change at Wendover...

The displacement of steam power by diesels had its impact at Wendover, Utah, on the east leg of the system. View, above, of Wendover roundhouse was taken by Guy L. Dunscomb in 1939. At that time the roundhouse had eight stalls and a 120-foot table capable of handling 401-class Challengers. Shortly before the retirement of the Wendover roundhouse, upper right, crews constructed a small diesel house for switch engine inspections. The two-story hotel-depot is to the left.
H. A. O'Rullian

During the 1950s and 1960s most heavy diesel repairs were handled at the Sacramento Shops. At right are two prime movers awaiting installation, while below is a view of truck dismantlement in the late 1940s.
Both: H. A. O'Rullian

At Sacramento Shops...

The old blacksmith shop at Sacramento saw progressively less activity with the coming of the diesels. It was gone by the early 1970s.
Author's Collection

Pounded and pummeled by some of the hardest jobs on rails, these Western Pacific F units rest at Stockton Shops, 1970. Dents, dirt, scrapes, cracks—these weary warhorses have them all, a badge of honor on a hardworking railroad. Units 918-A and 913-A are on the pit track, above, while we see the 3002, 758 and 913-A at right.

Both: Richard Steinheimer

Here we see the Sacramento Shops in the early 1970s, by which time they had become the chief car shops of the railroad.
Virgil Staff

Oakland Roundhouse ... Gone With the Zephyr

By the early 1960s the 10-stall #5 Adeline Street Roundhouse at Oakland was in a deteriorated state. The roof leaked, many windows were out, but the old place kept on until after the demise of the *California Zephyr*. Then, at 9:00 a.m. on July 20, 1970, the facility was taken out of service and ultimately torn down.
Virgil Staff

The *California Zephyr* normally received a wash job at Oakland and at Portola. Here, on December 2, 1947, we witness the 803 getting its face washed at the Oakland passenger facility. **Western Pacific: John H. Kaler** January 2, 1965, produced a holiday reprieve, below, for this selection of power resting between assignments at the Stockton roundhouse. **Virgil Staff**

Engineer Vern Brain, with 7,500 horsepower at the head end of the eastbound GGM, triumphantly climbs the .80 percent grade of the Altamont just west of MP 53 on May 10, 1970. Engine 915A heads up the train. **Virgil Staff**

By June 1944, the engines were being run up to 4,000 miles between maintenance periods, and on return to Oroville they were held as long as needed since they arrived for maintenance only three or four times a month. Ideally, not more than two locomotives per day were wanted at the roundhouse, but bunching sometimes occurred since diesels also ran back and forth from the Inside Gateway, and were sometimes turned back from Portola due to mechanical trouble.

Eastern and Western Division dispatchers were in regular contact, and in October 1944 there were numerous cases of turning diesels between Winnemucca and Portola in order to avoid bunching the power at Oroville. Holding the power in Oroville as long as was necessary was to be preferred to trying to rush it through in two or three hours which Cuyler considered detrimental to the efficiency of the men, and which generally had caused numerous other problems on a number of railroads.

In December 1944, it was decided that the mileage record was too difficult and cumbersome for the dispatchers to watch. Locomotives could now run for 12 days before returning to Oroville for maintenance and inspection. It was theorized that locomotives would be freshly serviced every 12 days, and Eastern Division dispatchers would get one locomotive back to Oroville every 24 hours, where it would be held for eight or nine hours. When a diesel was dispatched from Oroville, a telegram would be sent to the Eastern Division dispatcher informing him of the date the engine had to be returned for maintenance and federal inspection. If the engine arrived in Oroville but could not be completely serviced, it was placed on a run to Portola, but was not in any situation to be allowed to run further east. What actually was happening was that the diesels were making two 12-day trips out of Oroville and one six-day trip due to the ICC inspections.

On occasions the power ran up to 16 days and it was becoming difficult to hold anyone responsible at the maintenance pit when a unit failed due to material breakage or contacts becoming dirty. In July 1945, three 10-day periods per month were initiated. After that time the power working out of Oroville managed to arrive from three to five times a month for inspection and maintenance.

If the power was not spaced on the westbound trips, it tended to bunch at Oroville. It therefore became necessary to turn the power at Portola to avoid excessive delays and awaiting turn for servicing in Oroville. In an attempt not to bunch up at Oroville, some power typically ran from Oroville to Winnemucca, and then back to Portola for a run to Winnemucca as a Portola turn. In August 1945, there were numerous cases of turning diesels east at Portola, thus delaying Mikado steam power waiting to get out of Portola. Westbound business in August 1945 was exceedingly heavy and the railroad was running two diesels each day west out of Winnemucca and three west out of Wendover. In an attempt to get the power back onto longer runs, Duggan recommended that they again work the diesels between Oroville and Salt Lake, and in October 1945 they began running between Oroville and Salt Lake whenever the layover was not unreasonable.

The diesels would be used on the RT and CFS trains from Salt Lake City to Oroville which put them into Oroville about 12 hours apart. Out of Oroville they handled fruit blocks and other symbol trains into Salt Lake, but sometimes turned at Wendover and were sent west to avoid train delays at Wendover and long layovers at Salt Lake City. In all this hassle to build mileage and to get the power back to the terminal for maintenance, Cuyler concluded that 90 percent availability was about all that any railroad could expect to get. If a railroad had much higher availability over a period of years, either its records were inaccurate or the proper work was not being done which would show up on the records of failure.

8

Dynamic Brakes on the FT

OF CONSIDERABLE INTEREST has been the electric holding brake installed on the 901 Class of FT locomotives. This regenerative brake, or dynamic brake as it came to be called, employed the principle that a moving armature, being similar to moving a coil through a magnetic field, would generate voltage due to cutting magnetic lines of force set up by the traction motor field poles, when these were excited by current from the main generators. If a load or "grid" was connected to the armature circuit, current would flow causing the traction motor to "hold back" or resist rotation like any other generator. Mechanical power from the wheels was converted to electrical power and dissipated in the grids (resistors)—the final product being heat.

In regenerative braking, current was supplied only to the fields, and not to the fields and the armatures. Since the traction motors were then working as generators and not as motors, they acted as a drag. The power input was coming from the axles, and the axles were being turned by the weight of the locomotive and trailing consist descending the grade.

A DC motor suitably connected with its shaft being turned by another motor, will generate voltage. In dynamic braking, the resultant current was dissipated through heavy 7.44 ohm resistors in the form of grids so constructed as to provide a greater linear radiating surface. The amount of current that flowed was dependent upon the resistance of the grid, and a suitable grid would only allow a given amount of amperes. On the 901 Class, the Brake Warning Relay was set to pick up at 440 amperes and drop out at 430 amperes. This amperage could not be exceeded without burning out the air-cooled grids.

The 901 Class possessed a two-position electric holding brake with positions B-1 and B-2, in addition to controller

The dynamic brakes on the 901 class of FT were nothing but trouble. Cuyler had them disconnected.
H. A. O'Rullian

positions RUN and OFF. B-1 position was set for 36 mph and B-2 for 25 mph. Maximum speed in the Feather River Canyon was 30 mph, with engineers usually running from 25-30 mph in the summer, and 20-25 mph in the winter. The brake was considered adequate in the winter, but could not be used in the summer because the B-1 position was established too high, whereas the B-2 position was set too low. This brake was therefore too slow for maximum speeds in the canyon. B-1 would not hold a train below 33-39 mph, and B-2 was nonfunctional below 14 mph.

The brake was never very functional, and became a serious detriment to operation since the speed range was impractical. From the very beginning, the grids were constantly burning out due to their close clearance with the body of the unit. The grill, which sat over the grids, tended to sag from heat so that the two came in contact with consequent grounding and burning out of grids. All dynamic brakes were cut out in early 1943, the handles were removed, and signs posted: ELECTRIC BRAKE ON THIS LOCOMOTIVE CANNOT BE USED.

The chief reason this brake was discontinued was on account of the engineering design which had the high-voltage circuit or power circuit hooked on the dynamic brake circuit in such a way that any ground on the dynamic brake would also be on the power circuit. These units had established what Cuyler called a "floating ground condition that was only apparent when the locomotive was working to capacity." Ground relays tripped out, and generators and traction motors flashed. Moreover, the alkali dust and salt from the salt beds of the Eastern Division had settled on the grids, and heavy rains on the Western Division soaked the entire circuit. Salt and water is an excellent conductor, the effects of which undoubtedly caused grounds with consequent ground relay action and repeated detriment to generators and traction motors.

The 901 Class of FT locomotive possessed only one traction motor blower per truck, and was equipped with an inadequate grid blower motor. There was no dynamic brake interlock, and engineers who allowed the engine brakes to set up, while rolling in dynamic, learned the danger of sliding wheels when the dynamic brake and engine air brakes were used at the same time. Field loop jumpers enabled the control of all units from the cab, as long as the jumper had been removed from its receptacle at the rear of the rear unit, thus allowing the shorting bar to close the loop circuit.

The Western Pacific desired a rheostatic-controlled dynamic brake such as that possessed on the 904 Class. This variable electric holding brake was a much more sophisticated device than the old type of holding brake, and possessed both transition and electric brake control, as well as dynamic brake interlock. Additional to the usual power contactors and three brake contactors, the 904 Class power possessed a cam switch which enabled the complete isolation of brake and power circuits. In the position for power, the motor armatures and fields were connected to the main generator, while for braking the motor armatures were each separately connected to their grids, and the motor fields of each locomotive section were connected in series to the main generator armature, thus causing the two circuits to be isolated from one another. A selector switch was provided which was to be set to agree with the number of sections composing the locomotive.

Of great importance was the inability of the old-style, non-variable brake to operate with the new variable brake. If the Western Pacific operated 901 Class units without the two-position brake, there would be no dynamic braking for that train. If a rebuilt two-position brake was installed on the 901 Class, there could be no dynamic braking from these units should they be mixed with those of the 904 or 907 classes.

In 1950 and 1951, WP forces removed and retired all dynamic brake equipment on the 901 Class, and closed the dynamic brake louvers with solid plates. Following this removal, arrangements were made with Electro-Motive, and a variable-speed, grid-type dynamic brake was installed like that found on engines 904-912. Completion of this work took place in July 1954.

The new holding brake was considered to be conspicuously successful, and was used with air, and without retainers, on the third subdivision of the Feather River Canyon without any severe slack action. With respect to slack action, and contrary to what had been believed by many, the amount of tonnage had no bearing on the use of air and dynamic brake without retainers, although it was always necessary in the early years to employ retainers over certain portions of the fourth subdivision of the NCE regardless of the use of the dynamic brake.

Unit 903 was fresh out of the paint shop on September 18, 1947. Earlier paint had become badly deteriorated, and officials wanted to try a livery in Duco Orange 259-19151 with Duco Gloss Black roof and trucks as seen on this page and the preceding page. FT 901 was later completed in a slightly different orange. Note the Stimsonite reflector numbers and the treatment of accent lines.

H. A. O'Rullian

9

The Decline of Availability

IN JUNE 1942, after only five months of service, a serious trend was observed in the form of leaking cylinder liners on the 901 Class. When removed from the cylinders, it was noted that the liner seals appeared to be "dead," and to be composed of a kind of rubber without any elastic qualities. Original specifications had called for seal rings composed of neoprene, but the supply had become exhausted, and shut off by the War Production Board, and a Perbunen seal, which was not as good, had been substituted.

The Electro-Motive people appealed to the WPB for permission to return to the neoprene, but in the meantime the 901 Class had been assembled during the period of the Perbunen rings. Failure of the liner and cylinder head seals presented a very serious challenge considering the amount of business the railroad was compelled to handle.

As the engines became tied up in the shops for renewal of seals, O'Neill became increasingly annoyed that the company had not been notified of this condition so that it could have maintained a larger store of seals on hand. Ordinarily, an engine would run from Oroville to Salt Lake and return without adding water to the cooling system. But the power was losing water in the engine-cooling tanks, and delays became an everyday occurrence when it became necessary to water the diesels at every terminal, and sometimes more often.

While taking the 902 apart in July 1942, the machinists noted it possessed the old-style wrist pin bushings applied at the factory. These had been considered as unfit for use for a long time, and in their place a new bronze-type bushing had been developed which was considered very satisfactory. These would need to be ordered and progressively applied at Oroville, doing two to four cylinders every time a locomotive returned to Oroville for servicing and maintenance.

On the 902, the bushings had all been galled and there was as much as one-quarter of an inch wear in them due to this. Cuyler correctly assumed that these locomotives were equipped with a bushing in the gear train which within time would shell out. And while these locomotives were new, it would shortly become necessary to renew the gears and bushings in all of the engines, depending of course on how soon the old bushings wore out.

Engines were held for renewal of seals as soon as leakage was noted since there was fear that some other portion of the engine might become damaged. By September 1942, the Oroville forces had received at least two kinds of seals for replacement of the Perbunen variety—one of which was satisfactory, and the other of which was inferior to the Perbunen type. This latter type had the appearance of a moulded seal with a ridge. An order of these had been received some two months before, and when placed in the 903 had leaked so badly that it was necessary to again change them out.

In these early years, Cuyler's loyalty to Electro-Motive was always beyond reproach, but he did state on one occasion that he hoped EMD would send him only good seals. By this time the water systems were getting dirty, with seepage of oil and carbon into the water system from rings and cylinder head seals, and the water glasses were reported as becoming very dirty.

Some seals gave less than two weeks of service, and on one occasion they began leaking not more than two hours out of the terminal. To replace these seals it was necessary to remove the cylinder head and liner which took considerable labor and held the locomotive out of service for a considerable time since each locomotive contained 64 cylinders.

These rings were composed, at least in part, of synthetic rubber, with insufficient rubber to maintain elasticity. The mechanical department was informed that the substitute ring was a good ring, and it was suggested that perhaps they were not being installed correctly. Cuyler replied that there was only one way to apply these seals in an engine, and that one seal always appeared to be satisfactory, while the other did not.

In late April or early May 1943, a new trend began with the cracking of two cylinder heads on one of the 901 Class, and by November the Oroville forces were involved in wholesale removal of cylinder heads. At least initially the defective seal rings were considered responsible. Due to this condition the water from the cooling system was sucked out and blown up through the exhaust stacks, causing the engine to run low on water before it was discovered. This caused the cylinder heads to crack, and in addition became the direct cause of valves burning off at the valve head. Change-out of cylinder heads at this time contributed to a somewhat lower availability, although the heads had received between 150,000 and 190,000 miles before failure.

Finally, in August 1944, Electro-Motive informed railroads with 567 engines that they had discovered an unauthorized change in foundry practices that might have caused water leaks in the injector wells. These cylinder heads had been manufactured since June 1944, and a program of inspection was advised to prevent seepage of water with consequent pollution of the crankcase oil from such cracks. A new synthetic rubber seal ring had been perfected for installation beneath the head of the injector to prevent the possibility of water seepage up the injector well and into the lubricating oil. This change of design embodied a chill ring at the base of the injector well, and it was noted that these rings could be expected to cause water leaks at this point after an indefinite number of hours of operation.

By the middle of 1943, the Oroville forces were recording excessive amounts of leakage on the accessory end of all 567-A engines. These required constant attention and "tightening up," and had been largely remedied by Electro-Motive on engines built after November 1, by the installation of a baffle or deflector plate in the cylinder head cover frame. These were supplied free of charge and were applied to cylinder head covers at the blower end of the freight diesels. All 567-A engines had received these plates by the middle of June 1944 which remedied, at least temporarily, the leaking of oil from beneath the covers.

Then, in 1944, American railroads had an epidemic of broken compression rings which touched the Western Pacific upon delivery of the 907 Class in the summer of that year. Some locomotives ran on three units, while others were held at Oroville from 15 to 20 hours when broken rings were found on the pistons of these engines. The burden was chiefly on the maintenance crew since the railroad possessed only seven diesel machinists at Oroville. No problems appeared on the 901 Class, but the situation was awkward and detrimental to business since it was only with great difficulty that the engines could be prepared for service.

With the help of Electro-Motive, Western Pacific forces made the necessary corrections including the application of heavy wall compression rings which did not break, whereas the previous type of rings would break in one trip. EMD made an extensive study of this situation and decided that it was due to some condition which caused sufficient ring slapping to fracture the rings. One of the causes was the type of fuel being used at the time. Wartime limitations made it impossible to obtain fuel with the usual high-cetane ratings and low end point, and the fuel oil being delivered to the Western Pacific in 1944 went as low as 42 in cetane rating, with end point as high as 750.

The third step in obviating ring breakage was to apply a new-style, cast-iron ring that was wider and heavier than what was presently in use. This ring was most successful. Concurrently, all of the cylinder heads were defective and were likely to crack at any time. This was what happened to engine 907 which lost two units on September 10 due to cylinder heads being cracked on the units. Defective heads could not be found by inspection, and a cylinder head might crack one hour after it had left the maintenance terminal. It has already been noted that Electro-Motive developed a seal to be placed around the injector with the idea of trapping the water in the injector well, between the seal and the bottom seat of the injector. These were applied when received and apparently did aid in keeping the water in the engine from draining into the crankcase.

EMD tests had apparently shown that prewar fuel had a pressure of 100 to 140 pounds whereas the fuel in 1944 ran over 300 pounds in idling position. Poor fuels produced this "wallop" or sudden rise in pressure which was so severe that they caused a "flutter" or vibration that was believed would cause the rings to fracture. Electro-Motive research indicated that a stop or horseshoe on the power piston of the governor would decrease this rate of pressure, thus relieving the piston and rings of some of the sudden shock. This stop decreased the rate of pressure rise in the cylinder during injection and firing since it prevented the injector rack from opening to its previously set 5/8 wide-open rack position during transition or throttle movement, and thus inhibiting the engine from going into an overloading position, which it did formerly until the load had balanced between the engine and the generator. These horseshoes were supplied by Electro-Motive and applied at Oroville.

Mason watched the availability statistics with an eagle eye. His concern must have been considerable when in early September 1942 he received a letter from O'Neill stating his regret that it would be necessary to hold each of the 901 Class for from eight to 10 days to correct a defect in the gear train bushings and stub shafts of these locomotives. Investigation of the 903 had revealed that this locomotive possessed a soft stub shaft which seized and froze in the bushing.

Thin-walled, gear-shaft bushings had been applied whereas thick-walled bushings and carborized stub shafts for the idler gear were necessary. Thin-walled bushings were not sufficiently heavy for a 16-cylinder engine, and would shell out in time. Electro-Motive sent a representative to supervise this work, but in the meantime the Western Pacific was losing locomotive availability with some power in the shops and other power working on only three units.

10

How Much Can a Loco Lug?

SOME CONSIDERATION has previously been given to tonnage ratings and how they were developed on the Western Pacific. The second subdivision between Stockton and Oroville was the easiest for steam, and C-43 Consolidations frequently lugged 74-car freights, or heavier, between Oroville and Stockton. The MK-60-71 Mikados, and GS-64-77 Northerns would take 2,500 tons westbound over the Altamont, and between 1,800 and 1,900 tons up the Feather River Canyon. M-80 "Little Mallets" usually worked the Canyon with 2,200 tons and M-137-151 251 Class articulateds would drag 4,000 tons.

On the 2.2 percent grade between Greenville and Almanor, the 251 Class would handle 1,900 tons, or 2,200 tons southbound on the 1.80 percent from Little Valley to Halls Flat. These were drag ratings and ultimately were found to be somewhat slower than the longtime ratings of the diesels.

FT 908DC swings downgrade through the Altamont hills over Bridge 55.92 on July 17, 1959. Since the FTs tended to run in twos or fours, one can assume this train has not more than 2,750 tons trailing, or about 675 tons less than could be lugged by a brace of two F-7s.   **Don Hansen**

West of Portola station, the 336, one of 10 MK60-71 Big Tank Mikes, chomps off with the confidence of 71,300 pounds of tractive power. These bruisers could handle 6,000 tons on the Second Subdivision, but spent most of their years working between Portola and Winnemucca. The diesels which replaced these steamers were the subject of constant testing for lugging ability, as had been the steam power in earlier years. **Wilbur C. Whittaker**

In 1942 the railroad operated a series of tonnage tests to determine capabilities of the 5,400-hp locomotives. Electro-Motive's suggestions were initially followed, but the tests were made as soon after delivery as possible since the builder really didn't know what the power would do. Tonnage ratings established on the system timetables were usually drag ratings under the best possible conditions. North line winter ratings, based on experience, would be somewhat less. Moreover, North line ratings were somewhat less than when steam was gone since steam helpers operated best at lower speeds than the diesels were capable of running for any considerable length of time.

Cuyler always said that the builders had a tendency to overestimate the abilities of their diesels. When the first 5,400-hp diesels were delivered in late 1941 and early 1942, they were said to be worth between 4,870 and 4,920 tons up the one percent of the canyon. This figure was not taken very seriously by the Western Pacific, and in fact, O'Neill predicted they wouldn't "do it" without a great deal of trouble. Cuyler and the road foremen through the canyon found that this kind of tonnage might be possible if the power could be started at Oroville and run straight through into Portola. But with trains sidetracked frequently, one could expect damage to generators and traction motors when a train tried to move out of the siding. Summer ratings were set for 3,900 tons with 4,000 tons in winter. Ordinarily, 3,900 to 4,000 tons could be started in the third notch. Any more than this required bringing the throttle out to number five position which built up a high amperage in the electrical circuits and burned out the brushes on the commutators.

Cuyler and the road foremen had begun running tonnage tests in 1942 and decided the power, with 62:15 gear ratio, would not handle 4,920 tons up the canyon since there were difficulties in starting 4,000 tons. Reverse curves and the degree of curvature built up so much resistance that it became very difficult to start a train of over 4,000 tons. Cuyler's rating enabled trains to maintain 17-18 mph, whereas with 4,950 tons, the speed would drop to 15 mph or less. On one test train with 4,300 tons, the men couldn't get more than 14 mph out of the power. With the sustained grade of 117 miles, and temperatures being high in summer, the motors became so hot it became necessary to reduce the tonnage. Motors, in fact, began to smoke.

Limitation was therefore set at 3,900 tons in summer because of the heat which radiated from the rocks of the canyon. In winter the air was cooler, and the curves were damp which cut down the resistance.

On the 2.2 percent grade of the High Line, the rating was set at 2,000 tons since any greater tonnage would drag the speed down below 13-14 mph, and would burn out traction motors and cause flashovers. Eastern Division tonnage ratings were increased to 4,250 tons which could be maintained at 17 mph on the long and fairly straight one-percent grades of that division.

In 1948 a series of tonnage runs and tests took place over the railroad to again determine what kind of runs could be made at satisfactory speeds and without damage to electrical equipment. The first of these tests took place with train 53-NCE-22, engine 909, 81 loads, five empties, 6,535 tons, Winnemucca to Portola. At all times the 909 maintained a speed in excess of the danger point, with the lowest speed being 18 mph over Antelope Hill. Difficulty in starting this kind of tonnage on Antelope Hill could be expected, and Cuyler authorized 6,000 tons over the first and fourth subdivisions, westbound over the Eastern Division, if a road foreman was on board.

In August 1948, on the fourth subdivision of the Western Division, diesels were generally held to twice the Mallet tonnage. This was considered to be the most effective handling considering the fact that the small Mallet-type engines were being used as helpers. Through the canyon, eastbound fruit blocks usually were held to 3,700 tons, and other symbol trains were limited to 3,900 tons.

On September 15, 1948, Engineer C.G. Trumbo and Fireman J.F. Phillips handled train 1-61, engine 909, out of Salt Lake City with 55 loads, 38 empties, total 93, 5,568 tons. The 909 pulled out of Delle at 5:20 P.M. and arrived at MP 869, which is the top of the hill westbound, at 5:55 P.M., in a total time of 35 minutes. Continuous speed from Delle to MP 869 was 16 mph with throttle in run 8 transition 1. Train 1-61 never was in the overload area, and ran from Delle to Low in 41 minutes.

On the following day, train No. 78, engine 903, departed Wendover for Salt Lake City, with Engineer G.B. Gorham and Fireman L. Wakefield, on the head end of 89-5-94, 5,582 tons. No. 78 departed Wendover at 7:40 A.M. and reached the top of the hill at MP 864 at 9:27 A.M., arriving Low at 9:33 A.M. Total time consumed Clive to MP 864 was 30 minutes—Clive to west switch at Low, 33 minutes. Speed over the hill in No. 1 transition, run 8, was 17 mph, and at no time was the engine in or near the red overload area. A heavy wind was encountered from Delle to Lago which reduced the speed to about 38 mph.

Engine 909 on 1-62 with 90-4-94, 5,598 tons, ran the Eastern Division's third subdivision in November 1948 with its speed cut down to the minimum low speed or maximum load permitted on the traction motors. The tonnage rating in this territory was raised to 6,000 tons, so that this train had 400 tons under the new rating.

With the arrival of the 913 Class in 1950, a new series of tests was required. These F-7s possessed D-27 traction motors, allowing a minimum continuous speed of 11 mph as compared to the FT power with D7K traction motors allowing 15 mph in minimum continuous service. On March 31, 1950, engine 914ABCD departed Wendover westbound with 74-26-100, 6,434 actual tons. The train was mostly loads of steel and coal, which made an excessively long train for 100 cars, and was helped from Wendover to Spruce by the 901DC. After leaving Wendover, there was a strong wind, and some rain, but the power maintained a speed of 19 to 21 mph from Wendover to Silver Zone, with the throttle in No. 8, transition 1. Transition meter read from 565 to 600 amps but a greater part of the time it was precisely on 600 amps. The only time that this engine attempted to slip was on the sharp curves at Ola, Proctor, Clifside, and the Arnold's Loop, but when the throttle was reduced to No. 7 and sand was used on the curves, no more slipping was experienced. When this train was stopped at Elko to head into the crossover, its extreme length allowed it to hang over the two hogbacks so that Engineer Thompson was 10 minutes in trying to start again as he would come up against the load in No. 3 throttle and it would not move. In No. 4 throttle momentarily, the train still would not move so that slack had to be taken four or five times before the train was started.

On April 14, 1950, Engineer Seth Manca took engine 915ABCD out of Wendover on a heavy NCE. Leaving Wendover the train consisted of 91-9-100, 6,872 actual tons with two units of engine 906 helping to Shafter. There was no slipping up Wendover Hill, although some sand was used on the sharp curves. Speed of the train from Wendover to Silver Zone was 17 mph with the throttle in No. 8 position. The train was reduced at Shafter to 66 cars, 5,685 actual tons, and went single from Shafter to Hogan at a speed of 15 mph from the bottom of the hill up the one percent to Hogan.

Train 61-16 with 79-6-85, 6,484 actual, 6,759 friction tons, departed Wendover on May 17, 1950, with the 916ABCD. Highest ampere record of the 913 showed 775 where 825 was the danger point on continuous operation. The engine never operated within 50 points of this danger line, and it was not necessary to operate under the short time rating at any time. Road Foreman of Engines C.F. Fields rode this day and it was his opinion that he would not have been able to start this train if it had been stopped at any point on the grade.

Back on the first subdivision on March 28, 1950, Engineer Boyd R. Davis took a big train westbound out of Winnemucca consisting of 84-4-88, 6,828 actual, or 7,138 friction tons. No. 61 was in the clear at Jungo and started from the 74 car board east of Jungo with the engine working in No. 8 position, and bucking a heavy wind, all the way up Antelope Hill. Sand was used often but the engine never slipped. The F-7 made 14 mph all the way up the hill, and was 40 minutes making the climb.

April 6, 1950, brought the usual unsettled weather conditions to the fourth subdivision. Engine 919 on the first 153-6 GWS-4, with 60-12-72, 3,655 friction tons, slipped badly between Little Valley and Halls Flat, and finally stalled in the vicinity of K-79.5, after which the train was doubled into Halls Flat. Road Foreman Norman Roberts was on the engine and he recommended these engines be given less than 3,600 friction tons until a little later when weather conditions would be more settled. This was playing it very close but it does indicate something of the F-7 capability.

Enginemen considered the 913 Class to be somewhat slippery. Overall weight on the drivers was somewhat greater on the booster units than on the cabs, and there was considerable discussion about the cab unit weight not being effectively balanced over the drivers. According to Road Foreman G.M. Lorenz, "with heavy tonnage and these new engines pulling high amperage at low speed, there is a great tendency for slipping in throttle positions 8, 7, and 6 under adverse rail conditions, and I might state that there is no more helpless piece of machinery than one of these locomotives when they start slipping."

The last two units of a four-unit consist were inclined to be quite slippery, and this could be supposed to be caused by too great a volume of air emitted from sand pipes which was found to have a tendency to blow much of the sand off the rail. If it is true, as has often been stated, that on delivery only the sanders on the forward units were operational, then it can be understood why the rear units tended to be slippery since little sand would remain on the rail for the third and fourth units. Finally, Lorenz reported that "as one unit slips this puts a proportional load on the following unit which causes it to slip and the sequence is carried through on all four units. I have observed this action very closely."

The series of tests taking place on two round trips made between Keddie and Bieber in late May and early June 1950 were for the purpose of determining adhesion, and whether or not consideration should be given to so-called 65:12 gear ratios, in lieu of the 62:15, for the third and fourth subdivision power to be purchased on the next order. The railroad was represented by Superintendent of the Western Division G.W. Curtis, Assistant Superintendent of Motive Power Cuyler, Electrical Supervisor R.F. Carter, and Mechanical Supervisor R.E. Schriefer. Also along were three Electro-Motive representatives. A recording ammeter connected in the main generator circuit enabled the calculation of resistance on grades, and made possible the establishment of maximum tonnage ratings.

On May 27, 1950, Extra 919 East ran from Keddie to Bieber with 42 cars, 2,975 actual tons, 3,035 friction tons. Throttle position was No. 8, transition 1 for the entire ruling grade. The train left Greenville at 20 mph but speed on the 2.2 percent slowed to a low of 10.5 mph at K20, 21, 22 and 10 mph at K23.16 and K24. Amperes at K24 were at 830, or overloading the traction motors.

Train No. 153 with the 919ABCD ran from Bieber to Keddie on May 28, 1950, with 46-39-85, 3,781 actual tons, 4,056 friction tons. Ruling grade was 1.8 percent compensated between K95 and K78. On the entire ruling grade, throttle position was No. 8, transition 1. Speed was between 9.5 and 13.5 mph with amperage running between 660 and 825.

On the same day the 919DCBA ran from Keddie to Bieber on train No. 154 with 62-7-69, 3,298 actual tons, 3,493 friction tons. Ruling grade was 2.2 percent compensated from K15 to K25. Throttle position ran No. 8, transition 1 for the entire ruling grade. Percentage of adhesion, based on train resistance, was figured at 19.0 percent, with a factor of adhesion of 5.3 percent. Speed reached as low as 9 mph and ran in overload, at K23, with 875 amperes. More tonnage could have been handled but would only have increased the slipping and sanding.

On May 29, 1950, the 919ABCD handled train 153-GFS27 southbound out of Bieber with 52-44-96, 4,180 actual, 4,510 friction tons. Ruling grade was 1.8 percent compensated from K95 to K78. Throttle position was in No. 8, transition 1 for the entire ruling grade. Percentage of adhesion was figured at 19.7 percent with a factor of adhesion of 5.1 percent. Traction motors were overloaded most of the way with amperage usually running between 850 and 860, and speed getting down as low as 9 mph.

Prior to these test trips the Western Pacific was rating these engines at 2,500 friction tons eastward and 3,600 friction tons westward. Almost immediately, the ratings were raised to 3,500 friction tons eastward and 4,500 friction tons westward with these tonnages to be the absolute maximum friction tonnage rating to avoid excessive slipping and danger of damage to traction motors. This represented a considerable tonnage increase, and the chief dispatcher would regulate the individual train loads in accordance with conditions. If trains were ahead of time and the tonnage was available, they could be given the maximum. But if the trains were late, it would be necessary to hold somewhat under these ratings. Road foremen expended considerable time in that territory instructing enginemen on the proper handling of these locomotives with the heavier tonnage.

In July 1950, another series of tests was run with the F-7s to determine precisely what they could be expected to do up the Feather River Canyon between Oroville and Keddie. Train 2/54 with 104-5-109, 5,816 friction tons, departed Oroville Yard on July 19 with Engineer Herb Berg and Fireman Burk. Observers present were John Flynn, Carter, Cuyler, and T.D. Hunter. Engine 913 made a top speed of 30 mph at MP 206, ran 28 and 29 mph between MP 209 and 218 but started slowing at MP 219, and ran most of the way at 15 mph in No. 1 throttle, transition 1.

On July 20 the 913, with Engineer Kennedy and Fireman Bohannon, handled train No. 54 up the canyon with 115-7-122, 5,712 actual, 6,172 friction tons. Observers were Cuyler, Carter, Flynn, John McNally, and Norman T. Roberts. The fastest speed was 29 mph between Bidwell and MP 216, and they did 15 mph most of the trip, and continuously between MP 249-270. One stop was made at Paxton to test the ability to start on grade with this tonnage, and with very satisfactory results.

A third test was made out of Oroville on July 27, 1950, with 5,400-hp 909 on the 2/54. On this run, Engineer Herb Berg and Fireman O'Neill took 77-13-90, 4,472 actual tons, up the canyon with Carter, Cuyler, and Flynn as observers. With a considerable amount of slipping, the 909 pulled most of the hill in No. 8 throttle, transition 1, at a speed of 16 mph from MP 231 to Keddie. As a result of these tests, the tonnage was ultimately set for the canyon at 4,375 tons for the 5,400-hp locomotives, and at 5,500 tons for the 6,000-hp F-7s. North Line trains, with heavier tonnage than that already stated, would require helpers between Bieber and Halls Flat westbound, and between Keddie and Almanor eastbound.

Some adjustment of tonnage was required in the winter months due to icy condition of rails that prevailed throughout that period. Under storm conditions, several inches of snow and slush formed on the rail, and this was crushed under the wheels causing the engine to slip badly and lose momentum. When not storming, frost conditions could create the same problem. Trainmasters and road foremen watched this carefully and when weather conditions moderated, heavier tonnages were again handled. Tonnage ratings listed in the timetable were drag tonnages and were indications of about every pound that a locomotive could pull under the best conditions.

Helpers continued in use up the Inside Gateway, and Munson suggested a series of adhesion tests to learn precisely what a brace of five F-7s would do on the third and fourth subdivisions east out of Oroville.

On April 21-23, 1951, a series of three tests was run with a five-unit, 7,500-hp consist of the 916A, 918C, and 916BCD. Test No. 1 was uneventful, with Engineer Joe Burt taking the first 54-20 NCX19 with 107 loads and 17 empties, 7,136 actual tons, up the hill out of Oroville. Average speed was 14 mph, with some slipping throughout the entire distance, particularly in the vicinity of track oilers.

On Test No. 2, Engineer Bashford took the first 54-20 NCX19 out of Keddie with 71 loads and 17 empties, 4,247 actual tons. At the 48-car post west of Almanor they pulled the east drawbar from business car 105. All breaks were new but caused by flaws in the metal which finally caused it to fail under severe strain and heavy side-thrust each time the head end reversed direction on curves. Minimum speed on the 2.2 percent grade was below the minimum continuous rating, or approximately 9.6 mph, and 16.4 mph at K37 on the 1.5 percent grade. Total running time with the traction motors overloaded on the 2.2 percent grade was 35 minutes. Traction motors were overloaded on the entire 2.2 percent grade. Maximum load on traction motors, lead truck, was 930 amperes for the duration of five minutes. At that time the 916D was rated at 1,450 maximum horsepower output from the main generator, and average load on traction motors, lead truck, for this grade was 900 amperes, or 75 amperes over maximum continuous rating.

Test No. 3 saw Engineer Benz leaving Bieber on the first 153-22 GWS-20 with 88 loads and 13 empties, 5,135 actual tons. The train broke-in-two at K105, and again at K84.2—the first occurrence being a rear coupler knuckle seven cars back, and the second a draft pocket failure at the cheek plate, first car behind the locomotive. Examination revealed a 35 percent old fracture in the cheek plate. Two cars were set out and the train doubled to Halls Flat.

Traction motors were overloaded 90 percent of the time that the train was on the 1.8 percent grade, and the maximum load on the traction motors of the lead truck was 900 amperes for the duration of four minutes. Average load on the traction motors, lead truck 916D on this grade was 850 amperes, or 25 amperes over maximum continuous rating of this locomotive. The train made minimum speed of 13.1 mph on the 1.5 percent grade, and 9.6 mph on the 1.8 percent. Total time running with motors overloaded was 25 minutes on the 1.8 percent grade.

Gleason's comment, based on discussions with Cuyler, was that "it would appear that the tractive effort is reaching a critical pressure on drawbars and knuckles which would cause failure where undetectable weaknesses are present. As far as the locomotive and tonnage ratings set for this test trip are con-

Resting at Keddie between runs, F-7 913A awaits a call. This view, taken on December 30, 1972, looks west with Tunnel 1 of the NCE (leading to the Inside Gateway) to the far right, and the adjoining tracks leading to the wye and Tunnel 32.
Virgil Staff

cerned, the test indicates that the locomotive could successfully move these tonnages without danger to mechanical or electrical equipment. This test was very interesting from a standpoint of determining the practicability of using a locomotive consisting of more than four units and in determining whether or not knuckles and drawbars could withstand the terrific tractive effort exerted on heavy grades with heavy tonnages."

Basic conclusions derived from these tests were as follows: (1) It should be safe to drag rate five units on the third subdivision at 7,500 tons. The chief dispatcher's rating would permit 18-20 mph with 7,000 tons. (2) Test 2 train was obviously overloaded, and additional tests should be made with 4,200 or 4,300 friction tons. The drag rate on the 2.2 percent grade should be 4,100 tons, with the chief dispatcher's rating of perhaps 5,000 tons on the 1.8 percent grade between Little Valley and Halls Flat. Additional tests should probably be run, starting with 5,300 friction tons.

When the Morning Report brought bad news, Munson always searched out the causes. For example, on June 27, 1953, he wired to J.F. Lynch at Elko: "We are in bad repute because of performance of No. 17 [the *California Zephyr*] lately. Had another bad delay this morning at Garfield and Jungo. Let's get behind it and get them going again. Second CFS 26 breaking in two and doubling into Antelope did not help. JFL advise regarding actual tonnage on this train. What have tests shown in past as tonnage on Antelope hill westbound A-522."

Superintendent of the Eastern Division Jim Lynch immediately wired the following: "Second CFS-26 had 85-7-7208 actual 7,518 friction tons which is more tonnage than usually handled although no tonnage tests have been made on this subdivision. Train handled by engine 918DCBA which is rated at 8,000 tons. Train moving about 9 mph when drawbar broke at MP 492 on . . . third car behind engine. Conductor reports 33 PC old flaw. Engineer claims engine did not slip. This break-in-two occurred at point where there are reverse curves and weak drawbar would not stand the strain. B-305."

A second wire to Lynch then followed: "Is the rating on Antelope Hill westbound different from the rating on Wendover Hill westbound? Both appear to be compensated one percent and both long enough to preclude either being a velocity grade. A-136." Referring to the F7s, Lynch wired back: "D-239 Class engines have different rating westbound over Antelope Hill than they have on Wendover Hill. Westbound tonnage rating is 8,000 tons westbound on First Subdivision, 6,750 tons westbound on Third Subdivision. Antelope Hill is 9 miles long and presume tonnage rating established as it is with the idea that engines will not be required to work in red for excessive length of time even though overloaded. B-2." At this point Gleason terminated the exchange: "We agree with J.F. Lynch's B-2 [telegram] of July 1st, because as stated in our ETC-84 [telegram] of June 29th, the Antelope Hill westbound is only six miles in length according to contour maps that we have in this office, and a four-unit, D-239 Class engine should handle without difficulty as it would be operating in overload well within the short time rating. It has been our practice to take advantage of the short time overload rating on all short grades. ETC-88."

The question was renewed the following year. On April 1, 1954, Superintendent of Transportation Grant S. Allen wired Gleason: "Please advise circumstances on Extra 920-D West doubling the hill at Jungo. A-1." On the bottom of this mailgram is the following penciled note from Cuyler to Gleason: "Definitely nothing wrong with the engine—three units won't take 6,000 tons up that hill." Cuyler then wired Allen: "Your A-1 regarding Extra 920-D West doubling hill at Jungo. Train had 5,404 tons including friction. Tonnage rating for this district set at 8,000 tons for four units or 6,000 for three units. This was a three-unit locomotive. It is claimed that this rating is too high for the one percent, eight-mile Jungo hill. It will be necessary to make a test on this grade to determine proper tonnage, and I believe until this is done, tonnage rating should be reduced to 6,750 for four units in order to avoid delays of this nature. We will arrange to make tonnage test on this grade in the near future. ETC-33."

Allen replied: "According to the timetable the rating for four units of the 913 Class is 7,300 tons actual and with three units this would be 5,475 actual. Was the tonnage figured correctly?" Cuyler then informed Allen concerning the speed tractive effort specifications of the 901, 913 and 701 classes of diesel locomotives, and stated: ". . . the tractive effort is the same from 0 to 8 miles per hour and reduces after 8 miles an hour according to speed traveled. It is therefore our opinion that the figures given in our ETC-114 are correct."

Richard Shideler

11

Water and Other Problems

DURING WORLD WAR II, Western Pacific mechanical forces were so fully occupied with problems of maintenance and availability of steam and diesel power that little time was left for what might be termed "betterment." Terminals were jammed with tonnage, and delays were frequent on an essentially one-track main that carried trains in both directions rolling under authority of "19" and "31" orders. Enginemen going up the hill frequently found a train in every siding, and power was in such demand that it was not unusual for a big 251 Class 2-8-8-2 to lug its consist into Portola and then run back light to Oroville for a turn and another run up the canyon.

Steam of relatively small tractive effort frequently handled trains down the hill that could never have been budged in the other direction. With such huge tonnage tied on, easing into a water plug was of distressing importance since the missing of a plug by even a few inches meant cutting off and running to the next plug for water. Slides in the canyon caused crews to go dead and, on occasion, the crews sent out to replace them also went dead. Ed Cuyler's office was in Sacramento, but he was more likely to be found at Oroville, or Elko, or deep in the muck of the canyon on a derailment, or almost anywhere but Sacramento.

With the close of the war, a host of residual considerations demanded resolution, and interposition of new ones created a picture not unlike a jigsaw puzzle. Deferred maintenance, betterment, assignment of power, the construction and retirement of facilities relating to dieselization, and the necessary arrangements for faster schedules so close to the heart of President Whitman, all called for constructive, alert endeavor. Total mechanical forces during the first 15 days of January 1939 had been 589 for the Western Division and 203 for the Eastern.

Total forces in the mechanical department were undoubtedly at their high point during the first 15 days of January 1946 with 1,216 men on the Western Division and 435 on the Eastern. After this time, the reductions began to take their toll, with the first 15 days of February witnessing a drop to 1,620 men. These forces were spread as follows: Oakland 162, San Jose 7, Stockton 151, Sacramento 562, Oroville 261, Keddie 38, Westwood 7, Portola 132, Winnemucca 73, Elko 177, and Wendover 50.

The chief, immediate reductions which came with dieselization were at Keddie, Portola, Winnemucca, Elko, and Wendover, which dropped between 1948 and 1953 from 38 to 4, 87 to 55, 43 to 5, 120 to 74, and 35 to 2 respectively. These numbers continued to drop, helping preserve solvency during the low car-mile years of 1949, 1954, 1958, 1964, 1967, 1970, 1973, 1975, and 1976.

Equipment repair costs for the years 1948 through 1952 are indicative of mechanical department performance during the final years of dieselization. For steam locomotives, the average cost of repairs per locomotive mile stabilized at .6476, .4332, .4548, .5482, and .3803 respectively, with cost of repairs per pound of tractive effort at .1871, .1332, .0850, .0748, and .0876. For the diesels, during the same period, average cost of repairs per unit mile averaged .1092, .1430, .1174, .1303, and .1434 respectively, with cost of repairs per pound of tractive effort at .2093, .2515, .1854, .2038, and .2182 respectively. For the careful reader, these statistics should indicate something of why Western Pacific management continued its merciless drive toward complete dieselization.

WP's growing diesel fleet frequently became the subject of both major and minor adjustments. The enginemen had for some time been requesting that diesel locomotives be equipped with side window deflectors similar to those on steam power. Such deflectors would protect from rain and wind, and so prime windshield wings were applied on the FT locomotives between March 11 and May 9, 1946, and on 501, 504, 551 and 559 classes between June 5 and August 9, 1948. Windshield

In later years, power changes for the *California Zephyr* usually took place at Oroville. In this March 1, 1969, view, the 805-D will cut off from its train and the 804-D will move forward onto the main and then back to its passenger consist. When Oroville forces were overburdened, the westbound power would run into Oakland where it would be broken up at the roundhouse and placed in the stalls for work during the long layover. **Virgil Staff**

washers were applied on the 901, 904, 907, 913, 801 and 804 classes in 1950, with all classes of road power receiving left hand and right hand combined windshield wings and rear-view mirrors between June and August 1957.

Enginemen on the Western Division requested cab awnings for additional protection, and these were applied between February 1952 and February 1953. Addition of jump seats for swing brakemen became the norm, with first installations covering all cab units in the period between May and November 1952. A similar installation on all GP-7s and GP-9s was completed between August 23 and October 13, 1956.

Upon delivery of the first two classes of Alco switchers, the switchmen registered complaints that the hand holds did not provide sufficient body clearance, and were not in line with each other on account of one of each pair at each step being set in closer to the body of the locomotive. This arrangement was revised by bringing out this grab iron to be in line with the other, and setting grab irons apart so that sufficient body clearance would be maintained. Complete standardization with the Baldwins and EMDs was difficult since the step and body design were so different.

In September 1949, there continued to be complaints concerning the steps and hand holds on the 504 and 551 classes, and in October the 554 received a rearrangement on the steps and hand holds acceptable to the extent that all Alco switchers received the modification, including the later 559 and 563 classes at the factory. This modification placed the hand holds at the front and back steps in practically the same plane, set the bottom step tread outward about 7½ inches, and made the step flush with the end of the footboard.

Alco switch engines had been delivered with guard rails along running boards. This was not true of the Electro-Motive and Baldwin switchers, and in order to eliminate the possibility of injury, the railroad applied guard rails in the period between November 1955 and February 1956. Moreover, the radiator shutters on the top of the hoods of the Alco switchers were not of sufficient strength to support a man should he accidentally step on one of these while working on the hood. Therefore, a catwalk was applied over these shutters between September 1955 and June 1956.

The FT power possessed grab irons or hand holds not usually found on 5,400-hp locomotives. Two grabs were applied on each end of the FT locomotives; work was begun on September 23 and completed on November 25, 1947. This was a safety feature which placed additional hand holds above the ones already located on the sills so that a man could stand upright instead of in a crouched position when riding the pilot step. Between March 27, 1951, and July 8, 1952, the company took all covered wagons into the shops and applied additional grab irons and hand holds to the cab roofs and front ends of 55 cab units. The purpose of this modification was to provide safe and convenient hand holds for employees when washing windshields and performing other work on top of the cab roofs, and to enable switchmen and brakemen more ease and safety when riding the pilot step.

Between January 1955 and November 26, 1958, the Interstate Commerce Commission came up with its decision, *Ex Parte 174*, calling for application of emergency brake valves on the fireman's side of cab units, certain ladders, hand holds, steps and toe bars for enginemen to allow access to classification and headlights, and fuel cutoff valves—in the valve lines adjacent to the supply tank—which could be reset without crawling beneath the locomotive. Many of the items demanded by this decision were considered to be relatively unimportant and unnecessary on the Western Pacific, and required immense initial capital expenditures in addition to the considerable shop time when this power should have been on the road. In general it was believed that the alterations had little substantial relation to safety, and on the WP, most of the alterations necessary to the safety of the men had been completed between 1947 and 1951.

In this new work that began about September 1958 and was completed in October 1963, the company changed the position of each emergency brake valve on the fireman's side of the cab, and either installed or changed the position of another at the right rear end doors of the unit. Booster placement of these emergency brake valves tended to be on the rear lead and front trail, and all GP-7s and GP-9s received a brake valve on each side of the cab.

Modification of fuel cutoff valves took place on all covered wagons, including GP-7s and GP-9s. The FT locomotives received a nose ladder, while all other cab units received grabs along the side of the nose to enable cleaning of headlights and windshields. All covered wagons received end ladders at the right rear of each booster, and 913-924 Class engines had grabs and toe holds applied. An additional grab iron was installed on each end of engines 701-725, and on 2001-2010.

Prime 406 cab ventilators were installed on all cab units, in addition to the 701-732. These tended to be applied in the roof ahead of the horns, although on the 913 Class they were located off the center line. Where applicable Sacramento Northern power received the same modifications under *Ex Parte 174*, and WP switchers received ventilators if they did not already have louvered or screened openings in the front cab sheet

The Western Pacific diesel parade continued into second-generation power. Here is GP-40 3501 leading 3521, 3528, 3515, and U23B 2256 and 103 cars through Grays Flat on the pepper-hot morning of June 9, 1973.
Virgil Staff

Adjacent to Poe River Dam east of Pulga are six units of F-power working their way up the hill on January 24, 1971. This is 9,000 horsepower—a hefty powerhouse for some of the tonnages worked in the early 1970s.   **Virgil Staff**

forward of the engineer's seat. Application of ventilators was therefore included on all switchers of the American Locomotive Co.

Prior to the winter of 1947, the Western Pacific experienced continued difficulty with freezing of air lines in its 5,400-hp locomotives. This problem was not limited to the WP but was presenting a challenge to railroads in various parts of the United States. On November 3, 1947, a Westinghouse representative equipped engine 904 with eight thermocouples for measuring temperatures in the main reservoir system. The locomotive then worked between Oroville and Salt Lake City, with temperatures being recorded throughout the round trip. These tests indicated that the main reservoir system on the cab unit lacked approximately 30 degrees of cooling the air to atmospheric temperature. This last 30 degrees of cooling therefore took place in the brake pipe, and dropped a corresponding amount of water or ice into the pipe. On the booster unit the main reservoir system lacked about 28 degrees of cooling the air to atmospheric temperature. This last 28 degrees of cooling would take place in the main reservoir train line between the units, and the corresponding amount of water or ice would be deposited in this line. Investigation of the brake pipe showed water, slush ice, and eggshell ice as far as four cars back from the locomotive.

Authority was granted to equip the two cab units of the 901 Class with additional air cooler radiators, together with automatic drain valves, water traps, and necessary piping to interpose these into the air line between the compressor and the main reservoir. Booster units received installation of automatic drain valves to the main reservoirs. The work was begun on December 3, 1947, and completed February 6, 1948. This installation did make an improvement in the amount of moisture precipitated into the air trainline.

However, O'Neill believed that a very large part of this improvement might have been due to the electrical synchronization of the air compressors in the four units because, instead of only one of these compressors doing most of the work under the old method of synchronizing, all of the compressors were now doing an equal amount of work and thus operated for shorter periods and the air would be cooled by the existing radiation system at each compressor.

O'Neill felt that the arrangement as applied might be more elaborate and costly than was actually required to eliminate moisture from the train lines, and Cuyler had suggested the equipping of remaining 5,400-hp locomotives with electrical synchronization of air compressors by the use of magnetic unloader valves and automatic drain valves to the reservoirs, thus eliminating the arrangement of additional radiation appliances as installed on the 901. This work received a work order dated August 23, 1948, and it appears that the work was done with some haste in preparation for the winter of 1948-1949.

The winter of 1948-1949 showed considerable improvement in the correction of the recent difficulties. At that time, the biggest trouble was with the air hose freezing between the booster units on the freight diesels. An attempt was made to cope with this situation by raising the train line six feet on both units and having the air hose couple there instead of down below. There were also difficulties with the synchronization drain pipe freezing, and this pipe was moved so as to go down through the floor to a connection that would not come in contact with the outside atmosphere. As was the usual custom, the train line was blown out and the main reservoirs drained at each terminal.

In December 1948, the air lines of the 906 froze at Wendover, and on January 23, 1949, train CFS-12, engine 912, stalled at Belden because of a frozen air line. Westinghouse representatives were again called for consultation, and a test was made with diesel 906 equipped with synchronization and automatic drain valves only. Temperatures were taken off the air as it entered the brake pipe and compared with temperatures of the outside atmosphere. In this test it was found that the temperature of the air going into the brake pipe was 50 degrees higher than the outside temperatures, which indicated that it would be necessary to install radiators such as were installed on locomotive 901 in order to condition the air properly before it entered the brake pipe system of the train.

Another condition also existed in the air brake systems of freight trains which aggravated this condition and was not evident prior to 1949. This condition was brought about by the fact that the new AB brake valves, then in the process of being installed on freight cars, had developed leakage through the synthetic gaskets used in this valve. This leakage was very small and could only be detected by flame test on each car.

Cuyler had noticed that while a train would show a normal brake pipe leakage while standing at a terminal, it would show a greater leakage when moving at average train speeds during cold weather. This condition had a tendency to pull air out of the air brake system of the locomotive before it could be properly conditioned. That is to say, the air did not have an opportunity to cool off to a temperature nearer to outside temperatures and consequently precipitated water as it chilled going through the brake causing freeze-ups. The performance of the 901 made it appear that the amount of radiation placed in this locomotive was sufficient to condition the air so that it would even overcome the condition set up by this excessive leakage.

The Westinghouse people suggested that sufficient cooling surface be applied to cool the air to within seven degrees of atmospheric temperature and that sufficient drain valves be applied at frequent intervals along the cooling system to extract water as it was precipitated. This was the general arrangement on the 901, although not as extensively as now recommended. Recommendations to proceed with additional cooling surface and drain valves similar to those applied to the 901, but with increased area, brought authority to relocate the air-cooling radiators and rearrange the air brake piping on two cab units of Locomotive 904. The work order for this job was dated August 5, 1949. This work was considered to provide sufficient radiation, and the remainder of the FT locomotives received similar modifications by June 12, 1950.

The railroad also realized considerable trouble with the

This was power for the *Royal Gorge* in the 1950s. It features the 803-A and its diesel tender from the 171 class of 4-8-2 steam power in February 1950. Tenders 174, 175 and 177 were renumbered to 853, 851 and 852 with conversions completed on April 19, 1950.

H. A. O'Rullian

steam heat gauge line on the 801 Class which caused a false indication of pressure. Bill Stevens, at Oakland, rearranged this line from its location near the right cab steps, and placed a coil near the left cab heater, with the return line placed as much as possible in the warm portion of the cab. Return line drainage was provided so that water could run, instead of remaining motionless in the line.

In 1954 the Western Pacific considered the application of brake pipe flow indicators to its freight and passenger units. These indicators would provide a reliable indication of extraordinary brake pipe leakage or of a brake pipe application produced within or at the rear of the train. Application to F-3s, F-7s, and GP-9s was completed between December 22, 1955, and August 1956, with GP-7s included between April 24, 1964, and March 28, 1966. The FT locomotives were not included in this installation since by the middle of 1961 they were being programmed for replacement. Installation of this equipment allowed the engineer to know exactly when the train line was charged, and made it possible to move out in a shorter period of time after the brakes were released. The possibility of break-in-twos was minimized, and with a break-in-two there would be an immediate indication. Movement of trains out of terminals was considerably expedited by this installation, as was the restarting of trains after stopping.

Of interest has been the presence of small standby steam generators in booster units of the 5,400-hp locomotives. Opinions differed as to whether it was more economical to keep engines running, or shut them down and keep them warm during layover periods by the use of immersion or circulation heaters. All WP 1,350-hp locomotives were delivered with No. 4932-A-1 Vapor–Clarkson steam generating units which rested on a small water tank, and possessed a condensate return system from each of the engine cooling systems. These were forced-circulation, coil-type generating units with normal operating capacity of 300 pounds of water evaporation per hour at 25 to 50 pounds of steam pressure.

Locomotives of the 901 Class possessed one of these steam generators in the rear of the second booster unit, while 904 and 907 Class booster units each had a No. 4932-A-1. These "overnight heaters," as they were called, were difficult and expensive to maintain, and the railroad soon learned that they dare not be used since experience showed the steam to be detrimental to gaskets, seals, and radiators. Radiators, hose connections, hoses, pipe joints, cylinder head and liner seals started to leak. It was also clear that steam dried up the lubrication in the engines, and that after an engine had set idle for a time, the starting of this engine created a friction action before the oil spread to the moving parts.

Since government regulations required that the units be fully maintained as long as they were present in the boosters, the Western Pacific made use of annual or semiannual inspections to retire and remove them between 1950 and 1952. The oval-shaped water tanks on which the generators had rested were not removed, and according to Engineer Dennis Bright, holes were cut, and the tanks became the location for storage of tools.

All FT power was now required to remain idling while at a standstill in order to prevent freezing, and to prevent excessive expansion and contraction. On August 21, 1951, Gleason signed a work order providing authority to install a Vapor DF-64-4915-3 oil-fired standby heater in each of the units of engine 902. This unit heated and circulated the water of the engine coolant system, and possessed an output capacity of 150,000 BTUs per hour. The purpose of this installation was to determine if its application was as practical as claimed, and whether or not the potential annual savings of $909 could be actually realized.

Stevens noted that the cost of idling a locomotive must be placed against the cost of adequate help to stop and start engines, blowing out the combustion chambers, and checking the crankcase for water and oil. A crankshaft job was usually about a $10,000 outlay, and Stevens suggested that this problem warranted continued study since it was known that idling the engines would hold water leaks to a minimum, keep the engines from freezing, prevent any failure from starting or stopping the engines, and eliminate the cost of trained personnel, thus "practically assuring you of a job which you hope to do some other way." Installation was completed on October 31, 1951, but the heaters would not keep the engines warm because the water would not circulate properly. Removal took place about April 1957.

The subject of shutting down engines emerged again and again over the years. In March and April 1950, a series of running tests was instituted on various classes of diesel locomotives at the Sacramento Shops. These tests indicated that average fuel consumption during idling was 3.72 gallons per hour. Constant starting and stopping of these big engines was a heavy drain on the batteries which would not hold up under such a load, and failures occurred.

On the diesel freight engines, 16 cylinder-relief valves had to be opened on each unit, and the engine turned over by hand to dispose of the moisture in the cylinders. This meant 64 such valves would need to be opened on each four-unit locomotive, and following the test for water, the valves would be closed and the engine started. This operation would take one man at least 30 minutes after which the engines should be warmed to a temperature of at least 125 degrees before being placed under heavy load. Putting a heavy load on a cold engine was seen to be very detrimental as the working parts of the engine did not expand at the same rate, thus causing undue friction.

The main difficulty in the arrangement of the liner or separate cylinder seemed to be in maintaining a tight water seal between the liner and the water jacket of the engine, which seal must be watertight at all times whether the engine was hot or cold. The synthetic rubber or other compositions used for liner seals contracted and expanded rapidly when alternately heated and cooled, and also somewhat changed its form, and leakage of cooling water into the crankcase lubricating oil would cause crankcase failure. Leakage must be prevented to the fullest possible extent and the idling of the engine was believed to very largely prevent or minimize this difficulty. Condensation was also noted in the electrical parts, such as generators and traction motors, which occurred when the engines were shut down because no air passed through them to keep them dried out.

In the 567-C engine, as on the GP-9s, the builder changed the design in the engine so that the water seals were eliminated and there was apparently no danger of water entering the crankcase in this design. Whenever a crankcase needed overhauling, the mechanical department had the case converted to a "C" case as it was cheaper to have it converted than to restore it to its initial design. During the summer, engines which would ordinarily be shut down for less than two hours were ordered to remain idling, and in 1958 the interval was set at three hours. In January 1958, three passenger units at Oakland and two units at the Sacramento Shops were shut down at the end of their runs. The passenger units almost immediately started leaking through the liner seals, and the two units at Sacramento began leaking shortly after. Constant idling enabled the railroad to average about 12 years on batteries guaranteed for four years, and since the life of a battery was largely in proportion to the demand, experience indicated that shutting down engines would cut the service life of batteries by one-half, costing approximately $56,000 per year for replacements, in addition to numerous failures that would occur on the road through exhausted batteries.

design and increases in fuel costs were enabling or demanding some departure from the norm of the first 30 years of dieselization.

To return to the discussion of providing steam heat for passenger trains, it will be recalled that the Western Pacific found itself saddled with a 1,600-pound, DK-4516 steam-generating plant on each unit of its F-3, 801 Class passenger power. These steam generators were inadequate for the length of the train the railroad intended to pull. Each locomotive of the 801 Class consisted of one cab and two booster units, with each unit containing a DK-4516 steam generator. All steam generators rested on a 200-gallon water tank, but only the booster units possessed extra water supply in the form of one 1,200-gallon water tank each.

Arrival of the 804 Class of FP-7s ended the above problem, with power consists on the *California Zephyr* usually including

The summer of 1970 sees U30B 755 (later the 3055) on a heavy tonnage symbol freight at Almanor, California, at the top of the 2.2 percent grade—heaviest on the system. **Richard Shideler**

As fuel costs continued to rise, the subject took on added dimensions, and in August 1967 instructions went out to all terminals to shut down GP-20, GP-35, and GP-40 type units on a trial basis. These models did not have lower seals on the cylinder liners, and there was no chance for water to seep into the crankcase. But there remained the problem of water leakage into the cylinder head area, and if these were not blown out properly by turning the engine over and opening cylinder head cocks to make sure no water was present, there could be hydraulic action that might cause extensive damage.

On July 2, 1973, CMO R.W. Mustard ordered that between the hours of 8:00 A.M. and 12:00 midnight, Monday through Friday, all Electro–Motive locomotives not to be called for service in two hours after arrival, would be shut down and the battery switch pulled after the turbo pump stopped. Change in

an FP-7 on the point with one or more of the boosters being an F-3. The 804 Class possessed an A-B-A configuration, with 1,100 gallons in the boiler water tanks of each cab unit, and 1,400–1,600 gallons in the booster. All steam generators were of the 2,500-pound, OK-4625 variety which, when mixed with the 801 Class units, provided sufficient steam capacity for any train.

An FP-7 and its two 804 Class boosters carried 3,900 gallons of boiler water and provided 7,500 pounds per hour of steam, as compared to an 801 Class consist of 3,000 gallons per power consist of the usual three units, and 4,800 pounds of steam capacity per hour. As assurance against a shortage of boiler water between Eastern Division terminals, two 1,000-gallon tanks were installed beneath each baggage car of the *California Zephyr*. Taking advantage of the existing water transfer piping

Swinging downgrade in dynamic, the daily "G" west of MP 60, faces Stockton and points east. It's August 31, 1967, a magnificent day, and the "G" got out of Oakland at precisely 7:00 a.m. **Virgil Staff**

on the locomotives, a glad-hand coupling was connected to transfer piping inside the diaphragm of the baggage car. When the water in the baggage car tanks was needed in the locomotive, the fireman could go to the rear of the locomotive and close the pump motor switch, which was located inside the diaphragm at the end of the baggage car on the collision post. This was usually done at some regular or unscheduled stop, and the pumps then continued to operate until the fireman opened the switch at some other point where the train stopped. These tanks may not have been used after delivery of the 804 Class, but they were maintained for a number of years following that date as a precaution against delays.

Delivery of the 804 Class enabled the withdrawal of two, and often three, of the 801 Class cab units from *California Zephyr* service. The 803-A was always maintained as the unit that would go into standby, and at one time or another it traded its 57:20 passenger gearing for the 62:15 of freight service.

It will be recalled that the WP used the 801 Class cab units, retired off the *Californi Zephyr,* to dieselize secondary trains 1 and 2. Since the 801 Class cabs possessed only 200 gallons of boiler water, tenders 174, 175, and 177 from the 171 Class Mountains were fitted up as auxiliary water tanks, provided with water connections to the diesel water line, painted in the same scheme as the 801 Class, and given couplers in the place of drawbars. These tenders were known as tenders 853, 851, and 852 respectively, and were given not more than three feet of water out of Oakland which easily took trains 1 and 2 the entire length of the railroad. These ran on the *Royal Gorge* in its final days, being placed on the train in early March 1950, and continued in that service through early September when the rail diesel cars were placed in service.

In steam days, there had been standby locomotives at all major terminals, and passenger trains which lost their power were only temporarily delayed. Now, some kind of protection was still required for the railroad's four passenger trains, in addition to the need for power on numerous specials. In early March 1951, the Eastern Division began splitting some of its 6,000-hp F-7s of the 913 Class into two units each. These two-unit consists were found to be able to handle up to and including 13 cars each with sufficient water to run from terminal to terminal. Superintendent Jim Lynch calculated that not more than nine cars could be handled in zero weather, or more than six at −30°, but he suggested the possibility of additional water capacity to enable handling of 13 or 14 cars in any kind of weather.

The 913 Class of F-7s possessed one 4,000-pound OK-4740-74-DO-F steam generator, and one 1,200-gallon water tank in each "B" unit. Second boosters, or "C" units, possessed one 500-gallon and one 1,200-gallon water supply, but there were no cab installations. Because of axle load and space limitations, it was not possible to increase the boiler water capacity of the "B" units. But since an "A" unit would normally remain with the "B" unit when cutting these four-unit diesels in half for passenger service, it was decided to install a 700-gallon capacity tank in the "A" unit, thus providing water capacity in two units of 1,900 gallons. This would allow the use of two units without tying up a third in the handling of passenger trains between watering stations.

This work was done between September 1951 and June 1952, and included locomotives of the 922 Class. Boilers were fired up and tested every time these locomotives returned to Oroville for maintenance, which was sufficient to assure these boilers were ready for service in case of emergency. To assure against freezing, air connections were attached so that the system could be blown free of moisture. Water was at all times retained in the 1,200-gallon tanks, and was kept from freezing by reversing the engine cooling fans during the winter, and apparently by the installation of steam heat lines to the 700-gallon water tank.

At various times, Cuyler and O'Neill discussed the utility of equipping the 5,400-hp locomotives with automatic shutters. These had first been recommended on March 14, 1942, when the company placed its second order for diesel freight locomotives. However, due to wartime conditions it was impossible for the manufacturer to assemble the material for this application.

The 801 Class of F-3s were the first WP locomotives to be delivered with automatic shutter mechanisms, and all other diesel power possessed the manual arrangement controlled by the fireman. This was an intolerable situation since a fireman could not be expected to maintain engine temperatures in as uniform a manner as would be possible with automatic shutters. By closer control of engine temperatures, there would be attractive savings in cylinder heads, liners and pistons, in addition to better lubrication, better fuel combustion, and uniform expansion and contraction of material in the engines.

On the FT locomotives, the cooling systems were operated with the radiators full during warm weather, and with them at low level, or about 215 gallons, during the winter. Engine water thermometers ideally showed about 165°F., and recommended operating temperatures provided a latitude of 150–180°. Four 34-inch cooling fans per engine provided the necessary cooling, and temperatures were largely controlled by manually controlled shutters, and friction clutches in the cooling fan drives. Engine water thermometers were watched by the fireman, with high temperatures often indicating that the shutters were not sufficiently open, and low temperatures that they required some degree of closure. Friction clutches were engaged or disengaged based on seasonal temperatures.

In subzero weather when it became difficult to maintain the recommended engine temperature, the fans were shut down on the accessory end and the shutters closed, thus leaving the shutters at the other end to control the temperature range. Engine room temperatures could then be raised by removing the manhole covers at the accessory drive end, and allowing air to be drawn through the warm radiators into the engine room.

In late 1950 there were numerous reports of water loss from diesel freight units, especially on the Eastern Division. This was known to be largely due to the defective cylinder head seals which had been applied, and 768 of these seals were changed in the period from July 31, 1950, through about March 1951. Maintaining engine temperatures around 165° would aid the situation, and it was noted that when engines were dispatched from Oroville on the eastward trip to Portola, no problems were reported on the 116 miles of one-percent grade where the engines were working hard and maintaining a more constant temperature.

After a locomotive reached Portola the atmospheric temperatures were lower and consequently the engines had a tendency to cool, especially when the train was drifting downgrade and

On April 24, 1960, Don Hansen caught switcher 559 exiting Tunnel A in San Francisco, on the WP's orphan trackage. This was the old Ocean Shore Potrero Tunnel O, and consisted of 1,625 linear feet of timber lining. **Don Hansen**

shutters were not closed so that by the time the locomotive reached the bottom of the grade and started upgrade, the temperatures of the engines had fallen to around 130° or 140° after which the engines were again worked hard. This wide range of expansion and contraction further aggravated the trouble with defective seals and increasingly called attention to the need for automatic shutters for the control of engine water temperatures.

Engines 901-903 received the new equipment between November 7 and December 23, 1949. These shutters were thermostatically controlled with thermostats set to open shutters at 165°, and to close at 155°. At terminals, the shutters remained latched in the closed position, and upon leaving a terminal, both fans were placed in operation. Should two sets of fans cause engine temperatures to remain too low, one fan was then disengaged. These installations were notably successful, and the remaining 5,400-hp locomotives received similar installations prior to the middle of 1952. The 910-912, and possibly the others, received an automatic fan clutch in addition to controls which operated the fan clutch and shutters in steps from a vernatherm thermostat switch.

Between January and December 1957, the 501 and 504 Class switchers received the application of Minneapolis–Honeywell equipment, with the 551-562 receiving installations of Alco equipment between May 1960 and May 1961. In these latter engines, there were two arrangements of shutters.

The 551-558, possessing horizontal shutters, had the operating cylinders mounted outside on the top of the shutter housing. Locomotives 559-562 possessed vertical shutters, and on these the operating cylinder was placed inside the hood.

On April 7, 1945, Superintendent of the Eastern Division Jim Lynch passed the word to Cuyler that his men were complaining of their inability to determine beyond a reasonable doubt the correct number on an engine when it passed during high speed or heavy storm. This was of some significance since most of the railroad continued to run under the authority of train orders. Carbody number lights on the front sides of the bulldog nose were of small dimensions, and a set of 10-inch numbers, located in diagonally placed number boxes, were installed on each side of the cab roof of the 901 in early September 1945. The men liked this arrangement, and between December 16, 1947, and April 28, 1948, the remaining FT locomotives received a slightly modified indicator. Installations consisted of five-space diagonal indicator boxes with brackets and indicator lamps very much similar to those on the 481 Class of Lima Northern steam locomotives.

Each four-unit FT locomotive received boxes to the right and left roof at both ends, with each indicator consisting of five white opal glass cards, two blank metal cards, and three metal cards with figures about seven inches high to make up the locomotive numbers. The indicators were painted green to

The setting sun bathes Goecken Heights in golden splendor as the westbound AP, with the 919-D on the point, swings downgrade on January 15, 1967, through the Diablo Range via Altamont Pass. The whine of three units crowding the curvatures in dynamic was heard long before the orange nose made its appearance around the curve east of MP 54.
Virgil Staff

match the FT roofs, and the old engine numbers were temporarily retained.

In early February 1948, it was requested that these engine number indicators be changed from green to some other color, since the green color could be easily taken for a green metal flag, sign of a second section following. The number indicators had originally been painted green to match the roof, but now the railroad was painting the roof black, and there was no problem in similarly painting the indicators.

A more serious complaint concerned the location of the number lights in that they were said to interfere with switching and with receiving signals from the rear of the train. The light from the indicators was said to shine down into the engineer's eyes when he was doing a reverse move, or when looking back as he moved ahead. Reflections were said to be cast onto the wing windows when in use, and some men wanted built-in number boxes similar to those on the 801 Class of F-3 power. This would have been an expensive redesign job. To solve the problem economically, a flat plate was placed between the number lamp and its brackets, which projected outward sufficiently to prevent the rays of light from interfering with enginemen's view when looking back. This installation was made on the 901 and shortly to the remaining power.

Finally, in August 1948 complaints were received that the engine crews had no way of knowing whether the exterior classification lights were burning since there was no indication inside the cab. Cuyler believed this could be determined by the fireman when he arranged the colored glass in front of the light, but he agreed to have a hole drilled in the back of the classification lamps so that the fireman could determine whether or not the lights were burning by opening the door into the nose of the diesel. This work was completed between November 1948 and February 1949, and in addition the wattage was increased in the number and classification lights to increase their intensity.

About the same time, the mechanical forces installed ground lights on the 501, 504, 551 and 581 classes of switch engines, and on the "A" and "D" units of the 5,400-hp locomotives. Determination of engine speeds during the night was less obvious than with steam engines, and installations were completed in 1947 and 1952 respectively.

Until the late 1940s, the four-unit 5,400-hp FT locomotives were probably never broken into two sections of two units each. Any other combination was impossible since only cab units possessed batteries, and each cab and its booster was connected by a solid drawbar. In very late 1948 or early 1949 the Western Pacific began using two-unit combinations in ever-increasing numbers to increase the utilization of this power, dieselize helper, branch, and drag service, and thereby reduce operating costs. Only a limited number of units were so employed in the beginning, and steam locomotive headlights had been installed on the rear of such boosters with temporary wiring and an operating switch at the location of the backup light.

By at least May of 1953, all FT and F-7 boosters had received such headlights on one end including the switch and temporary wiring. However, these backup lights were not wired so they could be dimmed or turned off and on from the cab, and either the fireman or the engineer had to go back to the far end of the booster to operate the switch as then located. On January 7, 1954, President Whitman authorized the application of dimming and control devices in the cabs of all FT locomotives such as had always existed on steam locomotives, and application was completed between April and October 1954. Additional authorization was shortly granted, with the F-7s receiving such applications between March 1955 and March 1956—the F-3s being the final installations with cab applications in early 1958.

Of peculiar fascination to many have been the diesel locomotive headlights themselves. It would seem that all Western Pacific 5,400-hp locomotives were delivered with a 14-inch-diameter cluster light containing seven 50-candle bulbs, each with its own reflector. These could be focused manually, and initially some of the men attempted to produce what they considered to be the best possible focus for the run. This light produced a broad spectrum of visibility, but was nevertheless not to anyone's liking since the wartime quality of equipment was such that shorts developed and bulbs burned out quickly. These FT locomotives also had a 64-volt, $\frac{2}{3}$-kw dynamotor located in the hood to the left of the headlight. This dynamotor converted the battery voltage to 12.5 volts in bright, and 8 volts in dim. Burned-out bulbs required early replacement so as not to unequally discharge the two sides of the battery.

The Electro–Motive people were not very pleased with this light but wartime conditions made it impossible to obtain materials previously employed in earlier lights. A marker board was set up at Oroville in July 1942, where diesel freight engine lights could be regulated within the requirements of the law that a man be visible at 800 feet. These lights did considerably better than 800 feet, and for a time were considered to be successful. In the meantime, Electro–Motive was developing a single-bulb-type headlight which, however, appeared to possess many of the shortcomings of the cluster lamps.

Engine crews desired a light that would penetrate at a considerable distance, and concurrently would spread its rays so as to enable the crews to see fallen rocks and debris along the curves as they traversed the Feather River Canyon. The company attempted to meet this need by installing "elephant" lenses, for use in the canyon, which would cut the distance, but not under the required 800 feet, and allow the spread of this light as the men wanted. The so-called "elephant" lens was manufactured with ribs to diffuse the rays to the side, although in doing so it somewhat curtailed the distance.

All steam power was equipped with this type lens, and while there were certain objections, the crewmen considered this to be the best possible lens in the canyon. Some of them even believed the "elephant" lens would enable them to see around curves. What the men did not want on the third subdivision was a clear headlight lens, although on the first and second subdivisions, and on the Eastern Division, they preferred a clear lens since this enabled them to gain visibility for a greater distance.

About November 1944 the roundhouse foremen at Oroville were instructed to see that all headlights on third subdivision engines were equipped with an "elephant" lens. By 1949, this installation normally took place between November 1 and May 1 of each year with the "elephant" lens changed out on westbound trains at Oroville and again applied on eastbound trains. This was not such a chore as might be believed since most power turned at Oroville.

Power west of Oroville ran with what the men called a "clear lens" while between Oroville and Portola, during the months noted, one was most likely to see the "elephant" lens. "Elephant" lenses were changed out at Portola on eastbound trains and reapplied on those headed down the canyon, and there were apparently few complaints when the "elephant" lens was seen in the canyon during the summer months.

By the end of 1944, the Pyle–National Co. was manufacturing a single-bulb, 14-inch headlight that was interchangeable with the cluster-type headlight and would shortly replace it. This new headlight was a hinge-type, single-bulb, concentrated filament lamp with a crystal glass reflector, and arranged for a 250-watt, 32-volt, medium screw base lamp. The mechanical department was immediately interested in this new light and desired to replace all cluster-type lights with the new development. Pyle–National 250-watt, 32-volt lights had been standard on steam power for a number of years, and the 804 and 913 classes soon possessed the new hinge-type light, as would the later GP-7s, GP-9s, and GP-20s.

Sometime in the first half of the 1950s, a series of tests was made comparing the "elephant" lens with the "plain" lens and it was concluded that the difference in diffusion of light was not sufficient to warrant continuation of two different lenses. During 1955 the "elephant" lenses were changed out as they became defective. In November 1955, a series of sophisticated tests was made on Western Pacific headlights, with the conclusion that the large single-reflector type headlight was as good as anything found among competitors. All classes of power were checked, and all headlights conformed with specifications requiring them to be of sufficient illumination to pick up the figure of a man at a distance of 800 feet. In fact, the Pyle- National headlight, which had been tested at Wayne, Illinois, on July 19, 1953, is said to have produced 475,000 candlepower with the crystal silvered glass, and would pick up objects at 1,250 feet.

The two RDC cars were equipped with the only sealed-beam lights on the railroad. These lights are said to have possessed maximum candlepower of 390,000 with a pickup distance of 1,180 feet. The chief problem with the early sealed-beam light was dark spots that appeared sometime after the light had been in service. The mechanical department kept a careful watch on the RDC sealed beams but was not about to replace its crystal silvered glass reflectors with an inferior sealed beam as some individuals wanted. The Pyle–National light was considered superior to the sealed beams on neighboring railroads, and oscillating lights were not believed to be of any particular aid to the engineer. Engine headlights were checked for proper focus at least every 30 days, and the company would not begin to install sealed-beam lights until it had evidence that the new,

A generation after the dawn of the diesel age on the Western Pacific, GP-40-2 3545 and mates put in an appearance with the TOF at Paxton, just west of MP 278. It is 10:25 a.m. on July 10, 1980. The 3545 class lacks oscillating lights on the hood, although they are present on the 3550 class. **Virgil Staff**

revised sealed beams were a distinct improvement over the early ones.

All GP-35s and all GP-40s through unit 3516 received Pyle–National C-195-CZ hinged aluminum reflector type headlights on each end, but starting with the third order of GP-40s, all locomotives of this model received 200-watt, 30-volt Electro-Motive twin sealed beams at each end, with a Pyle–National 20585 dual sealed beam oscillating signal light with white and red roundels on the front end only. These oscillating lights had manual control for the white and red roundel, and automatic control for the latter when actuated by a decrease in brake pipe pressure.

General Electric power came with GE 400-watt, 30-volt headlights consisting of two 200-watt, 30-volt lamps at front and rear, and all GE power, with the exception of the U23Bs, possessed a Pyle–National 20585-DCFV red and white oscillating light at the front of the locomotive on the operator's cab. The SW-1500s possessed Electro–Motive twin-sealed beams on either end, and the 711 and 712 were the first low-horsepower geeps to receive the twin-sealed beam installations (in 1971). All other GP-7s and GP-9s received such installations between December 1974 and January 1976.

By 1977, most road power possessed twin-sealed beams, although some power continued temporarily to possess a Pyle–National "ashcan" light on the rear. Safety flasher lights had been installed on 12 switchers in 1970, and by the end of 1977 it could be said that Western Pacific light systems continued to be thoroughly modern.

12
The Faster Handling of Trains

WHEN THE FIRST 5,400-hp locomotives were delivered in 1941 and 1942, there were no permanent diesel-fueling facilities on the railroad. System tank cars, containing diesel fuel, were located at Oakland, Oroville, Keddie and Elko, with fuel transfer expedited by Granco pumps of 100-gallon-per-minute capacity. On eastbound runs, the 901 Class departed Oroville with full tanks of fuel. At Elko they were refueled for the run into Salt Lake City and return to Elko where they were fueled for return to Oroville. By March 1942, it was possible to take fuel at the Rio Grande facility in Salt Lake City should the westbound power out of Salt Lake be turned at Wendover for a return run. Tank cars 1061, 1065, 1167 and 1179 were assigned to Eastern Division diesel oil service, and since the Rio Grande was short of tank cars, one of these floated between the Utah Oil Refinery and the Rio Grande at Salt Lake.

As additional diesels came onto the property, the increasing number of tank cars in diesel fuel oil interchange service made it imperative to easily establish identity between these and the majority of those with bunker fuel. Many railroads experienced sticking injectors which seemed to indicate that their tank cars may not have been completely clean. The Western Pacific, from almost the beginning, took some of its tank cars, cleaned them thoroughly, painted the domes yellow, and stenciled on each dome: DIESEL FUEL OIL ONLY. These tanks were also cleaned and inspected before again being filled with fuel. In this manner the company maintained its fuel in first-class condition, and did not experience the problem of sticking injectors so prevalent on a number of other lines.

Permanent installations of 20,000-gallon diesel oil storage tanks were authorized for Stockton, Oroville and Keddie in the summer of 1942, in addition to two 20,000-gallon storage tanks for Elko. Permanent oil storage at Stockton would shortly allow the movement of the 501 Class to that terminal, and the Keddie installation would provide for any number of 5,400-hp runs on the North Line. A 20,000-gallon installation was completed at South Sacramento in March 1945, which eased the assignment of the 501 Class, or other switching power, at that point for many years to come. Construction of 72,000-gallon fuel storage tanks for South Sacramento and Wendover received authorization about the same time, with the Wendover facility being constructed primarily to avoid any necessity of fueling at Salt Lake.

From the beginning, the mechanical department had been concerned about the fuel oil gravity gauges on the 5,400-hp locomotives. These were rather crude instruments which did not provide precise information as to the amount of fuel remaining in the tanks. At the very end of 1944, or beginning of 1945, the company began the application of a bayonet-type gauge to each tank, and located this gauge just below the gravity gauge inside the engine room. As the average consumption per mile was figured at 6.2 gallons, the engine crew could determine by reading the gauge whether or not there was sufficient fuel to make the next terminal. Eastbound power out of Oroville always fueled at Elko, but a unit cutting out, excessive time on the road, tonnage, and weather conditions would have a bearing on fuel consumption.

There had never been an intention to fuel road units at Winnemucca since this would only increase the terminal delay.

Cloaking the skies with a veil of black, a consist of Burlington Northern pool power thunders eastbound through Almanor on the drowsy afternoon of August 26, 1977.   **Virgil Staff**

But before the middle of 1945, fueling was possible by gravity from tank cars. This tied up cars, caused extra switching and labor, and delayed the servicing of locomotives. By July 1945, Cuyler had noted that dispatchers were increasingly running the power back and forth between Portola and Winnemucca, and he feared the locomotives might run out of fuel after being dispatched from Winnemucca in either direction.

A 20,000-gallon oil facility at Winnemucca, such as existed at Oroville and Keddie, would reduce any delay and assure sufficient fuel. On November 7, 1945, Master Mechanic William Parry notified Road Foremen Williams and McKay that as of that date all diesels eastbound through Winnemucca would carry at least 10 inches of fuel. Should it be necessary to fuel, the units should not be filled but given sufficient to bring the oil level to approximately 12 or 13 inches. Diesel engines having 10 inches or more of fuel oil would go on through into Elko.

Additional diesel engine fuel oil facilities were authorized for Elko in 1945, and coach watering and diesel fuel oil facilities for Oakland in 1946. Fuel and water facilities received authorization for Winnemucca in 1947, and Portola received its new diesel-fueling station in 1947-1948. The Wendover facility continued to receive repeated use, especially on westbound trains, and a 100,000-gallon capacity (actually a series of 20,000-gallon tanks) was installed during the same years. San Francisco, Oakland, Stockton Yard, Sacramento Shops, and Keddie all received diesel oil columns and additional fueling facilities in 1949 similar to those recently installed at Portola, Winnemucca, and Wendover. In 1952, with complete dieselization near, President Whitman authorized changes in oil storage at Oakland and San Francisco; installation of two new 20,000-gallon tanks and relocation of another to provide 60,000 gallons of diesel oil storage at Stockton; the 420,000-gallon tank at Portola was moved to Oroville, and two 20,000-gallon tanks in addition to the installation of an additional 20,000-gallon tank provided Portola with 60,000 gallons; two 20,000-gallon tanks were installed at Keddie, and one old-style tank was retired. Finally, Elko received an additional 500,000 gallons of storage, with San Jose receiving a 20,000-gallon tank shortly afterward, thus completing, for some years to come, the program of providing and standardizing fuel oil storage over the railroad.

In early 1947, before the new tanks for Winnemucca and Wendover had arrived, O'Neill was showing concern that the new 801 Class, when it arrived, might not make it all the way from Oakland to Salt Lake with 18 cars on train No. 40. Indeed, the tanks were not quite ready, so that No. 40 fueled at Elko, because of the canyon pull, and No. 39 departed Salt

Awaiting a crew change on July 14, 1973, an eastbound freight tarries momentarily with GP-35 3005 and GP-40s 3511, 3542 and 3518. No clearance is required at Winnemucca for movement to the Sixth Subdivision, so the symbol freight will shortly move out for the paired trackage (WP and SP) upon receiving verbal authority from the dispatcher. **Virgil Staff**

Lake with full tanks. Watering of locomotives, both directions, took place at Oakland, Oroville, Winnemucca, and Salt Lake.

Western Pacific covered wagons came equipped with 1,200-gallon fuel tanks which did not allow sufficient oil for freight units to run between Oroville and Salt Lake. Some experimentation was required, and in 1949 freight diesels were fully fueled at Winnemucca in both directions. The mechanical department figured that a 5,400-hp locomotive loaded down with tonnage should make it from Winnemucca into Salt Lake, but then be fueled at Wendover on the westbound run. Westbound units out of Wendover could probably make Elko on a quarter tank but this was taking a chance. Moreover, no one wanted to take fuel at Elko, but preferred to use Winnemucca in both directions. Wendover also seemed the logical place to take fuel in either or both directions. An eastbound stop made directly at the diesel-fueling risers allowed the opportunity to take fuel for 10 or 15 minutes while changing crews, replenishing drinking water, and while trainmen were getting ready to move. This would reduce the time during westward fueling, and would allow the units to reach Winnemucca where sufficient fuel must be taken to assure that the power had better than 400 gallons out of Portola since it was known that unit fuel consumption down the canyon to Oroville averaged about 50 gallons per unit.

When the *California Zephyr* began operation on March 20, 1949, the 801 Class power ran from Oakland to Salt Lake and return with all maintenance taking place at Oakland. The small capacity steam generator water tanks did not allow for extended runs, and initially not all the belly tanks under the baggage cars had been installed. This work was being rushed to completion, and any baggage cars with tanks were immediately employed to complement the boiler water in the booster units. An electrician rode each train at least partway, and on train No. 18 he switched on the baggage pump at Virgilia and switched it off at Portola. On train No. 17, he threw the double knife switch at Stockton, and shut it off at Niles. The steam trainline gauge was maintained at 150 lbs. or better at all times since this appeared to be the minimum pressure at which the needs of the diners could be served.

On the *California Zephyr,* the power left Oakland with full tanks of fuel and water. Should the baggage car belly tanks be installed and operational, no engine or baggage car water would be taken at Oroville or Wendover. On No. 17 at Salt Lake, the 801 Class power would be waiting with full tanks, and the Rio Grande would fill the baggage car tanks with as much water as there was time to permit. This provided additional emergency water into Winnemucca and cut the time for filling up at that point. By September 1949, the forces had the watering of the train at Oroville down to four minutes, but when the automatic operation of the baggage water tanks was not in service, the filling of booster units took an additional two or three minutes.

Man and nature combined to make this scene. Bridge 314.36 feels the weight of a doomed *California Zephyr* on a pleasant morning in March of 1970. This is Clio, California, and the *Zephyr* would expire on March 22. **Joseph Ward**

On occasion, No. 17 arrived in Salt Lake with the water supply pipe from the baggage car frozen. This necessitated taking boiler water at Wendover in order to make Winnemucca. In December 1949, a copper pipe was installed from the steam trainline pipe on each baggage car to the steam generator water supply pipe. The taking of boiler water at Wendover was then discontinued, and the boilers were filled only at Winnemucca and Oakland. In January 1950, the forces began filling the baggage supply tanks to full capacity at Oroville, although the water tanks on the boosters were allowed to go through if the water was not lower than 12 inches from the top of the tank. This minimized the delay at Oroville but allowed the greatest possible amount of water to be taken in the time allowed.

Beginning February 8, 1950, No. 18 began changing power at Oroville, with maintenance to be at that point rather than at Oakland. The power then ran round trip to Salt Lake and Oakland, and was cut out at Oroville on the eastbound run out of Oakland. The arrival of the new 804 Class, with larger boiler water capacity, enabled the power to limit its watering en route to Winnemucca in either direction. This was not always the mode of operation, and at a later time when the power on No. 17 was cut off at Oroville, the units on No. 18 were watered as was the train. Unlike the 801 Class, the 804 Class possessed water fillers on the sides of cab units as well as boosters, which temporarily delayed Nos. 17 and 18 at Winnemucca since the water hydrants at the east and west ends of the depot were located for watering of two F-3 booster units in addition to the baggage water tanks.

In late 1949, all eastbound freight power was fully fueled at Winnemucca, and under ordinary circumstances the diesels ran through to Salt Lake and were not fueled until arrival at Wendover on the westbound run. This limited delays to eastbound fruit blocks and provided sufficient fuel for the westbound run into Portola. It was earlier noted that the presence of defective cylinder liner seals created monumental problems on numerous railroads at this time. The defective seals were changed out progressively at every opportunity but unfortunately the new seals were themselves defective, and FT and 801 Class units were losing cooling water from the engine so fast that some freight power found it necessary to take water at such emergency watering places as Delle, Shafter, Wells, Carlin, Beowawe, Winnemucca, Jungo, Gerlach, and Doyle.

In the early 1950s, President Whitman and General Manager Munson were applying pressure to speed up schedules and get the trains over the road faster. This was largely becoming possible due to CTC installations on the Eastern Division, lengthening of sidings in CTC territory, and by shortening of terminal delays. On May 24, 1950, Engineer A.W. Fuller took engine 916ABCD out of Gerlach with the 1-61 and 2-61, 7,186 tons. The units had not been fueled at Winnemucca, and the 916D showed 12 inches of fuel on the gauges. Between

Scotts and Chilcoot, the 916D failed for fuel, thus badly delaying No. 78 at Chilcoot, but with sufficient time to squeeze into Chilcoot for No. 18. Fuller suggested that Winnemucca forces be officially instructed to fuel the diesels on heavy westbound trains, and on May 29, 1950, Superintendent John Duggan ordered that all heavy tonnage westbound drags be oiled for fear they might not make Portola.

After delivery of the 804 Class with increased steam capacity and larger boiler-water storage, the baggage car belly tanks were seldom used although they were temporarily maintained and filled as protection for heating the train in case of delay during subzero weather. During winter storm and snow conditions, No. 17's engine was normally watered at Portola as an additional provision for heat should the train be delayed by a slide. With early March, the power ceased to take boiler water at Portola, and depended on the full replenishment received at Winnemucca. By early 1952 the baggage car tanks were not generally in use, and the engine tanks were replenished on No. 17 at Winnemucca and Oroville. At various times, and often for long periods, No. 17's power was fueled at Salt Lake so as to cut the fueling delay at Winnemucca.

In 1951, the mechanical department had for sometime been toying with the idea of enlarging the 1,200-gallon fuel tanks on the covered wagons. Mechanical Engineer William B. Wolverton was deeply involved in this project, and it was determined that it should be possible to increase the size of the fuel tanks by 300 gallons which was proven practical after installation on a single test unit. The plan had always been to regularly operate eastbound out of Oroville to Elko, take fuel at Elko, run to Salt Lake and return to Elko for refueling. With the limited capacity of the fuel tanks this had seldom been possible. Power fueled at Winnemucca, turned at Salt Lake, and then fueled westbound at Wendover, with no fueling at Elko. This situation perpetuated the need for hostlers and hostler helpers at the two points, whereas the taking of fuel at Elko could be absorbed by the forces already at that point. This would also speed the trains on their way since the only significant delay at Winnemucca and Wendover would be to change cabooses and crews.

The work took place in two installments with the 901-924 receiving tanks between August 22, 1951, and September 10, 1953, and the 801-805 receiving installations between January and August 1954. This extra 300 gallons per tank was accomplished by the application of "blisters" to the sides and ends of the existing fuel tanks. Determination of whether a tank had been enlarged was always easy since the skirt over the tank was altered so as to be practically flush with the side of the unit. Also, at the ends of the tank one could notice that the tanks had been extended by welding an end section onto the original tank. These installations eventually made it possible for freight power to fuel at Elko, and for the *California Zephyr* power to run through Winnemucca to Salt Lake.

California Zephyr locomotives then fueled at Oakland, Salt Lake, and Oroville on the eastbound run where engines were changed, with water being taken for the steam generators at Elko and Portola in both directions. This was accomplished without added delay to the train as the time formerly used at Winnemucca was divided between Elko and Portola. At this point Gleason gave up the idea of any further use for the baggage car belly tanks since, on occasion, transfer lines tended

to freeze when on foreign trackage, and the pumps frequently lost their prime.

To illustrate, power being turned at Wendover, Elko, or Winnemucca was fueled before being dispatched, and No. 17 was frequently fueled at Winnemucca to the extent that dead time permitted as established by the timetable. Under this arrangement the passenger power normally arrived in Oakland with about 450 gallons per unit which was considered a sufficient margin of safety. This servicing at Winnemucca was necessitated by low water pressure at Portola, and by lack of sufficient water risers at Portola and Elko. These were rushed to completion for watering of Nos. 17 and 18 at Portola and Elko, and went into operation with the new time card effective April 24, 1955.

In February 1955, Munson was applying pressure to assure that the crews be able to make the newly inaugurated faster

Early May 1974 catches the WPE with units 3525, 3008, 3022 and 2001 working tonnage up the Canyon near Pulga. This was a daily-except-Sunday symbol handling short traffic and doing local work between Stockton and Salt Lake City.
Virgil Staff

handling of trains through Elko by reason of changes in inspection, and he made it clear that the company could not afford the "luxury" of relay power during the heavy business season, or of any evidence of inactive handling of trains through the terminals. Time was of the essence, and effective April 24, 1955, Nos. 17 and 18 were allowed three minutes at Winnemucca, and five minutes each at Portola and Elko for watering. Portola was thought to be an essential watering point, and it was considered doubtful that the power carried sufficient water to bypass Portola as a watering point, at least in the winter months. On July 31, 1956, the forces discontinued watering the diesels at Portola, and by June 1957 they had watering time at Oroville down to six minutes.

In early 1958, a prolonged discussion began concerning the possibility of eastbound perishable schedules being cut to the fifth morning at midwest points from California, with ultimate application of a fifth day schedule likewise to westbound traffic. Fueling and inspection had to be done at some location en route, and whatever procedure would allow such schedules would become the necessity. Numerous schedules would be getting faster, and in the process of eliminating the greatest possible number of delays, Elko came to be downgraded as a fueling facility for through power, with Salt Lake City taking its place.

Road Foreman of Engines M.W. Hammond instructed his enginemen that the new merchandise train, to be known as the *Advanced CFS* must have its fuel cisterns full on leaving Roper Yard. Based on a test with the FB141, it was clear that any power that ran through Elko must of necessity take fuel at Winnemucca. Past experience had shown that the bottom 200 gallons of fuel could not be figured in the total available fuel on a unit because when the level got below 200 gallons the suction

THE FASTER HANDLING OF TRAINS 101

was broken when going around curves due to the fuel sloshing around in the tank. This would cause an engine to starve for fuel, and ultimately to stop.

Cuyler explained to Munson that permitting five units to go through without fueling would put the power very close to failure. A delay, or a mistake in tonnage, or possibly added tonnage en route would place the power in danger of failing. The test had shown that four of five units must be fueled at Winnemucca if they were to run through Elko. The fueling at Winnemucca would not take very much time, and five minutes of replenishing would assure the locomotive would not fail for lack of fuel.

Regarding the fueling of eastbound trains at Winnemucca after inauguration of the fast schedule, fuel consumption tests were made on the eastbound GGM trains Nos. 3-7 and 10-14, and PC trains, Nos. 3-7 and 10-14 during May 1958. Instructions were then issued that it would not be necessary to fuel westbound trains at Winnemucca with tonnage less than 4,200 tons. Eastbound trains had to be fueled at that point to assure these trains would reach Salt Lake without difficulty. During the tests, the average eastbound train showed that if fuel was not taken at Winnemucca there would only be 61 gallons in each unit on arrival at Salt Lake. Tanks need not be fueled to capacity at Winnemucca but should be fueled during the time the units were at that point.

Until August 1958, plans had been under consideration for additional fueling facilities at Elko. These were now set aside and Winnemucca and Salt Lake City came to be accepted as permanent fueling points. In August, freight and passenger units were already being given a nominal amount of fuel at

A Portola-bound manifest heads through the Plumas National Forest on the late morning of October 9, 1977, crossing Bridge 288.76 at Quincy, California. **Virgil Staff**

Winnemucca while changing crews, and in February 1959, Superintendent J.F. Lynch issued instructions to discontinue fueling eastbound freight engines at Winnemucca if the train had less than 3,500 tons. At this time, no trains of over 3,500 tons were being fueled if the train possessed five units. Some fueling of westbound trains took place at Winnemucca for fear they might run out of fuel or have problems in the canyon. Fueling was possible at Portola but this would cause additional delays.

In the interests of expediting the TOF, no fuel was taken en route to Salt Lake when tonnage was below 2,000 tons. Fuel measurements at Elko showed that the units had 12 inches of fuel which was adequate to get them into Salt Lake without fueling at Wendover. In April 1959, Cuyler established a 2,400-ton limit for eastbound trains. Symbol trains heavier than this had to be fueled at Winnemucca, with time consumed not to exceed 10 minutes. This was usually adequate to make Salt Lake, with fueling at Wendover only in emergency. Most of the earlier fueling problems were allayed during the 1960s with delivery of bigger power with larger capacity fuel tanks. The GP-7s and GP-9s possessed only 1,600-gallon fuel tanks but the GP-20s, delivered in 1959-60, featured a fuel tank capacity of 2,350 gallons. GP-35s carried 2,600 gallons each, and all GEs and GP-40s carried 3,250 and 3,600 gallons, respectively. Probably the last trains to be regularly fueled at Winnemucca were the *GGM* and the *FB*. Mechanical forces for fueling were removed from Winnemucca by early March 1967, and all power east out of Oroville had to be assured of full tanks since fueling at Winnemucca was discontinued as of about March 7 or 8, 1967.

Eastbound for Portola, the 3533, 3054, 3007, 3503 and 3543 hustle a train headed up by a brace of containers onto the western end of the Willow Creek Viaduct. This location is roughly 5½ miles from the upper (east) end of the Feather River Canyon. It is 9:20 a.m., May 12, 1974. **Virgil Staff**

13

Maintenance and Fuel Ratings

WE HAVE PREVIOUSLY observed a certain amount of ring breakage due to low cetane rating and high end point of fuel procured during World War II. Low cetane fuel was smoky and sooty, and tended to wax during cold weather. Wax gathered on the surface of the fuel, and tended to plug the filters causing engines to starve for fuel. During subzero temperatures through Nevada and Utah, the wax sometimes became almost as heavy as scum, and seemed to affect the suction lines to the engine injectors. During the winter of 1945-46, the railroad was obtaining 52 cetane and 600 end point with less wax content, and no problems appeared in -20° weather. This fuel had a lower pour point and was consequently more expensive. The possibility of using heaters, which might be cheaper than the higher cost of oil, was considered and it will be recalled that the mechanical department tested such equipment but found it wanting.

Prior to the war, and during the very early part of the war, the cost of diesel fuel had been low. In fact, this had been one of the points argued in favor of diesels as compared to steam. But fuel costs began to rise during the war and generally continued to rise following the conflict. By August 1948, the power was burning a somewhat lower quality fuel than previously, and Cuyler studied the records carefully to learn if a high sulphur content and high end point would indeed be detrimental to the service life of parts. In 1953 the company continued to buy some straight run diesel fuel, but the cetane rating was down and Cuyler and Gleason showed great concern for the difficulties which might be expected with the use of so-called "economy fuels."

The Western Pacific began using Class "B" distillate fuels —often known as economy fuel—in the late summer or early autumn of 1954. These fuels were heavier than regular diesel fuels but not in the category of a very heavy fuel oil. Western Pacific's fuel was a mixture of catalytic cracked and straight run. An additive, known as SR-158-D, was used to maintain stability when the fuels were mixed or stored for any length of time in storage tanks. By 1956 the cetane rating was as low as 34 and Cuyler recommended discontinuance of derated fuels.

Diesel engines would not fully burn this fuel and the unburned part found its way into the crankcase lubricating oil, causing sludging detrimental to the service life of parts. By June 1956, WP units were beginning to show sludging, and additional time was being required to remove the heavy deposits. The cost of maintenance was running at .134 cents per unit mile, but this could not continue for long. Oil radiators were becoming plugged to the extent that effective cooling was impossible, and a program was established to remove all radiators and clean them in an effort to eliminate this condition.

It was decided that in the future, oil coolers would require removal and cleaning at least once each year, and change of Michiana filters would be reduced from 30 to 10 days. In 1956 an increased reduction in the life of liners, pistons, rings, heads, valves, and injectors was noted, and on July 1, 1956, Flynn reported that in 1954, 54 percent of the liners removed were scrapped because of wear. So far, in 1956, 80 percent of the liners removed had required scrapping. Moreover, he would need more help. Cuyler figured that if he could get through 1957 without excessive trouble, the company could use derated fuel at a true savings. Maintenance costs due to derated fuels were up in 1956 by $49,044 but fuel savings, over what they would have been, were at $197,000. Myron Christy provided figures indicating that fuel consumption was about the same, except for the passenger units. This interested Cuyler since it had been supposed by many, but never by him, that the economy fuels possessed sufficient BTU's to enable the burning of less fuel for the same amount of work. His view had always been that most of the BTU's, which it was originally felt would be utilized, were wasted through smoking at the stack, and through soot that went into the crankcase. This was mainly, he felt, because the diesel engine was not capable of burning this fuel. In fact, he had often speculated that it might require more of a given amount of economy fuel than of regular fuel to accomplish a given amount of work, and Christy's statistics indicated that more economy fuel was indeed being used per gross ton mile when comparing 1954 with 1956.

Fuel costs continued to rise, and in March 1957, Munson reminded Superintendent G.W. Curtis that the company couldn't do much about the price but might be able to control consumption through fewer train miles and employment of fewer switch engine shifts. "Whenever you do either, you should always remember that the savings you bring about have a sort of double-barreled favorable effect on our operating expenses."

A better grade of fuel was used at switching terminals to cut the smoking of switch engines to a minimum. In 1958, and probably considerably before, Burnzall Conditioner was added to the "cat-cracked fuels" to control possible carbon emission. Additives were not required for stabilization since, at least by 1961, fuels being delivered from Salt Lake contained Nalco treatment which stabilized the fuel so that the heavy ends when burned in the combustion chamber did not produce as much carbon as the unstabilized fuel. In 1965 the company was using a regular run diesel fuel which was considered stable, and which minimized carbon deposits in the combustion chamber. The railroad had therefore come almost full circle: not quite so good as before the war, but greatly improved over wartime and post-wartime usage.

Nubieber, California, at the north end of the NCE (Inside Gateway), sees the interline BN170 fresh off the Western Pacific with a WP crew still in command. The train will continue north over Burlington Northern rails with a power consist of 3546 on the point and the 3541, 3529, 3008, 3014 and 3059 following. It is July 8, 1980. **Virgil Staff**

14

A Matter of Oil

BACK IN EARLY 1942, the Western Pacific had no experience with what the lubrication oil drain periods should be on its road diesels. Samples went through regularly for chemical analysis to a lab in Los Angeles, and it was a simple matter to thumb through the reports showing the present state of knowledge concerning the lubricating oils and their drainage intervals. The object of these chemical analyses was not only to determine how well the oil was meeting expectations, but the length of time that it could be expected to do so. Based on experience, the drain period was initially set at 12,000 miles in April 1942, and 15,000 miles in February 1943. Condemning limit in July 1943 was 20,000 miles, 25,000 in October, and 30,000 in December. By November 1944, the condemning limit was set at 40,000 miles, with 50,000 miles established in early 1946.

The oil under test was Texaco URSA X-40-2-Star, and was of great satisfaction to the railroad. This oil contained an additive, which makes the Western Pacific probably the first railroad to use an additive oil in its road-freight diesels. It was a generally held opinion at that time that freight engines would accumulate carbon due to long periods of idling. On the WP, between Portola and Oroville, a locomotive would be 10 to 16 hours on the road, with the engine idling up to 95 percent of the time. The purpose of the additive was to cut the carbon, and at one time or another, visitors from foreign roads remarked that the Western Pacific engines were clean inside.

No oil was reclaimed, and a viscosity test for fuel dilution was made every trip on the road locomotives and every week on the switch engines. A "Visgage" was used for this test, and all results were registered on a chart for future reference. Water was easily detected because oils with detergents will turn yellow when mixed with water, and the condition of the oil in regards to gummy material, corrosion and dead filters was accurately checked by using the blotter test. These tests took only about 15 minutes per unit, which included obtaining

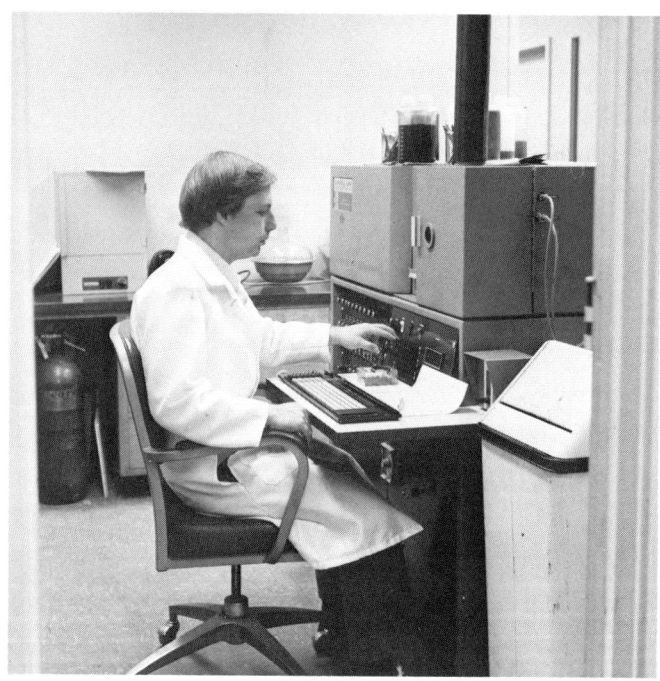

Chemist Richard Hurst works at the Atomic Emission Direct Reading Spectrometer in a corner of the lubrication laboratory of the WP at Stockton, 1976.
Virgil Staff

the samples from the engine and completing the tests. Most lube oil changes took place at Oroville and Elko, and surprisingly, the bigger oil consumption was at Elko. In these years, the power was being operated greatly in excess of the distances or times recommended, but the engines were clean inside, the oil when removed remained tolerably good, and O'Neill gave the major credit to the presence of detergent in the oil.

From the beginning there was some perplexity as to the means of disposal for used crankcase oil. The oil remained good and it was felt should be put to some use. By late 1942 this oil was used for free oiling of freight cars, and the oiling of the machinery on steam locomotives, but at no time was it ever used in the journal boxes of locomotives or rolling stock. In May 1943, the company was using storage tank No. 5 at Oroville for mixing four parts of crankcase oil with one part of Shell's "cold weather oil"—the two oils being blended by use of an air-operated device.

Some oil was reclaimed at Oakland in 1945, but Cuyler feared that after the double-strength additives had been mixed with the reclaimed oil, he would have a second-class oil that was only slightly less expensive than the new URSA oil, and that the railroad would be confronted with the fact that it was taking chances with its diesel locomotives. The oil was therefore used for other purposes, such as free oiling of locomotives and cars, oiling of all shop line shafting, switchpoints, or other track oiling. Contaminated oil never reached tank No. 5 but was dumped into the crude fuel oil sump and burned along with the other crude oil.

As the company acquired additional diesels, the problem increasingly had to be faced of how to dispose of the used crankcase oil. In 1949 the mechanical department began to think in terms of reclaiming its own oil, and in 1950 it completed an authorization for expenditure of funds to construct a lube oil "Refinoil" plant at the Sacramento Shops. This plant operated until May 1958, and, as an example of productive capacity, is known to have reclaimed 45,091 gallons between

East of Proctor, the WPE sings in dynamic as it keeps its 11:35 a.m. appointment with milepost 784. The proper handling of locomotive lubricating oil was still a priority item when this photo was made on June 23, 1976. **Virgil Staff**

May 1, 1957, and April 30, 1958. At the time that the plant was discontinued, the cost of reclamation was at .401 cents per gallon, as compared to .5574 for new oil. The opportunity to purchase back the reclaimed oil for .299 cents per gallon was accepted, and the Western Pacific used a considerable amount of this reclaimed oil until September 1959 when it lost two crankshafts due to the oxidized condition of the reclaimed oil that was being purchased.

In 1953, and probably as early as 1949, the policy had come around to scheduled oil changes at the annual and semiannual ICC inspection. By laboratory analysis of the oil, made at frequent intervals, the drain period had been extended to between 50,000 and 60,000 miles after which time the oil should be changed. Periodic checks were made to determine if any change should be made in this arrangement, and since the power accumulated about this much mileage in a six-month period, it was decided to change the oil on inspection dates when the locomotives were out of service for repairs, thus eliminating any out-of-service time for changing oil.

By this time, some railroads were not changing their oil, as a matter of policy, but only adding oil as it was required. This might be acceptable if one found it necessary to frequently tear the engines down, since this would require a new crankcase of oil. But Cuyler didn't expect this kind of maintenance in any amount, and he feared dirty crankcases with the expected increased maintenance cost. Dirty oil caused crankshafts and cylinder liners to score, and until the loss of two crankshafts resulting from the oxidized reclaimed oil, the WP never lost a crankshaft because of impurities in the oil. Moreover, to extend the interval over six months caused a more rapid change of oil filters, which at the time were more expensive than the oil. Filters usually lasted about 30 days, and some engines ran up to 12,000 miles before a filter change was necessary.

Sometime prior to March 1965, the policy was changed to a three-month drain period. For reasons unknown to the writer, a two-month period was temporarily instituted in March with filters changed about every two weeks. Lube oil samples for outside analysis were regular and frequent. Cuyler asked Bill Stevens and Richard Shideler to get deeply involved in the study of what was transpiring within these engines. Using March 1969 as an example, the oil analysis reports for that month showed 11 units requiring attention: two with lead increase, six with small water leaks, two with dirt in the oil, and one with fuel dilution. None of these was a covered wagon, but seven were GP-35s and GP-40s.

Cuyler retired as chief mechanical officer on April 14, 1970, but became a consultant until January 1, 1973. At the time that D.F. Pilkinton took his place on April 15, 1970, monthly lube oil samples were being taken from most of the power, with some power receiving analysis at more frequent intervals. Lubrication oil, like diesel fuel, was becoming prohibitively expensive, and on June 22, 1970, Pilkinton announced that henceforth all switch engines, covered wagons, GP-7s and GP-9s would participate in the new extended lube oil periods of annual oil change intervals with samples to be taken every 30 days. All bigger power would have semiannual oil changes, with sample intervals of 30 days for the GP-20s, and 15 days for the U-30Bs, GP-35s, and GP-40s. Thirty-day sample intervals would correlate with ICC inspection and 15-day intervals with truck lubes.

Lubrication oil analyses were expensive, when done off the railroad property, and required a minimum of three to four days before a given analysis was returned. Alfred E. Perlman became president of the Western Pacific on December 1, 1970, and R.G. Flannery took the office of executive vice president on January 1, 1971. The story goes that these two almost immediately indicated interest in a company-owned lube oil laboratory—in fact, demanded one. This is not difficult to believe in view of Perlman's lifetime interest in the scientific evaluation of lubrication. Such a laboratory was quickly set up.

An atomic absorption spectrophotometer was installed in the laboratory, and lube oil analysis commenced operation about the end of November 1971. The new laboratory immediately realized significant savings for the company, but the spectrophotometer possessed certain characteristics which impeded the rapid analysis of samples. Precise dilution of each sample in a special solvent was time consuming, and since the machine used different setups for different elements, it was always necessary to run the samples in batches. Results were therefore delayed, and immediate information on a given engine was not available when needed. On December 7, 1972, Perlman approved the retirement of the atomic absorption spectrophotometer, and its replacement by an atomic emission direct reading spectrometer which simplified operation, detected metals like tin and nickel—which the first machine would not—detected minute concentrations of lead and copper, and made it possible for chemist Richard Hurst to run individual samples when immediate samples on units were needed.

On January 10, 1974, Superintendent of Locomotives John S. Miller ordered that all oil changes were to be totally directed out of Stockton. At this time, all arbitrary oil changes were discontinued, and all changes became laboratory directed. A long-term series of sophisticated tests on two new lubricating oils was begun about August in which five U-23s, six GP-40s, and 11 controls were involved. About the end of 1976 or early 1977, one of these oils, PED 5022, was accepted as the new "house oil," although the test continued on after that date.

Virgil Staff

John S. Miller
A change in the way oil was changed.

15

The Death of Steam

DIESEL POWER assignments in the early 1940s have been previously discussed. Switchers were spread around the system so as to receive the maximum use, with those of 1,000 horsepower taking the heaviest assignments. Wherever possible, steam was placed on standby, and following the war a considerable number of fantails were stored. Until completion of Dieselization Plan "A," dieselizing the Eastern Division, the mainline freight service west of Oroville was chiefly with steam power. The *Exposition Flyer* was dieselized by the 801 Class, with the *Royal Gorge* essentially dieselized by arrival of the FP-7s in 1950. Specials continued to receive steam power, but this arrangement was largely terminated shortly after arrival of the 913 Class in the same year.

By at least April 1948, the Baldwins were temporarily handling the Trevarno and River Rock locals and the 508 was assigned to yard service at San Jose. In April, Duggan attempted unsuccessfully to dieselize the Reno local with the 557, but gave up the idea in May and again in June when the Baldwins were unable to pull the tonnage normally handled by a consolidation. This situation was compromised in June by running a Baldwin when the train was light, and putting on steam when the tonnage was heavier. By early 1949 the Del Paso turn was dieselized by a Baldwin, and the San Jose branch by a 504 and 551 Class in January. Sacramento turns were dieselized in May 1949.

Arrival of the 913 Class in early 1950 dieselized all mainline service east of Portola, and most service east of Oroville. The

C-43 class, No. 60, one of 65 Consolidations built new for the Western Pacific, trudges up the old line east of Oroville on November 28, 1937. These engines were rated at 1,250 tons up the one percent, or theoretically 250 tons more than a single unit of FT diesel over the Third Subdivision.
Wilbur C. Whittaker

It was taken for granted that the new diesels would power the varnish, but getting full utilization of the new engines in freight service was a trickier matter. From the East Portal of Tunnel 2 one could usually catch this view of the *Zephyr* at about 2:15 in the afternoon. Here's No. 17 coming at us on April 17, 1966. And with a little patience and a modicum of luck, there would be a westbound AP not far behind! **Virgil Staff**

The 559 class was the first to take over diesel switching chores on the Eastern Division, but the GP-40 proved to be the ultimate inheritor of these utilitarian tasks. The Rowley Local switches the magnesium plant at Rowley, Utah, on the early afternoon of June 21, 1977, at the end of the Delle Branch some 11.1 miles northeast of Delle.
Virgil Staff

power started running through Keddie on the NCX and SWG trains on February 8 or 9, and the B&L local and the Keddie–Portola local received the 585 a few days later. About February 20, engine 907 was cut-in-two and used in shuttle and helper service on the third and fourth subdivisions. Tracks at Keddie were filled with two-unit diesels, and Roundhouse Foreman O.M. Beard was anxious to get the steam power moved out permanently. After January, the oil-burning steam power was being moved off the Eastern Division, with most of it receiving assignment at Stockton.

Arrival of the 559 Class completely dieselized all switching assignments on the Eastern Division. With completion of Dieselization Plan "A," three two-unit FT consists provided helper service out of Wendover and Elko, and about the same time the Tooele Valley local was dieselized. Up to August 1950, the Baldwins had seen service at Oakland, Stockton, Sacramento, Oroville, Keddie, Portola, and Salt Lake City, but had never worked Bieber, Wendover, Elko, or Winnemucca.

The RDC cars released two of the F-3 cab units for back-to-back pool freight service between Oroville and Stockton, and engine 803A became assigned to the San Jose local in late September, and ran into March 1951. These engines were not operated on the other Western Division branches since they were restricted from certain industry tracks. Tenders, which had accompanied these diesels, were maintained at Oroville, Stockton, and Oakland Yards for emergency use. All three of the cab units remained on the first and second subdivisions for passenger train protection.

Minimum continuous speed rating on the 801 Class was 22½ mph, so that every attempt was made to keep these off the long continuous grades. The 801A and 802A, back to back on the second subdivision, hauled about the same tonnage as a Mikado, and the 803A is said to have handled as high as 2,100 tons on the San Jose local.

With the falling off of business in late November 1950, the diesel road units which normally would have been on the Eastern Division were turned west at Oroville, with others taking fourth subdivision helper service, or service on the Keddie–Portola shuttle. Munson made a surprise visit to the Oroville roundhouse one night in early December 1950 and found considerable steam in use, with diesel road power idling. Munson considered this to be an intolerable situation, and it may have been at this time that he began to consider a more positive method of controlling the handling of diesel power. To look ahead, in April 1952 the auditing department figured that on an Oroville–Oakland turn, a Mikado cost $1.65 per mile in addition to the helper trips over the Altamont which ran at $2.02 per mile on the eastward trips and $1.29 on the westbound. Diesel power costs, for a three-unit diesel, without helpers, was figured at $1.32 per mile, so that there were considerable savings each time the diesel could be employed.

In January 1951, the 551 and 581 classes were being tried on the Keddie–Westwood turn, and in a sudden spurt of business, the railroad found itself with more tonnage than it could immediately handle. Engines were run light to assignments, and steam was placed back in service. When an excess of tonnage showed up at Bieber, the 260 was tied up indefinitely at Oroville, and Portola no longer kept standby steam power laying for an occasional emergency. Power was taken off runs for other runs, and the chiefs cooperated to the fullest extent with the Eastern Division in turning power back at Portola.

Superintendent G.W. Curtis suggested on January 24, 1951, that a joint meeting be held at Portola on January 30 to discuss the entire problem. Out of this discussion came Munson's decision to authorize a power coordinator, who would be Larry Contri from the Sacramento dispatcher's office, and who would receive morning reports, reports of all diesel movements, reports showing the power located at each point and when it was ready for service, or if tied up for what reason and when it was expected to be available. This position became effective February 1, 1951, and was held by Contri for 19 years. Prior to being named to this job, the assignments were determined by the chief dispatchers. But as Contri once told the writer: "Mr. Munson was hot to get the diesels moving." This job, then, lasted 19 years after which time it became a function of the superintendent of transportation in the reign of General Manager MacLeod.

There was never any shortage of problems, an example of which transpired about February 11, 1951. Engine 920 on a westbound train was the only four-unit diesel in sight for train 2/54, and four units were needed to handle 2/54's tonnage up the canyon. This power would have reached Oroville Yard around 5:00 P.M. had it not been for slide difficulties at two points. The roundhouse foreman had advised that he could service and turn the engine in about one hour, so that no excessive delay was anticipated.

Due to the slides, engine 920 did not reach Oroville Yard and turn into the roundhouse until 9:40 P.M. At 9:50 P.M. the roundhouse foreman informed the yardmaster that he could have engine 920 at 10:50 P.M. The crew was called for 11:15 P.M. and the delays thereafter were as follows: 15 minutes to get the air; 20 minutes meeting Extra 914 West, 35 minutes for a break-in-two in two places because of unknown parties stepping on the pin lifters; 20 minutes waiting for a meet with No. 2.

Eastbound at the western entrance to the Feather River Canyon, the 33 speaks softly as it walks through Oroville with the potential for 43,300 pounds of tractive power. It was May 30, 1938, and steam was secure on its throne.
Wilbur C. Whittaker

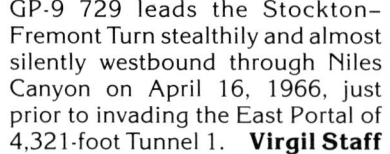

GP-9 729 leads the Stockton–Fremont Turn stealthily and almost silently westbound through Niles Canyon on April 16, 1966, just prior to invading the East Portal of 4,321-foot Tunnel 1. **Virgil Staff**

Munson, always the gentleman, could be very tough. Naturally, he wanted the details. The slides were not avoidable, and Superintendent G.W. Curtis reminded him that the foreman had given the engine to the yardmaster for call within 10 minutes after it stopped on the tieup track. But in view of the requirement that crews be given one hour, 30 minutes call, the call time could not have been earlier than 11:15 P.M. He assured Munson that they were not having repeater trouble with transients stepping on the pin lifters at Oroville Yard, and Gleason suggested that the roundhouse foreman used the time he needed since these men knew they were required to turn out locomotives that they were relatively sure would make successful trips.

Following this discussion, Munson authorized the roundhouse foremen to give the dispatcher a figure on availability of incoming diesel power without first seeing the diesel, with the transportation department accepting responsibility for any delays in case something was found amiss with the power. Actually, there had been such an understanding with the master mechanic for a number of years but on this night the chips just didn't seem to stack right.

In May 1951, the 551 replaced the 581 Class engine at Portola, with the Baldwin receiving assignment to the Portola–Keddie local. This dieselized the local, with engine 30 remaining at Portola to protect the times when the stationary boilers were shut down, and engine 26 used out of Portola Yard en route to Stockton Yard. The 506 and the 552 respectively were used on work trains on the third and fourth subdivisions in June, with the 585 known to have been on the

Oroville–Keddie local on June 11. Essentially all trains through the canyon were now dieselized. The 559-560, and the 560-562, were used in helper service from Keddie to Almanor in early 1951, but the engines tended to heat and to lose water so that both were uncoupled and placed back in yard service.

A picture of the extent to which dieselization had taken place by July 1951 can be seen in the roster of steam locomotives then at various terminals: none at Salt Lake City, Wendover, Winnemucca, or Keddie; seven 401 Class stored unserviceable at Elko; the No. 30 at Portola in standby stationary boiler service; 15 at Oroville, at least 13 of which were in storage; 10 at Sacramento Shops, 25 at Stockton, and seven at Oakland. Much of this stored power was being carried by two-unit diesel combinations which, in August, could be found the length of the railroad.

During the summer of 1951, two of the 559 Class switch engines were tried on the Westwood Turn. This was not simply a test since it should be remembered that the consolidations were no longer working east of Oroville, and there was insufficient power to give the turn the excessive horsepower of two units of FT. All the Alco road switchers through the 559 Class possessed Blunt trucks which nosed badly and tended to spread the rail. In late November, the nosing was so bad with the 559-561 on the turn that the 564 was placed on the point and the 561 was sent to the Sacramento Shops.

The arrival of the six SW-9s in June and July 1952 released 1,000-hp Alcos from work train and local service for assignment as follows: Oakland two, Stockton three, Oroville one. This essentially released steam engines 163 and 165 at Oakland; 40, 41, 164 and 166 at Stockton; and No. 1 at Oroville. All yard operations were thereby dieselized with additional yard assignments protected by steam. The 601 Class of SW-9s initially worked their way in sets of two between Elko and Oroville in drag service. For the remainder of 1952 they worked assignments on the Keddie–Westwood local, San Jose local, Reno local, Oroville–Keddie, and Portola–Keddie turns.

Arrival of the two orders of GP-7s between June 1952 and April 1953 released the 601 Class for various other switching, local, and work train assignments, with engines of the 701 or 601 Classes finally and completely dieselizing the Trevarno and River Rock locals by early 1953. By July 1, 1953, the 708 was on the Trevarno local, 710 on the Tooele local, the 712 and 713 were in the Wendover helper service, and the remainder worked east and west out of Portola. Except for the TS-132 in standby service at Stockton, the Western Pacific just didn't need the old steamers anymore. The railroad was now dieselized and the mechanical department could concern itself with other problems.

The Great Northern had shown interest in dieselizing the California–Seattle symbol trains in 1951 with power to be furnished from a pool provided by the GN, SP&S, and WP. This pool would provide substantial savings, and would avoid the presence of large diesels standing idle at junction points such as at Bieber, Bend, and Vancouver. The Western Pacific was interested in this proposed operation, but was not sufficiently dieselized in September 1951 to allocate the necessary diesel units without penalizing other operations. The arrival of the second order of GP-7s in April 1953 enabled such changes

It is unspeakably hot on the afternoon of July 16, 1979, the radiation of the sun's rays rebounding from the salty desert in visible waves. And U30B 3068 leads the 3521, 3519 and 3515 westbound at Salduro, Utah, with a freight for Wendover. Only in the early morning are the salt flats comfortable in summer. **Virgil Staff**

in assignment that a portion of the proposed pool was now possible, and the new operation became effective June 1, 1953, with the engine arriving at Bieber on the NCX during the evening of May 31. Western Pacific power now went through to Klamath Falls, Oregon. The problem of power running through Bieber, with changed designation in both directions, was handled by the GN in early 1954 by a new timetable which used similar train numbers to those used on the Western Pacific.

Western Pacific's excellent showing in diesel utilization in 1952 and 1953 was made possible by the presence of a power coordinator with complete responsibility and authority in the placement of power. Reliable studies indicated that this plan increased utilization by at least 10 percent over what it had been previously when the dispatchers handled the power. Cuyler was convinced that without this plan it would not have been possible to operate without the use of steam in 1953.

The power coordinator also operated very closely with the mechanical department in order to assure that locomotives were sent to the shop when due for ICC inspections, or when return was necessary to the central maintenance point at Oroville for running repairs. The mechanical department released the locomotives for 10 days, which allowed the power coordinator to have the locomotive for that period of time, and allowed him sufficient time to make advance arrangements for its proper return.

Availability continued to equal about 80 to 90 percent of the hours per month by taking advantage of the characteristics of the business on the Western Pacific, and performing most of the maintenance work during the comparatively long interval during which there was no demand for the unit. During a period of 50 percent utilization, the number of road units on the railroad enabled an 80 percent availability to provide sufficient power for all needs, thus enabling the use of a smaller shop force. In periods of higher utilization, an increase in availability meant larger forces, but this added expense was supposed to be offset by the increased mileage made by the units.

16

The RDC Experiment

TOWARDS THE END of 1949, the losses on the secondary passenger train, the *Royal Gorge,* were sufficient to cause the elimination of its sleepers and diners. Application was made for total discontinuance, and the WP prepared for its next move should such application be rejected. In fact, the various public utility commissions did authorize the discontinuance of daily operation but required the substitution of a triweekly service between Oakland and Salt Lake City.

Concurrently, the Western Pacific considered the purchase of a Budd rail diesel car to substitute for the short steam trains that had been so expensive on the *Royal Gorge.* An RDC-1, for experimental purposes, arrived at Salt Lake City about Decem-

Ultimately, the *Zephyrette* proved there was no need for a secondary passenger train on the Western Pacific. Still, the RDC cars performed nobly on what was probably the longest "doodlebug" run in the U.S. Here is car 375 on October 1, 1960, in front of the Oakland station finishing up the final run of Train No. 1. There were no crowds, and there was no fanfare. **Don Hansen**

Budd car 376 is spotted in its home at the Zephyrette shops in Oakland on June 25, 1959. The unit has only about 15 months of service remaining on the WP. **Don Hansen**

ber 15, 1949, but was delayed at Winnemucca due to failure of an idler journal bearing. The car then moved to Portola on December 17, from whence it ran through to Oakland as train 2/17.

This car was powered by two 275-hp GM6-110 diesel engines. Both were mounted beneath the carbody, one at each truck. A drive shaft was connected through means of a torque converter and reduction gears between each engine and the inside axles of each truck. The inside wheels were the drivers and the outside wheels were the idlers. The torque converter was used in lieu of a clutch, and was essentially the same drive used in army tanks during the war. This provided a very smooth drive, and a rough start was almost an impossibility. These cars were fully reversible, and possessed controls at each end.

Their day on the Western Pacific done, Budd cars 375 and 376 wait patiently at the Oakland Shops for a purchaser. One appeared, finally, and the cars were sold for further service on the Northern Pacific.
Tom Irion Collection

116 D-DAY ON THE WESTERN PACIFIC

The car was inspected by almost everyone of importance, and impressed its riders with the smooth, rapid ability to accelerate and decelerate. The fundamental question was how it would perform on Nos. 1 and 2. On these trains there would be need for a baggage compartment and pilot, and the mechanical forces, with Budd approval, temporarily modified the RDC-1 with a head-end compartment so as to run as Nos. 1 and 2 for a few days. Pilots were installed at the expense of the Budd Company, and mail and express were transferred between standard equipment and the RDC for the five round trips taking place between January 17-26, Portola to Salt Lake and return.

The WP was generally pleased with this car although there were those who believed it better fitted for commuter service than for long runs such as between Oakland and Salt Lake City. The first purchase order for an RDC-2 was placed with the Budd Co. on January 23, 1950, and a second car was authorized by the board of directors on June 1—the two being received on May 25 and July 19, 1950, respectively.

The two new self-propelled baggage coaches, numbered 375 and 376, measured 85'0" across the couplers, and each contained two model 61801 GM engines with 5.6x5" stroke and bore. Each of the two engines had a rating of 258 horsepower at 1,800 rpm, and there were two hydraulic torque converters per car. Both cars were delivered with 33" wheels, but the railroad changed this to 34" in 1953. Truck brakes were a model CF Budd disc with Rolokron bearings, and drive was by model 8 Spicer axle drives—two per unit. Control brakes consisted of a modified HSC braking system with an M-23 brake valve, D-22-AR control valve, and an A-3 independent brake valve.

After delivery the cars were put through a series of tests, which resulted in many modifications over the years, both by Budd and by the Western Pacific. Mechanical Engineer W.B. Wolverton participated in all of these, and was undoubtedly the chief authority on the railroad concerning the RDCs and their problems. Over 90 significant modifications were instituted prior to 1954, and a few are listed below:

1. Installations of nine two-passenger reclining seats immediately behind the baggage compartment for the comfort of revenue passengers.

2. Installation of a second toilet in the small compartment adjacent to the baggage compartment.

3. Installation of a conductor's desk at the small jump seat near the end of the car opposite the baggage compartment.

4. Installation of a body-mounted pilot to both ends of the car.

5. Installation of diagonal number lights, two per end, at each end of the car.

6. Installation of wiring and plug-in receptacles at each end of the car for jumper equipment to furnish power for lights and air conditioning when the car was being hauled by a diesel locomotive.

7. Installation of an additional air horn at each end of the car with each new horn installed to blow signals toward the opposite end of the car. These horns were used for signaling to the rear, for recalling flagmen, and for extra effects.

8. A red Gyralite was applied on the rear end door and a white one on the front. This was to provide an oscillating red light at the rear which latter was standard on all Western Pacific passenger trains.

Car 376 was given 1,164 miles of operational tests between July 21-24, 1950, and the operation was without any of the mechanical or operational difficulties previously experienced with the RDC-1 demonstrator. A test run was made with the 375 as a work train between South Sacramento and the Altamont on August 21, and another between Sacramento and Oakland on August 28. A final pre-inaugural test, conducted between Sacramento and Oakland on September 12, provided the final braking tests. White flags were placed for test stops at mileposts 118.4, 113.0, 106.4, 99.0, 81.5, and at 67.25, and measurements were made of stopping distances from these flags.

Reduction in service by trains 1 and 2 from daily to tri-weekly became effective with the departure of a Budd car eastbound from Oakland Pier on Friday, September 15, 1950, and westbound from Salt Lake City on Sunday, September 17. These cars ran with baggage compartment to the front, and were fueled at Oakland, Oroville, Portola, Winnemucca, and Wendover. During times of heavier business, Nos. 1 and 2 often ran with an F-3 on the point, followed by the water tender, a baggage car, and an RDC to the rear. In later years, specials were frequently consolidated with trains 1 or 2. The Budd car then went out with the special, and either returned on its own, or was coupled in behind the water tender, or behind a brace of F-7s should they have been employed on the special. Performance of the RDC rendered a maximum speed in torque conversion of 55 mph, with cruising speed direct of 70 mph at 55 percent of the available horsepower. The car would do 62 mph on a one percent grade, and seldom lacked for power except on those rare occasions when limping into a terminal on one engine.

The mechanical department had pondered how the RDC would do under gale conditions. On January 18, 1951, Road Foreman of Engines C.F. Fields rode the 375 on No. 2 from Winnemucca to Salt Lake City in a very severe snowstorm with winds of almost gale intensity. The engines operated normally although the complete bottom of the car and engine housing were a mass of snow and ice. "At the first cut west of Boaz and through Boaz snow had drifted over the rails to a depth of 12 to 15 inches and I would estimate that at places the snowdrifts were one-fourth mile in length as it was very hard to tell how far they extended as the snow has a tendency to fly right back on the windows and we were unable to see out until we were through the snowbank. Speed of engine on entering snowbank was 60 mph and when it emerged the speed was about 35 mph with throttle wide open," reported Fields.

In regular operation, additional problems made their appearance. Pilots were refastened and strengthened, and trimmed sloping upward to the outside to insure sufficient clearance. Air capacity was increased by increasing the compressor speed and installing higher horsepower motors. Automatic drain valves and air radiators were applied to furnish dry air to the sanders and brake system.

To assure reliable shunting of coded track circuits, copper shunt shoes were applied against the wheels. These were modified from time to time as the forces gained additional experience with the cars. In late 1951 the mechanical department very successfully employed its own design of a steel-welded and fabricated back with cast copper renewable contact shoes riveted to the steel back. A No. 1/0 bonding wire was run between the shunt blocks on the car, with pressure on the shoes being experimentally varied between 30 and 40 pounds. Eventually the WP settled on cast-iron shunts which were adequate but less expensive. In coming to a stop, the engineer always closed the sanders at least two car lengths from the stopping point to assure that the car would not be resting on its own sand.

Early in the lifespan of the 375, it was noticed that when this car passed through a heavy rainstorm, the control circuits became grounded, thus affecting engine temperature control and oil pressure which shut the engines down. Nevertheless, the car was regularly dispatched since this was believed to be the more economical way of determining the trouble that shut down the No. 1 engine. Wolverton and others made a careful study to learn what improvement could be made so that the wiring would be protected when the cars passed through heavy rainstorms.

Finally, because of the alkali dust and the many weeds blowing around underneath the cars in Nevada and Utah, the forces installed air filters at each end of the diesel engine housings, and closed off the louvred side openings of the engine compartments. This aided considerably in keeping the engine compartments clean and took much of the air cleaning load off the oil bath engine air filters.

In spite of the deficiencies, the Western Pacific considered the roughly 10-year RDC experiment to be a success. Yearly savings from Budd car service were estimated at $700,000, and the relationship with the Budd Co. indicated that firm's serious interest in producing the most trouble-free car possible. However, rising costs and poor revenues on trains 1 and 2 finally caused management to request abandonment. By 1957 there was little deadheading of train and engine crews on trains 1 and 2, and company mail could be carried on the locals, as was already being done, or on trains 17 and 18, the *California Zephyr*. The store department was using its own equipment, and arrangements for employees needing transportation could be handled by other means.

The Western Pacific had tried cutting passenger fares but there was always a regular loss on this train. By 1959 the traffic was such that very little revenue was collected between October 1 and June 1. On the Eastern Division, few employees used this train, except on weekends, and the express business had fallen off to the extent that extra baggage cars were no longer generally required during the heavy Christmas movements. Direct out-of-pocket losses during 1959 amounted to approximately $255,000, and in April 1960 the company filed for abandonment which became effective October 1, 1960. The Western Pacific now had only the *California Zephyr* in passenger service, and cab units 801A and 802A now regularly ran in freight service with a gear ratio of 62:15.

And then there was one—after October 1, 1960, only the *California Zephyr* carried revenue passengers on the Western Pacific. With cabmates 801-A and 802-A already in freight service, the 804-A wheels No. 18 through Sunol on March 29, 1969.   **Virgil Staff**

People Make a Railroad

Modern Machinery is mighty nice, but it takes people to make the railroad move. On the Western Pacific, as on other roads, every job is important. In this salute to the men and women of WP, we start with Conductor Whitey Fisher of the *California Zephyr*. In top photo, Whitey, right, compares watches with Engineer Louis Fischer as departure time nears Oakland. It's highball time for Whitey, left, and Brakeman Sam Heath, center photo, at Oakland on April 15, 1968. At Sacramento, bottom, Whitey is on the ground again to signal departure. Whitey functioned in the best of a trainman's tradition, and he often went far beyond the call of duty in being courteous and helpful. To Whitey, the Western Pacific always came first. **All: Virgil Staff**

PEOPLE MAKE A RAILROAD 119

One Man's Locomotive: Engineer Vern Brain is about to take the 921-D back to its train.

M.D. Aydlotte leans on a switch-stand as he critically eyes the lineup in the Oakland New Yards in October of 1966.

Bobby Grubbs, famed over the entire railroad for his smooth air applications, was one of the best-liked hoggers on the WP. Below, he relaxes momentarily prior to the departure of Train 18 out of Oakland in January of 1966. **All: Virgil Staff**

Dispatcher Clayton L. Foss works the first trick at one of the two Eastern Division boards in Sacramento, May 19, 1974. These machines were built by Union Switch & Signal, and employed the 506A coding as does the present system built by Safetran Corp. At the time of this photo, the 5-6 subdivision console seen here was about to be retired in favor of the new system already in service on the Western Division.

The late afternoon sun pierces the soft shadows of the old No. 5 Adeline Street roundhouse in Oakland as Clifton J. Conley concentrates. Conley was roundhouse foreman on the day this photo was taken, February 2, 1969, but both he and his roundhouse were nearing retirement.

Both: Virgil Staff

PEOPLE MAKE A RAILROAD 121

17

The Navy Grows Old

THE WESTERN PACIFIC'S "navy" was growing old, and between 1951 and 1953, the rail-road comprehensively studied the fundamental needs of its aging fleet of vessels on San Francisco Bay. This fleet consisted of two steam tugs—the *Hercules* (built 1907 and the *Humaconna* (1919)—two uncompartmentalized wooden deck barges (1909), and the steel-riveted deck barge No. 3 (1928).

The initial consideration was to dieselize the tug *Humaconna* in 1954 and purchase a steel car barge in 1955 to replace the two wooden barges. The wooden barges had a capacity of 10 to 14 cars, depending on their length and weight, and might be replaced by a longer steel barge capable of carrying more cars than the existing barges, and that would reduce the large annual outlays necessary to keep these old wooden barges in service.

Since there was no intention of purchasing new tugs, the new barge would need to be small enough to be handled by the existing tugs. There were those who talked of a barge that would haul 28 cars, but would either of the Western Pacific tugs be capable of manipulating such a long barge, especially in windy and inclement weather?

On May 11, 1951, Superintendent G.W. Curtis wrote to Oakland Terminal Superintendent Henry Stapp that while the company could undoubtedly get by for a number of years if it

The MV *Las Plumas* turns just outside its Oakland slip on the dreary morning of November 11, 1966. This vessel was fast and beautiful, and at a distance was often misidentified as an aircraft carrier. **Virgil Staff**

Steam tug *Hercules* in the Moore drydock for repairs on January 12, 1940. The *Hercules* possessed 150 horsepower more than the *Humaconna*'s 850, and its draft of 15.5 feet was one foot less.

Gabriel Moulin

patched up the two old wooden barges, it occurred to him that their small capacities were costing extra money. A self-propelled barge, twice the car capacity of the wooden barges, would greatly reduce operating costs and at the same time improve the service. A larger capacity barge would cut the number of daily trips to a given slip, and would speed the operation across the bay. The two wooden barges in addition to one tug could then be scrapped or disposed of, and the remaining tug, and barge No. 3, could be retained for standby and extra service. Indeed, after months of study and discussion, this is precisely what happened.

Could a loaded barge in excess of 325 feet be handled by WP tugs? Surveyor R.H. Boyt for Pillsbury & Martignoni answered that this would depend as much on the ability of the Master of the tug as on the power of the vessel, but he doubted the ability of the present tugs to handle such a loaded barge, particularly at the San Francisco Powell Street slip. This factor was not discouraging to G.W. Curtis, superintendent of the Western Division, since he was now convinced that the new barge should be self-propelled. The two wooden barges were "fast running out their useful life, and every time it is necessary to drydock them the repair costs are extremely heavy and constantly increasing due to rotting of the wood," said Curtis. Barge No. 3 could be continued in service indefinitely, but the tugs were another story. The *Hercules* was an all-steel vessel but because of its age required continuous replacement of hull sheets and other parts to meet Marine regulations. Tug *Humaconna* was in generally better condition, except that the two boilers in the *Humaconna* had developed progressively long cracks in their front heads. These cracks were welded each time they extended, but the time would arrive when renewal or replacement of these boilers would be necessary, and the time out of service would be prohibitive to say nothing of the costs.

In May 1952, Wolverton made the initial specification estimates for a self-propelled barge to carry 28 or 29 cars. Phillip Wyche, of the engineering department, had already made a thorough study of the state of the fleet which seems to have convinced Gleason that dieselization of the tugs could be accomplished at a much lesser cost than the construction of new vessels. General Manager Harry Munson pointed out that dieselization of one of the tugboats would not solve the barge problems, and Gleason asked the firm of Pillsbury & Martignoni to study the problem, and to provide recommendations and cost figures. By at least May 1954, Gleason had come around to believing in a self-propelled car barge, and Pillsbury & Martignoni were asked on August 16, 1954, to start a preliminary study relative to designing such a barge.

Only the Western Pacific seems to have believed in the wisdom of such a car ferry, and reputable shipbuilders in the Bay Area seem to have shared a belief that a self-propelled car barge of approximately 350-foot length would be unwieldy and costly to operate, that it would be too narrow when compared to the overall length, and that wind resistances and tide conditions would greatly interfere with satisfactory maneuverability. Gleason did not believe this at all, and Western Pacific's Myron Christy, who had been placed in charge of these studies, and who was something of an "old salt," concluded in August 1954 that a "single self-propelled unit can perform from a service standpoint as well as or better than tugs and barges in handling our transbay business." In fact, the larger

Three-cylinder locomotive 4472, a left-hand-drive Pacific of notable repute, rides San Francisco Bay aboard the MV *Las Plumas*. This is the first leg of a journey home, and the *Flying Scotsman* will depart Oakland on the following day for temporary quarters in Stockton. It is August 12, 1972. **Virgil Staff**

barge could do a given amount of work as fast as or faster than the two barges each with half its capacity, but would lose some of the flexibility of the two smaller barges, although studies indicated that such loss of flexibility would not delay deliveries.

On March 22, 1955, Munson requested L.C. Norgaard & Associates at Pier 5, San Francisco, to undertake a preliminary design of a self-propelled car-float suitable for transbay operations. According to Mr. Christy, the effective average weight of cars lifted in company transbay freight car ferry operations should be taken at about 48 tons per car. This figure was based on the actual weighted average gross weight of all cars lifted westbound during 1954. Westbound movements were considered controlling because of the preponderance of loaded cars and heavier movement in terms of total cars lifted.

Maximum barge load that would present itself would be a full loading of loaded hopper cars about 95 tons each. Actual design tonnage developed should be figured at 67.2 tons as the average car weight, which was equal to 60 long tons per car. This meant that the vessel would be designed for about 1,900 short tons capacity of optimum loaded draft, and that it could easily handle 19 fully loaded 70-ton-capacity cars, versus 11 such cars on the then-present barges. Heavier loads would be possible, but with some proportional sacrifice of speed and fuel economy.

A new self-propelled vessel was authorized by the board of directors on February 27, 1956. President Whitman was pushing Munson to get construction moving, since maintenance and repair expenses for the present fleet would ultimately be

The WP toehold on San Francisco starts at this ferry slip where cars were loaded onto the MV *Las Plumas* in this 1960-era photo. A trio of S-2 switchers await the call to action, and the flatcars on the right-hand track are "idlers" that will be used to nudge freight cars aboard the vessel. **Richard Steinheimer**

wasted money. The proper bow design was of great importance, and Cuyler worked closely with the engineering department in its study of the slips to be used by the new *Feather River*. L.C. Norgaard & Associates became the architect, and an agreement dated March 27, 1956, authorized this firm to complete the preliminary drawings authorized on March 22, 1955.

The new car ferry was built by the Albina Engine and Machine Works of Portland, Oregon, and was of all-welded steel construction—framed longitudinally with hull, below deck, divided by eight transverse watertight bulkheads and by five non-watertight. The vessel possessed a canted stem and a square stern, and measured 375 feet in length by 59.1 feet in breadth. A superstructure bridged the four tracks, and was fitted out 'midships to provide a navigation bridge and day quarters for the crew.

Propulsion was by three 84-inch propellers at the stern connected to the port main, center main and starboard main engines, each of which was an Enterprise model DMG-38 direct reversible, eight-cylinder supercharged diesel marine engine with 12-inch bore and 15-inch stroke. Each engine was rated at 700 bhp at 300 rpm and provided the vessel with a

The *Humaconna* rests beside its barge on January 9, 1941. *Humaconna's* overall length was 151.7 feet compared to its sister's overall length of 145.8. Built in 1919, she was 12 years younger than the *Hercules*.
Western Pacific Collection

The steam tug *Humaconna* brings the No. 3 deck barge into its slip. Net register tonnage was 190, or 70 tons over that of the *Hercules*.
Western Pacific Collection

mean speed of about 10 knots. The bow was fitted with a 250-bhp Murray and Tregurtha Harbormaster propulsion unit for bow steering and maneuverability. This unit was powered by one GM6-110 engine, and took oil from a bow tank of 3,824 gallons. Four deep tanks of 9,630 gallons each provided fuel storage for the three Enterprise engines.

Car capacity was established at 27, 70-ton cars, and draft was 6'6" light and 10'0" loaded. Sperry Gyroscope Co. built the steering equipment, and the minimum turning basin requirement was 750 feet. The vessel possessed telegraph, radio, and radar systems, and was as modern as could be produced at that time. Construction was based on "Design No. 303 WP" dated September 25, 1956.

Original plans had been to name the new car ferry the *Feather River*, but as of May 23, 1956, the name was changed to *M.V. Las Plumas*. Mrs. Whitman smashed a bottle of champagne against the *Las Plumas* at Portland, and a customs license for operation was issued at the Port of Portland and the vessel sailed for home on July 7, 1957. Captain Steve King handled the vessel on her own power between Portland and San Francisco Bay, and Western Pacific's Captain Gustav A. Bergman and Chief Engineer Harold Clifford were aboard for experience and additional instruction.

Since the *Las Plumas* did not have accommodations for the crew, the writer believes one standard Pullman sleeping car, and business cars 105 and 106, in addition to a tank car, were carried on deck. On San Francisco Bay the *Las Plumas* was welcomed by the *Humaconna*, and by a host of yachts and fireboats. Acceptance trials took place on July 12, 1957, which included radius turns and crash stops. At 07:30 on July 29, 1957, the *Las Plumas* went into regular service on a three-shift operation with a seven-man crew.

Barges 1 and 2 were sold in June and September, respectively, 1957, and the East Bay Dredging Co. took the steam tug *Humaconna* away on her own power on July 9, 1958. The steam tug *Hercules* and Barge No. 3 would remain on standby for sometime, but maintenance of the *Hercules*, for standby service, became so excessive that it was sold to Thomas & Brown Shipbuilding, Inc., in September 1961. The Southern Pacific withdrew its last transbay ferry boat on July 28, 1958, and from this date Western Pacific passengers crossed to and from San Francisco by bus. But the *Las Plumas* would continue to ply the waters of the estuary and San Francisco Bay, and Western Pacific management was visibly gratified by the substantially lower operating costs, and by the improved service possible to its shippers.

18

How Much Power is Required?

FINAL DIESELIZATION, accompanied by completion between 1953 and 1955 of an ever-changing dispatching system, became the pivot around which a new kind of railroad materialized that could be scarcely recognizable to those who had worked the road in earlier years.

The majority of structures along the right-of-way were pulled down, sidings were extended, and signals relocated to provide greater braking distance for anticipated freight train speeds. The "31" order was discontinued as of March 1, 1952, and an interesting concomitant of the new TCS system in early 1953 was the surprising rise in gross ton miles per train hour on the Eastern Division.

Dieselization ultimately made possible longer and heavier trains without helpers over most districts. Few helpers were used over the Altamont, none up the canyon, east out of Portola, over Sand Pass, west of Gerlach over Sand Pass or Chilcoot hills, or east or west over Antelope Hill. Trains only infrequently received a help over Delle Hill to Clive. The helper at Wendover was eliminated in December 1963, and the final help over the NCE took place on September 24, 1971, when Engineer Bob Larson, with the 703-914D, boosted No. 54 out of Keddie.

In 1953, eastbound symbol trains out of Oroville usually ran with three or four units, but west of Oroville many trains ran with two units into Stockton, and two or three units over the Altamont into Oakland. In late 1954, three and sometimes four units were working on the PC, CFS, FB and SWG symbol trains west of Oroville in order to expedite the movement of these trains and fulfill their schedules. Two-unit engines could handle all of these trains on the second subdivision west of Oroville, and could sometimes make the schedule. But three units handled them 20 to 30 minutes faster. On the first subdivision west of Stockton, three units were generally needed to handle the heavy westbound tonnage trains over Altamont Hill, particularly the PC and CFS trains.

Three units were used on the FMS to make the schedule and provide power for No. 62 the following morning out of Oakland which generally was a heavy tonnage train and most of the time required three units. This handling normally eliminated helpers in both directions.

There was a major discussion at this time between General Manager Harry Munson, Superintendent of Transportation Grant S. Allen, and Power Coordinator Larry Contri concerning the transportation ratio and the adverse effect on it by reason of "overpowering" certain trains. It should be recalled that Oroville was a turning point for most power into or out of the lake. Four-unit trains westbound into Oroville frequently received two-unit consists to Stockton, and three-unit consists from Stockton to Oakland. Contri's view was that if the symbol trains were handled with units according to their tonnage, most symbol trains would not make their schedule, and on the first subdivision there might be the necessity of doubling the Altamont because of weather conditions.

By using three units all the way from Oroville to Oakland on the PC and CFS trains, there would be a reduction of the initial and final terminal delay at Stockton Yard which would save about 20 minutes on an engine change when it became necessary to add tonnage at Stockton Yard, or when the train was too heavy for two units into Oakland. Three units would maintain schedules and eliminate the need for helpers which would far overshadow any cost of extra units.

Cuyler, who became the CMO upon retirement of Elbert E. Gleason on October 31, 1954, often stated that the "overpowering" of trains would correspondingly reduce wear as it would relieve the load on the other units. Cuyler noted that the wear rate increased as the load factor increased, and that the frequency of repairs to a diesel unit operating under full load was much more rapid than if the unit was operating under conditions of lesser load. Fuel consumption should not vary in great amount since it took a certain amount of fuel to move a given amount of tonnage. The use of extra units had raised the average speed about nine percent, and since higher speed was desired, more power would need to be employed per ton haul in order to accomplish this.

Allen pointed out that in 1953 a concerted effort had been made to get along without using any steam power for the busy season. This proved successful, but had required the use of diesel helpers at Wendover and Stockton with consequent low mileage on helper engines, and a greater number of light miles. A great number of trains were operated on the Eastern Division in 1953 with three units requiring helpers at Wendover. Moreover, three units did not function as well in maintaining the schedules. West of Oroville most trains operated with two units requiring helpers at Stockton. Again these trains did not perform as well as they should.

During the middle and latter half of 1954, most through trains received three units which eliminated helpers and speeded the movements, and Allen was of the opinion that the power was being used to best advantage.

High Line trains were regularly receiving four units which ran through to Klamath Falls, and effective May 10, 1955, the Western Pacific furnished pool cabooses to protect symbol trains operating between Keddie and Klamath Falls. One Great Northern yard engine was eliminated at Bieber on the same date, and a second one shortly after. The GN enginehouse force, car force, and office force were similarly abolished at Bieber, and all enginehouse or car force work which could not be eliminated, and which previously was handled at Bieber, was now performed at Klamath Falls.

By June 1955, business was sufficiently heavy to cause Munson to think in terms of five-unit power consists, particularly on trains between Oroville and Bieber, and possibly on the PC and CFS trains out of Salt Lake. The Expediter and SWG, both North Line trains, were getting too heavy for the four-unit consists, and the trains were losing time with the tonnage they were handling. Both the SWG and Expediter received helpers between Keddie and Norvell, and a few trains received help between Bieber and Halls Flat.

It was thought that increasing the number of units to five would eliminate the helper crew at Wendover which was used primarily to help the PC and CFS, and occasionally a drag over Wendover Hill. There would be very few occasions where the tonnage would exceed that which could be handled by five units on the PC and CFS trains and it could be regulated on drags not to exceed the tonnage of five units.

Cuyler figured that the addition of a fifth unit westbound over Wendover Hill would increase the speed from 18 mph to 22.5 mph with the usual 4,000 tons. Certainly it was worth a test. As G.W. Curtis saw it, the chief problem would be to find sufficient booster units to make up five units for these trains without detriment to other eastbound trains.

Under then-current instructions, when the Expediter had over 2,500 tons in 50 loads, the train was given a helper from Keddie to Norvell. Allen estimated that five units would ease the ability to make the schedule, and enable an increase in tonnage of the Expediter above the 50 cars. Five units would not increase the tonnage particularly on the SWG or NCX but would eliminate helpers from Keddie to Norvell on about 50 percent of the northbound trains. A few tests were to be made between Oroville and Klamath Falls to learn how the plan would work out in actual practice, and a number of test runs would be made between Oroville and Salt Lake.

The first test run took place with the SWG-7 between Oroville and Bieber on September 8, 1955. The train had five F-7s, with 49 loads and 16 empties, 3,395 actual tons. Total running time was eight hours, five minutes. Minimum speed on the one percent of the canyon was 24 mph in transition 2 at full throttle. On the 2.2 percent out of Greenville the train made 11.1 mph in transition 1 at full throttle. At no time was the locomotive overloaded, and no difficulty was encountered in starting.

A second test train, on the SWG-14, ran out of Oroville on September 15 with 64 loads and 14 empties, 3,810 actual tons. Total running time was eight hours, 29 minutes, and minimum speeds were 21.4 mph full throttle through the canyon, and 10.0 mph on the 2.2 percent north of Greenville. A momentary maximum of 1,600 hp per unit, 8,000 hp per locomotive, was reached when starting the train up the 1.5 percent

Covered wagons near Sacramento. **Richard Steinheimer**

grade out of Keddie. The F-7s were not overloaded for any appreciable length of time, although the average load on the traction motors over the 2.2 percent grade was the maximum continuous rating of 825 amperes.

A third and final test took place between Oroville and Bieber on October 6, 1955, with five units of the 913 Class taking the SWG-5 out of Oroville with 67 loads and six empties, 4,195 tons. Helper 732, one of the newly delivered GP-9s, was cut in 19 cars behind the five point units, and ran between Keddie and Norvell. Total running time was 8 hours, 26 minutes. Minimum speeds were 20.6 mph in full throttle on the one percent, 12.2 mph on the 2.2 percent with the 732, and 15.7 mph on the 1.5 percent grade without the 732. At no time were the units overloaded.

Superintendent of the Eastern Division J.F. Lynch studied Cuyler's report of the three test trips and concluded that he would have little use for five units on the Eastern Division. Between Portola and Roper, even four units were not needed except to help expedite movements of eastbound trains over Sand Pass, Antelope, Hogan, Silver Zone and Low, and westward similarly. In his estimation, five units would be a considerable waste of power as the Eastern Division at that time could not handle sufficient tonnage for five units due to the length of sidings.

In the meantime, the eight GP-9s had been delivered at Burmester between September 14-20, 1955. The GP-9 was a 1,750-hp locomotive with a 567C engine, and possessed a main generator similar to that of the GP-7. The rpm was increased by 35 over that of earlier models, thus producing an additional 190 kw out of the D12 generator. The D37 traction motors were rated at 900 amps, kilowatt capacity was raised by 26 over that of the D27 motor, and CFM remained at 2,400, or similar to that of the F-7.

Unlike the earlier GP-7s, they possessed an anti-sluing device allowing the use of this type locomotive in more than two unit combinations without causing excessive side stresses on the rail. Unlike the GP-7s, they had shunting, but their chief weakness, according to General Diesel Supervisor William F. Stevens, was that they were overfueled with insufficient air. The GP-9s immediately made possible the reassignment of the 601 Class of SW-9s then in work train, local, and shuttle service on the main line.

The SW-9s had been purchased to use in mainline service, but on delivery it became evident that their severe lateral movement above speeds of 30 mph made them unfit for such operation. In helper service they tended to heat since the radiator was pointed forward from the front of the unit. The SW-9s also possessed a rigid truck, and the engineering department began to make noises when it found its main line being thrown out of alignment. Cuyler had hoped to place swing-hanger trucks beneath these units, but no deal could be worked out with the builder, which forced the railroad to generally assign these units to switching service.

During the years of 1954-1955, Munson applied pressure to get the trains over the road with more dispatch. Terminal delays were always the chief problem, and there were always more delays when business was good due to the longer time required to prepare trains for departure, and the fact that more drag trains were operated which had a tendency to increase rather than decrease the delays.

Siding limitations through the canyon increased the difficulty of making connections, and the longest trains tended to be westbound with eastbound trains going into the hole. Westbound tonnage was greater than eastbound, and the movement of such tonnage in early 1956 was complicated by a tonnage rating for the 913 Class of 6,175 tons between Wendover and Shafter, while for the same class, a four-unit locomotive could take only 5,500 tons up the hill between Oroville and Portola. Maximum grade on both districts was one percent but the tonnage rating was higher between Wendover and Shafter because the curvature was less than between Oroville and Portola.

Numerous tests, not mentioned in this study, had been run at various times and it had been found that any freight train up the canyon with over 5,500 tons was difficult to start, especially if the train was sitting on two or three curves, some of which were in the reverse direction. In such trains, the possibility of drawbar breakage was greatly increased, and tonnage was reduced to take care of this situation.

Curtis had run some 165 car freight trains up the canyon,

Roper Yard of the D&RGW at Salt Lake City in July 1973. This was the end of the line for most WP power, and these units await a westbound run for Stockton or Oakland.
Virgil Staff

Early afternoon outside the West Portal of Tunnel 3 on April 21, 1968, provides the setting for three westbound GP-20s climbing the final stretch of 1.0 percent grade about one mile east of the summit.
Virgil Staff

but there had been too many break-in-twos per train on the reverse curves of the canyon, and it was concluded that the Feather River Canyon was not the place for trains of excessive length.

In late 1957 and early 1958, increased use was made of five-unit locomotives on the NCE in an effort to reduce both helper engine and train miles. Five units were also of particular value westbound out of Bieber where there was no economical way to provide regular helper service to Halls Flat. Westbound schedules out of Salt Lake City also came under consideration since the SLW, and especially the PC, were losing time due to their being heavier than the other manifests out of the lake.

On April 10, 1958, Fruit Block 129 out of Oroville began running with a fifth unit in order that this unit would be available out of Roper for the PC. Five units were available bearing in mind that NCE trains had to be protected in addition to some symbols west of Oroville with this type of power. During periods of slackened business, four units were sufficient. Additionally, it was the practice to use five units on the Fruit Block eastbound and on the PBF westbound. In times of a tight power situation, such as in April 1959, both trains ran with four units with the PBF tonnage regulated accordingly so that no delays would be experienced because of this reduction in power.

These compromises did not basically affect the early 1958 agreement with the Rio Grande and midwestern railroads to furnish faster service to forwarders and for house merchandise between Chicago and the West Coast. This faster service resulted in trains arriving in the San Francisco Bay Area on the fourth day out of Chicago, ready for a fifth morning spot. The Western Pacific used five units on its symbol trains PC (Pacific Coaster) from Roper Yard to Oroville, with the train trimmed

Former *Zephyr* unit 805-A, at the head of 7,500 horses and five units, rolls downgrade on an eastbound run up the NCE (Inside Gateway) with Nubieber and points north as its destination. This is Bridge 6.73, just east of the east switch at Moccasin in December of 1970. **Joe Ward**

to 3,500 tons, and a two-unit pusher used westbound for 53 miles out of Wendover. Train SLW (St. Louis–Western Pacific) also operated on a faster schedule but the running time was not so critical and a four-unit locomotive usually handled its 3,800 tons. The third manifest, the CFS (California Freight Special) had a somewhat slower schedule than the other two symbol trains and usually operated with approximately 4,500 tons. North Line trains operated with five units on the head end, and the southbound GWS and CAL usually ran with five units.

The question of maximum utilization of road switchers constantly perplexed the management. Cuyler and Contri agreed that they could handle considerably more business without additional units. Additional business would reduce standby time. Engines 701-713 and 725-732 were used mostly on locals, as helpers, and in shuttle service. Five-unit locomotives and lighter tonnage decreased the use of helpers, but helper power had to be assigned even though not utilized on all trains.

Cuyler feared that the company would be faced always by low utilization on road switchers because of the nature of their service. The 701 Class averaged 16.4 miles per hour in 1958 against 13.7 miles per hour in 1957. Local, helper, and shuttle service did not result in a favorable utilization figure since there was no way of moving the majority of these engines into a connecting run in order to build up their utilization. Contri noted that such service resulted in long layover periods at terminals between the arrival and departure of schedule runs, sometimes as much as 12 hours a day and for longer periods on weekends and holidays. The use of five units and scheduled arrival of trains at Roper and Oakland resulted in long layovers of 901-924 Class locomotives, and the 801-805 Class locomotives, used almost exclusively in passenger service, again because of schedules, suffered long layovers both at Salt Lake and at Oakland.

Faster schedules resulted in units arriving at terminals earlier thereby causing a longer layover before the next train. Power was sometimes sent to Salt Lake City to protect trains reported for arrival at a certain time, but due to various reasons the train did not always arrive as figured which resulted in these units laying over for longer periods than anticipated. Fewer units on these trains could improve the statistics but would be undesirable because of the resulting delays to important trains. When hours available increased faster than hours worked or assigned, this also resulted in poorer utilization.

The eastbound COFC crawls through Garfield on the outskirts of Salt Lake City on June 20, 1978. This is a Sealand Container train running from Oakland to Salt Lake and thence to Elizabeth, N.J. **Virgil Staff**

The Western Pacific's D.L. Loftus tried to explain why utilization (measured in hours) might be so poor when train miles were up substantially. "While total hours worked by the 800 and 900 Class engines were up only 2.2 percent during the third quarter," he said, "unit miles [and train miles] were up over 10 percent. This of course reflects the faster average train speeds [up 8.5 percent] and suggests that miles per unit hour worked should also be considered along with hours worked."

It may be of interest that Rio Grande and Western Pacific often exchanged power for short turns to avoid delays due to derailments or other interruptions of traffic, and at least between 1954 and 1961, WP road power laying over at Roper (Salt Lake City) was sometimes used to haul heavy cuts, especially to the Union Pacific interchange on the Rio Grande. Pooling of power with the Rio Grande was not considered practicable, and in 1959 all five westbound Rio Grande trains ran through to Ogden, with eastbound trains running through Roper with only very light terminal delay at that point.

Like many railroads, the WP flirted with internal combustion early. B.L. McNeill and Edwin B. Allison stand by gasoline motor inspection car 601 on August 27, 1939. This unit was built in 1922 from a Model T truck chassis, and could handle up to 14 passengers. Actually, the car was always something of an anachronism on the railroad, but it lasted until after Allison retired on December 26, 1950.
E. B. Allison Collection

132 D-DAY ON THE WESTERN PACIFIC

WP Weathers the Winter

Although the Western Pacific does not climb over the top of the Sierra Nevada, as does the Southern Pacific, the furies of winter are nevertheless well known to the men of the WP. The mountains of the Plumas tower over the Canyon, the tracks climb and cling, and nearly every year the snows come. The battle against the elements is then renewed. This folio portrays the WP in the tide of winter, working always to keep traffic moving.

PRECEDING PAGE: Jordan Spreader No. 7 and a lashup behind the 915-D at Keddie, California, in December 1971. Since retirement of the last rotary plow, most snow removal has been by nose plow or via one of the Jordans. **Tom Moungovan**

THIS PAGE AND NEXT: A blanket of snow muffles the passage of an eastbound freight at Portola. **Richard Steinheimer**

Rotary 3 at the ready at Oroville, November 1949.
H. A. O'Rullian

The drifting snows of mid-January 1952 decorated the equipment in a storm remembered by an entire generation of railroaders. One of the 801 class takes a breather at Mason on the Bieber line. This class of F-3 was used in helper, rotary and spreader service in those days, and the morning reports on this date showed gale winds accompanied by snow levels of 204 inches at Norvell.
Grant Evans Collection

The stars are out this quiet, crisp night at Portola, as the rotary and GP-35 3012 share the moonlight. **Richard Steinheimer**

WP WEATHERS THE WINTER 137

19

The Search for Replacement Power

IT WAS DURING late 1958 or early 1959 that the Western Pacific considered the acquisition of new locomotives with greater tractive effort and increased horsepower. In September 1959, a study was made of the road diesel locomotive requirements by the research, operating, and mechanical departments. The conclusion was that because of several changes in freight schedules, the first of which occurred in early 1958, there must of necessity be greater power needs per train and/or reduction in tonnage of trains which would mean running more trains because of the lower horsepower of the diesel units available. Furthermore, the then-present age of the FT units, Class 901-912, made these units economically obsolete, and because of these two factors a replacement program should be considered.

As a result of this study, six Electro-Motive GP-20s were ordered for delivery in 1959 and a program was established for the replacement of FT units by sending them in to be rebuilt by EMD into additional 2,000-hp type units. These GP-20s would possess an improved distribution of weight on the drivers, larger fuel tank capacity, and would have unencumbered vision on both sides, both front and rear. Better flexibility would ease the breaking up and making up of locomotive consists, and this power would make ideal replacement for a number of aging 5,400-hp units that could then be retired.

It was considered that the railroad should start rebuilding 16 FTs into GP-20s and this program was started by sending four FT units back to EMD at La Grange, Illinois, for rebuilding to GP-20s. This reduced the fleet of 48 units of FTs to 44. Shortly thereafter this program was halted because of a possible impending corporate merger. In the meantime both orders, to work their way west on tonnage trains out of Lincoln, Nebraska, were accepted by Mechanical Supervisor R.E. Schriefer at Lincoln—engines 2001-2006 being received on December 2, 1959, and 2007-2010 on August 5, 1960.

The original plan was to replace the 16 FTs by the end of 1963, with the remainder to be rebuilt by the end of 1967. At that time it was estimated that 36 GP-20s would be required to replace the 48 FT units. Shortly after trading in four of the FT units on GP-20s, a change of plan called for tentative replacement of the 44 remaining FT units with 27 of the new type 2,250-hp, Electro-Motive GP-30 diesels providing, of course, that this did not reduce the fleet to the extent that engine assignments were not covered.

At approximately the same time, a number of new models had made their appearance on the market, and management indicated great interest in testing them. Between May 7-11, 1959, a 2,400-hp EMD SD-24, demonstrator No. 5579, was tested and thought not to be quite the equal of two units of FT power. Cuyler feared serious design defects in the SD-24 which would undoubtedly be remedied in time but which in the meantime would create serious maintenance problems for the railroad.

Design defects were to be expected, according to Cuyler, because of the radical change in design and the increase in horsepower developed out of the same engine used in the 1,500 and 1,750-hp units. This increase of horsepower could be expected to increase the generation of heat with consequent metallurgic problems where heat could not be radiated rapidly and absorbed in the cooling system. What Cuyler wanted was the 2,000-hp GP-20 locomotive which sustained very little horsepower load increase on the engine. On the GP-20 this had been made possible by eliminating the horsepower used to drive the blowers when the throttle was increased over the fourth notch and substituting the turbocharger operated by exhaust gases.

The 567D2 engine of the GP-20 operated at 835 rpm, and possessed a D22 main generator rated at 1,400 kw. The D47 traction motors had a similar amperage rating to that of the GP-9s, but could theoretically accept forty additional kilowatts over that of the D37 of the GP-9. CFM traction motor blower capacity was increased by 200.

American Locomotive Co. was anxious to have WP test its new 1,800-hp DL-701 road switcher, and Cuyler saw this as a chance for an interesting comparison with the 1,750-hp GP-9. Four units were borrowed from the Southern Pacific and operated on test runs starting December 13, 1959. Recording electric meters were installed on one of the four units to record main generator power output, and fuel meters were installed on two of the four units. Time, speed, and throttle position were recorded at each milepost except during periods of extended dynamic braking.

Train SWG-13 departed Stockton Yard on December 13 with Alco units SP5869, 5855, 5857, and 5866 trailing 2,276 tons. Average speed between Stockton and Oroville was 36.6 mph, and 25.0 mph between Oroville and Keddie. Out of Keddie, on test No. 2, tonnage was increased to 3,549 tons, with average speed between Keddie and Willow Springs being 22.8 mph. Termination of the run was at Willow Springs instead of Bieber due to the practice of exchanging power with westbound trains at the meeting points. The return trip on the CAL-13 was with 4,087 tons into Keddie, and 3,472 tons into Stockton Yard. Average speed between Willow Springs and Stockton Yard was 30.8 mph, with average speed in both directions of the SWG-13 and CAL-13 being 28.8 mph.

The same power then took train GGM-15 between Stockton Yard and Roper, with maximum tonnage of 3,618 tons between Oroville Yard and Winnemucca. Between Winnemucca and Salt Lake, tonnage consisted of 43 loads and 43 empties, 3,508 tons. Average speed up the canyon was 23.1 mph, and 43.6 mph between Elko and Wendover. On the return leg, the four units ran on the CFS-17 with 4,600 tons between Roper and Elko, and lesser tonnage into Stockton. Average speed between Wendover and Elko was 32.8 mph, and 42.5 mph between Winnemucca and Portola. No helpers were used on any of the test trains.

In January 1960, comparative tests were made with four WP GP-20 units, Nos. 2003, 2005, 2001, and 2004. These test runs were essentially similar to the runs with the DL-701 power except that the North Line trip ran into Bieber. To keep the tests comparable, testing on the northbound trip above Willow Springs was excluded from the total picture. SWG-24-25, out of Stockton Yard, handled 2,274 tons up the canyon to Keddie with an average speed of 21.7 mph. These results must have been tinctured by a blanket slow order through the canyon. However, the run between Keddie and Willow Springs averaged 25.4 mph with 3,625 tons. Return trip on the GWS-25 was with various tonnages, and average speed between Willow Springs and Stockton Yard was 33.0 mph. Average speed on both trains was 29.7 mph.

The four GP-20s then handled train GGM-27 between Stockton Yard and Roper, with 4,032 tons between Oroville and Portola at an average speed of 22.6 mph. Again, as in the previous trip, there was a blanket slow order through the

Four-stroke cycle General Electric U30B thumpers ascend the Third Subdivision at Rich Bar on the clay-cold morning of February 14, 1971. The 763 was later numbered 3063, and was one result of the Western Pacific's search for replacement diesel power. **Virgil Staff**

canyon. Between Portola and Roper, the GGM-27 had 60 loads and 19 empties, 3,974 tons, and ran between Elko and Wendover at an average speed of 46.5 mph. On return, the PBF-28 lugged 3,693 tons between Wendover and Portola with an average speed between Wendover and Elko of 41.4 mph, and 49.6 mph between Winnemucca and Portola.

After carefully studying the test results, Cuyler concluded that both power consists operated well at high altitudes, and both types gave a good account of themselves in generating the horsepower at which they were rated. The Alco claim that its units possessed a lower fuel consumption was true in comparing Alco turbocharged 1,800-hp units with the GP-9 unaspirated engine. However, the turbocharger on the GP-20, according to the test results, placed it equally if not better on fuel consumption than the turbocharged Alco units, and it was Cuyler's conclusion that the GP-20s were superior from the standpoint of speed, acceleration, and fuel consumption.

Alco representatives apparently advised that their engines should be disassembled on a four-year maintenance interval, which would have been very costly and would not have fit in with WP practices of obtaining maximum service life of parts. A large expenditure for increase of stock in parts above the then-present inventory would add additional expenses, and an extensive education program in order to train personnel in operation and maintenance of this power would increase the burdens. In Cuyler's opinion, the test results clearly indicated that the 2,000-hp diesel unit would handle more tonnage at a faster speed than the Alco 1,800-hp unit and at a lesser maintenance cost.

To complete this battery of road tests, three Alco 2,400-hp DL-640s were delivered at Stockton during the week of April 17, 1960. These units, numbered 640-1, 640-2, and 640-3, were 75-mph units with a continuous rating of 17 mph. Because of their high continuous rating, these four-motor units were not considered practical for the NCE on a test basis, and so only ran on test runs on the east-west line. Running out of Stockton Yard on train GGM-19, the three units handled 3,744 tons between Oroville and Portola with an average speed of 22.8 mph. Between Portola and Roper they ran with 57 loads and 27 empties, 3,794 tons. Average speed between Portola and Winnemucca was 46.4 mph, and 43.1 mph between Elko and Wendover. Average speed between Stockton

GP-40 3509 heads the westbound mail train as it clatters over the Southern Pacific crossing at Niles Tower in mid-1971.
Virgil Staff

Yard and Roper was 39.2 mph with total running time between the two terminals of 21 hours, 25 minutes.

On the return trip the DL-640s ran into Portola on train 1-PBF-20 with 38 loads and eight empties, 2,229 tons. No readings were taken between Portola and Oroville on account of dynamic braking, but 2,254 tons were taken from Oroville Yard to Stockton Yard with an average speed of 43.8 mph. Average speed between Wendover and Elko was 45.2 mph, and 51.2 mph between Winnemucca and Portola. The total running time between Roper and Stockton Yard was 14 hours, 41 minutes, with an average speed of 49.4 mph. In the tests so far noted, average speeds have been included between Oroville and Portola, Wendover and Elko, and Winnemucca and Portola because of the heavy gradients found on those districts.

President Whitman and General Manager Munson were insistent that these tests be as unbiased as possible, and that there be no partiality on Western Pacific's part toward one manufacturer over the other. When the reports were in, Christy, Cuyler, Road Foremen J.C. Lusar, J.C. Currier, Jr., Norman F. Roberts, and others, provided essentially similar evaluations. The DL-640 was a good performer in high-speed, minimum-grade territory, but in mountain-grade territory its performance was less than that realized with Western Pacific's GP-9 or GP-20 locomotives.

In such territory, acceleration was poor, its speed with approximately equal tonnage was less, and wheel slippage was a problem. In fact, in the acceleration test the DL-640 was slower even than the Alco 1,800-hp units. Unit performance was equal only to the 1,800-hp units, and less than equal to the GP-20 Electro-Motive units on certain phases of this test. This was accounted for by the failure of the Alco 2,400-hp units to deliver the rated horsepower which, it was felt, was lost through wheel slippage that occurred on grades.

The problem of carrying additional parts inventory was also significant, as was the expectation of problems with gear trains, camshafts, and frames. A recommended arbitrary three to four-year overhaul period for these units would increase the expense in cost-per-mile figures, and it was finally concluded that this power would show excellent performance on a level-grade railroad, but since these were not dual-purpose locomotives, a small railroad such as the Western Pacific could not afford or have a place for special purpose road locomotives such as the DL-640.

Beginning April 16, 1961, the Western Pacific conducted a series of tests using four General Electric 2,500-hp U25B demonstration units numbered 753 through 756. The test runs consisted of one round-trip Stockton to Klamath Falls and return, and another from Stockton to Salt Lake and return. The run to Bieber was made on train NCX-16 with two loads and 146 empties going up the 2.2 percent out of Greenville. Average speed between Keddie and Willow Springs was 27.2 mph. Return to Stockton was on April 17 with 4,225 tons on train GWS-16 out of Willow Springs, and 3,798 tons into Stockton Yard. On April 18 these units handled train GGM-18 with 4,490 tons, and returned to Stockton on April 21 with train PBF-19 with 3,040 tons. Between Elko and Wendover train GGM moved 55-50-4530 tons at an average speed of 43.8 mph. Between Wendover and Elko, train PBF handled 58-8-3078 tons at an average speed of 45.8 mph.

The general feeling toward these units was friendly, although Road Foreman J.C. Currier, Jr., felt that five GP-20s would have done just as well on the North Line, and would have provided more adequate braking than would be possible with four units descending a grade. In fact, on the descending grades there was considerably more use of air brakes to control the speed than would have been necessary with additional units. Cuyler noted that these four units developed 10,000 horsepower as advertised, but felt the high continuous rating of 15 mph would confine unit use, in spite of horsepower, to about the same tonnages as that of a lesser horsepower locomotive on heavy grades.

Cuyler was dubious about the service life of the Cooper-Bessemer engine, and while he realized that these engines had been newly designed, he preferred to give them time to prove their worth. There were many features of these engines toward which he was very favorable, but he questioned their service life, especially where they had cast the cylinder head and liner as an integral unit. For if anything happened to either the head or the liner, the entire assembly would require scrapping and replacement.

It was his recommendation that before consideration be given to these units, the company wait until some of them had been placed in service for sufficient time to determine their service life. Loftus viewed the test results in a generally favorable light and noted that "the experience of the last couple of years indicates [that] speed almost dictates that during the 1960s we must go to higher and higher horsepower units. It is simply not economical in the long run to consistently use five, six and even seven units where a fewer number could do the job." Finally, Cuyler commented on the need for another competitor to the one substantial manufacturer (Electro-Motive) then involved in locomotive construction. Feeling that this was not a healthy situation, he hoped the company would ultimately come to some equitable arrangement with G.E.

Cuyler proposed, in February 1963, the reinstatement of the locomotive retirement program to cover a period of three years. Many of the parts in the FT units were original from delivery, and some of these parts were beginning to show signs of failing. These included generators, traction motors, engines and body parts which had been obsolete to the builder's manufacturing lines for approximately five years. The mechanical department experienced increasing difficulty in obtaining material, and it was expected that units would have to be held out of service for longer periods before repairs could be made. Despite all efforts to keep the costs down, they gradually increased because of the age of the components and because the service life was now short and there would be increasing need for replacement in order to assure dependability of operation.

In October 1963, Electro-Motive began production of a new 2,500-hp GP-35 locomotive, and Western Pacific began purchase of this model with 10 units, Nos. 3001-3010 accepted at Elko between November 30 and December 7, 1963. General Electric power at this time still had not been seriously considered since it was believed that the two-cycle engine would be more economical to operate than GE's four-cycle. Four-cycle engines, because of their designs, were composed of heavier parts which it was expected would require more elaborate facilities for easy maintenance. Out-of-service time on the four-cycle engines was expected to be higher than that for the two-cycle, and availability would be decreased.

Furthermore, the handling of two different classes of power at the same terminal was expected to increase maintenance problems, and the considerable additions to store stock would increase costs. Just as the two-cycle engine, when first designed, had required several years to cope with design problems, it was believed that the same would be true of an improved four-cycle, and that the builder would require time to make such an engine a dependable unit of power.

The 2,500-hp, 567D3A turbocharged engine of the GP-35 operated with an additional 65 rpm over that of the GP20, and possessed a D32 generator capable of producing 1,740 kw—340 kw over that of the GP-20. D67 traction motors were rated at 1,000 amps, 357 kw, or 435 kw above 18.5 mph. Traction motor blower capacity was increased to 2,800 cfm, or 200 cfm over that on the GP-20.

On September 21, 1963, a serious derailment was experienced at Beowawe, Nevada, which involved westbound units 924D, 2003, 730, 916A and 916B. The 916B, being the least damaged, was retained but the remaining units were so seriously damaged that the four remaining units were replaced with two additional GP-35s, Nos. 3011-3012. These were accepted at Elko in late November or early December 1964.

In late April or early May 1964, a performance test was made on the Eastern Division using 9,500 horsepower to handle a train of 5,000 tons. The purpose of this test was to compare the difference between the same horsepower, but with a train of 4,000 tons which had been previously tested. On this test it was learned that 9,500 horsepower would handle a train of 5,000 tons on level track at the same track speed as was accomplished with same horsepower and 4,000 tons. On Wendover Hill, the average speed from start to top of the hill was about 22 mph, but was about 25 mph after speed had been obtained. This resulted in about 4 mph slower speed, but in the overall time the 5,000-ton train was only about 10 minutes slower in reaching the top of the grade. All concerned had the opinion that it was entirely feasible to operate trains of 5,000 tons with 9,500 horsepower.

Alco tried again in early 1964, discussing with Christy the possibility of trying out the Alco Century 628, six-motor, 2,750-hp demonstrators. In June 1964, units 628-3, 4, 2, 1 handled train GGM-14 from Stockton Yard to Roper, with 58-41-99, 4,486 tons between Oroville Yard and Winnemucca, and with 57-41-98, 4,410 tons between Winnemucca and Roper. Average speed up the canyon was 28 mph, and 49.4 mph between Elko and Wendover.

These tests were interrupted because of a cracked turbocharger casing at MP 857 so that further testing with four units was impossible. The return trip to Stockton was made with 628-3, 4, 2 handling train 1-PBF-15 with 63-3-66, 3,396 tons. Average speed between Roper and Wendover was 47.4 mph, and 43.8 mph between Wendover and Elko. These locomotives were considered to have put on a very good performance as long as they were operating, and Cuyler was impressed by what the added 250 horsepower, over that of the GP-20, would do in the acceleration test. But he was apprehensive, for numerous reasons, about the maintenance cost of this type locomotive, which was the same view he had of the U25 previously tested.

In early 1964 Cuyler consulted with Jim Lynch, L.D. Michelson, K.V. Plummer and Larry Contri about further motive power needs. It was agreed at this time that at least 10 additional GP-35s should be purchased in 1965 as this would enable the retirement of up to 16 FT-type units. Savings in maintenance would be considerable and it was estimated that tonnage could then be increased on trains by at least 10 percent. This would reduce train miles by permitting heavier train loads. A further advantage of this latest power was that it might enable trains to run through without fueling from Stockton to Salt Lake City, and from Salt Lake City to Stockton with a saving of at least 30 minutes on the schedule. Cuyler stressed that shopping of FT units would be expensive and he did not recommend such a reconditioning program as the railroad would not then have the horsepower required to meet the schedules. In order to avoid out-of-control repair costs and have dependable units of adequate horsepower to handle the competitive schedules, it was recommended to Christy that the locomotive replacement program should be continued. An order was then placed for 10 additional GP-35s, engines 3013-3022, with acceptance at Elko taking place between April 7 and May 7, 1965.

Electro–Motive began building regular production models of the GP-40 in November 1965, and Western Pacific's first order of these, numbered 3501-3510, was accepted at Elko between May 27 and June 1, 1966. All previous WP power from Electro–Motive had featured 567 designs, and this was the first power to have the new 645 engine with similar 10-inch stroke, as in the 567 varieties, but with the new $9\frac{1}{16}''$ bore. Electro–Motive is said to have felt that the 567 series engine had reached its developmental limit, and the demands for higher horsepower were now made possible by increased piston displacement per cylinder, thus enabling an increase in displacement on 16-cylinder engines from 9,072 cubic inches to 10,320 cubic inches.

Electro–Motive avoided the use of heavy, bulky components, and parts interchangeability with the 567 series engine was generally retained. Generally, the cylinder liner and piston were the only wearing parts not interchangeable with the 567. Most 645 parts would fit 567C and 567D models. The new "E" model crankcase looked identical to the 567D crankcase from the outside, but on the inside, the structural and load-carrying sections were strengthened. Improvements were made in the exhaust manifold, power assembly, and turbocharger, and the GP-40 appeared to be a superior model to the GP-35.

Tests began November 4, 1966, using four 3,000-hp GE U30Bs numbered GE 301, 302, 303, 304. Test runs consisted of one round trip Roper (Salt Lake City) to Stockton and return, one trip from Roper to Stockton, and one round trip Stockton to Bieber and return. On the run to Bieber with 12,000-hp on the head end, the U30Bs lugged 42-54-96, 4,150 trailing tons up the 2.2 percent between K15-25. Rail conditions were ideal, and the grade brought the train down to 16 mph between K20 and K25.

Among the items of criticism noted by various individuals were the dynamic brakes on the U30s, their rough-riding qualities, general shoddiness of door fittings which would be noticeable in cold weather, and the degree of amperage drop before the final buildup of amperage in new throttle positions.

The *Expeditor* moves eastbound out of Oroville over Bridge 210.82 on September 16, 1967, in the care of blue-and-yellow General Electric U33B demonstrators. **Virgil Staff**

No one seemed to believe the GEs were any better than the 3500 Class of GP-40s.

Cuyler felt the U30s would give an excellent operating performance when they were out of the shop. His only question was whether or not the engines in them would hold up under constant general service, and whether they would be an economical unit to operate. Both Michelson and Cuyler were anxious to compare these with the GP-40s, and to bring such tests to a conclusion since the management, to this point, remained undecided on who should build the next order of locomotives.

Testing of the four GP-40s began December 20, 1966, with 3502, 3503, 3504, and 3508 making an eastbound run from Oroville to Bieber on train SWG20, and one westbound run from Bieber to Stockton on the GWS20. Consist up the hill was 49-26-4122 trailing tons. The four units in tandem were rated at 12,000 horsepower but drag duty performance control gave 8,400 hp. Acceleration and fuel consumption figures were considered of great importance, but the test results were not conclusive since rail conditions were not comparable to those with the U30Bs. The rails were covered with a thick layer of ice, and snow flurries cut visibility. Condition of the rail caused slipping and loss of adhesion between Greenville and Almanor. The GP-40s hit milepost K15 at 38 mph but had slowed to 18 mph at K18. At K18.3 they stalled, and had to double the hill to K25.

A single, center-cab, 1,500-hp Alco Century 415 was employed in tests on the Fremont local beginning February 1, 1967. Observers aboard were two Alco representatives and Western Pacific's K.B. Schulthies. Shideler later noted that the locomotive generally gave a good account of itself, and took curved rail extremely well. High adhesion was demonstrated as no wheel slip was encountered at any point on the test. But the cab layout was considered very poor. Visibility was considered less satisfactory than on the GP-7s, although was greatly improved with the engineer standing.

Engineer Woods and Fireman Grummett believed the performance was somewhat better than on the GP-7s but approximately equal to the GP-9s. The unit appeared to be economical in fuel consumption since only 160 gallons were consumed after 13 hours of service which included 132 road miles, 1,010 trailing tons over the Altamont, and numerous switching movements consisting mostly of hopper cars with sand or gravel lading. Maximum speed obtained on comparatively level tangent track with 864 trailing tons after accelerating for four miles was 44 mph. The chief doubt was whether or not the Alco-251 diesel would hold up in general railroad service.

Three SD-45s were arranged for runs in February 1967. The 10,800-hp lashup had 69-1-70, 4,140 trailing tons up the 2.2 percent on February 24. This train hit the hill at milepost K14 doing 34.3 mph. By K20 the speed was down to 14 mph, and at K20.6 a knuckle was broken and the crew had to double the hill to K25. February 26 brought the three SD-45s back to the 2.2 percent with 64-25-89, 4,625 trailing tons. Train SWG hit

THE SEARCH FOR REPLACEMENT POWER 143

K15 at 19 mph, and ran from K17-23 most of the way at 11 mph. General Manager L.D. Michelson and Cuyler were greatly impressed by this performance of locomotives 4352, 4353, and 4354 since it indicated three of these units would handle the same train as six F-7s or five GP-40s.

Fuel consumption figures on these tests showed the F-7s in NCE service used 2.58 gallons per MGTM vs. 2.466 gallons on the SD45s. The 20-cylinder engine would be slightly more expensive to maintain, and would increase the costs of wheel work compared with the GP-40s. A penciled note in Cuyler's handwriting indicates some possibilty of increased maintenance costs over those figured for tighter tolerances and increased length of the 20-cylinder engine, but while somewhat decreased availability and increased rail wear might be expected, it was believed that the savings in using the larger locomotive would override this cost, assuming the quality of engineering in both types of units was equal.

Six new GP-40s, Nos. 3511-3516, were shipped between March 16-20, 1967, and on March 31, 1967, the last six 1,350-hp units were consolidated at Oroville and sent out on a "drag east" for the EMD plant at La Grange, Illinois. Barring destruction of more modern units on WP or foreign trackage, future trade-ins or sales would be of F-7s, with booster units going first, and cab units at a later date. Some uncertainty prevailed as to whether the next order of power should include six-axle, 3,600-hp SD-45s or their equivalent in four-axle, 3,000-hp U30Bs. The final decision was made during the summer of 1967, and the Western Pacific placed in service its first U30Bs, Nos. 751-755, by the close of October 1, 1967.

Just prior to delivery of the 751 Class to the railroad, a series of tests was conducted in September with 3,300-hp U33B General Electric demonstrators Nos. 301, 302, 303, 304. Road Foreman R.K. Harrison came down the canyon with these four units on train AP-3 with 75-9-84, 5,074 tons. The four units "were hard put to hold 5,074 tons working maximum dynamic brake," he said, and while they were supposed to be rated at 850 amperes maximum dynamic brake strength, the top strength ever drawn on this, or any future run, was 775 amperes.

These U33B locomotives were rated at 3,300 hp per unit, or 825 hp per traction motor. Each was basically similar to the 3,000-hp U30B type then on order, but they possessed an in-

Alco Century 636 demonstrators eastbound with train on February 1, 1969. Cuyler was not terribly impressed with Alco road power, and the Western Pacific never did purchase any.   **Western Pacific Collection**

The morning sun touches the Advance CMS with General Electric U30B 752 on the point as it slices its way westbound through Knolls, Utah, on July 2, 1972. This is near the eastern edge of the Great Salt Lake Desert, and at the eastern threshold to the salt flats. **Virgil Staff**

creased cooling capacity, 25 more rpm at throttle 8, and an increase in BMEP achieved through a modified turbocharger and fuel setting. These units were not equipped with drag duty performance control as were the GP-40s, and 3,300 hp to the traction motors was delivered at all running speeds while in throttle 8 position.

During these tests, unit 303 was taken out of service for several days due to a hole in the radiator, and GP-40 No. 3509 was substituted in its place. On September 9, 1967, the 3509 went up the canyon with No. 6 and No. 7 throttle position, maintaining track speed all the way to Keddie. No. 3509 was on the point with three U33Bs trailing. Up the hill out of Greenville, the front truck of the GP-40 sanded all the way. Consist on this train EXP-9 was 66-9-75, 4,686 gross tons. No slippage was indicataed on the load meters at any point on any unit, and the GP-40 did not approach its short time limits. This power hit the 2.2 percent grade at 35 mph and had slowed to 18.6 mph on arrival at milepost K22.

From K16-25 the 3509 was showing approximately 900 amps, with the GEs running between 850-1,250 amps in the 50-minute short time limit between K17-19. Between K19-25, the GE units were running 1,200 to 1,350 amps for approximately 14 minutes in the 12-minute short time limit. The highest continuous amperage these U30Bs might operate was 1,200 amps.

September 10, 1967, brought the same power westbound out of Bieber on the CAL-8 with 72-25-95, 5,543 gross tons, and the GP-40 trailing the three U33Bs. Between Little Valley and Halls Flat on the 1.8 percent grade, all trucks were sanding, and there was some slippage at milepost K79-80. At no time did the GP-40 approach its short time limits. Locomotive 3509 was running approximately 950 amps between K93 and the top of the hill at K77, whereas the U33Bs ran almost continuously in the 12 and six-minute short time limits for 26 minutes—eight minutes in the four-minute short time limit, and three minutes in the 12-minute short time limit. At this point, the GE traction motors were beginning to smoke on all three units.

On the following day, the SWG-10 left Oroville for Keddie with units 301, 302, 304, 3509 and 51-42-93, 4,616 tons. Track speed of 35 mph was maintained between Oroville and Keddie, and the power could do 38 mph, or slightly better than track speed, from Oroville to just west of Poe. On the following run up the canyon with the EXP-16, the 302, 303, 301, 304 ran to Bieber with 62-0-62, 3,435 tons. The train easily made track speed from Oroville to Keddie using only variances of 5½ to 6½ throttle position once track speed was obtained. On the 2.2 percent between K20-24, they rolled uphill at 26 mph and amperage at 1,050 or in the continuous rating. Shideler observed this run and recalled that on one point on the 2.2 percent grade, the speed dropped to 24 mph and the amps reached 1,100 momentarily.

On return with the CAL-15, the 304, 303, 301, 302 handled their consist from Bieber to Keddie with 58-37-95, 4,571 trailing tons or 5,111 gross tons. Between K78-89 on the 1.8 percent grade, a speed was generally maintained between 19-24 mph with amperage between 1,050-1,150, or within the continuous rating of the traction motors. These were 1,200-amp

THE SEARCH FOR REPLACEMENT POWER 145

continuous rated motors and Shideler observed the 1,200-amp figure was approached several times, but not exceeded into short time ratings.

Of considerable interest in these tests were the runs with one GP-40, No. 3509. GP-40 units were equipped with a load control cutback feature for the purpose of making them more compatible with units of lesser horsepower. This device cut in at 23 mph so as to cut back the horsepower and match the tractive effort capabilities of earlier locomotives. At 12 mph, 2,100 hp would be produced with a 62:15 gear ratio. When MU'd with lower horsepower units, this prevented units of higher horsepower from taking all the load.

The U33Bs were not equipped with this device, and did not cut back in horsepower at drag speeds, thus assuming a greater proportion of the tonnage. For this reason the GE units were well into the short time ratings, while the GP-40 remained in normal ratings at drag speeds below approximately 20 mph. Since the U33Bs tended to overload first, it was suggested that they be kept on the point when subjected to heavy trains. This same overloading would also occur with Western Pacific's new U30Bs MU'd with GP-40s unless the U30B operated in power match. Cuyler concluded that the new U30Bs on order should perform as well as the U33s since the new units would weigh some 18,000 lbs. heavier.

Based on test results, it was believed that 3,300 hp was an excessive amount for four traction motors at drag speed, but the new 3,000-hp U30Bs shortly to be delivered should not present this problem. Although the U33B was not considered by some to be a good drag locomotive, General Manager L.D. Michelson informed President Christy that the GE locomotive compared favorably with the GP-40, and that its overall performance was very good, particularly under load, under acceleration, and when attempting to make track time. Fuel consumption on runs was very good compared to the GP-40 although the latter was said to have used less when idling.

On October 9, 1967, Christy informed Michelson that he would like an "in-depth comparison with EMD GP-40 units . . . to help guide our future purchase decisions." These performance tests were run in the first half of 1968. Tests included three GP-40 test runs in which the power contained IDAC (Instantaneous Detection and Correction) equipment, one trip with the U30Bs on Almanor Hill, one round trip with the U30Bs, and a partial run using GP-40s without IDAC equipment.

On the three runs with IDAC equipment, between Keddie and Almanor, consists included 4,058 trailing tons on train 1-SWG-29, 4,116 trailing tons on the 1-SWG-6, and 4,283 trailing tons on the 1-SWG-13. On westbound runs over the 1.8 percent grade between Little Valley and Halls Flat, the GP-40s handled 4,460 trailing tons on train CAL-29, 4,654 trailing tons on the Extra-3508 West, and 4,435 trailing tons on the CAL-12. The four GP-40s not IDAC-equipped were not able to handle 4,419 trailing tons on dry rail, and finally stalled at milepost K20-7/8. Graphing of these runs indicated that the IDAC-equipped GP-40s easily outperformed those units not so equipped.

The IDAC equipment operated on the principle of electrically detecting and correcting wheel slippage through minimal reduction of generator current, by sensing the rate of change in current flow between the traction motors, thereby momentarily reducing the main generator excitation. Rapid wheel slips signaled for sanding in addition to excitation reduction. On trip 3, the drag duty performance was altered according to Electro–Motive specifications so that a minimum of 2,500 hp was produced at a continuous speed of 13.8 mph.

As built, specifications were set at 2,100 hp at a continuous speed of 11.1 mph—these settings being used for trips 1 and 2. A full 3,000 hp was available at approximately 23 mph and over, with either setting. The reasoning behind a smaller horsepower reduction as in trip 3 was to raise balancing speed with a reduction in adhesion requirements which results in a higher usable horsepower per unit in relation to speed. Calculations showed that actual horsepower at continuous speed with the altered drag duty performance was somewhat less than that anticipated, and in several cases horsepower fell much lower than expected where IDAC limitations were made by reducing generator current because of wheel slip. This test 3 was not considered a good performance because of the almost continuous slipping that was evidenced from the meter indicators hunting back and forth.

Performance of the 751 Class, the success of the U33Bs on the line, and perhaps other factors figured in the order of four additional U30Bs delivered as the 756 Class between September 20-29, 1968. Like other WP U30Bs, past or future, these possessed Electro–Motive trucks, and the heaviest axle loadings on the railroad. Western Pacific's main line did not seem universally suited for a six-wheel truck, and extra truck maintenance in addition to additional curve and flange wear caused the railroad to standardize on the four-wheel truck, and to further limit maintenance problems by using only Electro–Motive trucks under its road power. On the North Line, tractive effort was deemed more important than horsepower, thus the limitation of power requirements to 3,000 horsepower.

In late 1968, Cuyler asked WP's Norman Anderson to compile materials and test results in a series of locomotive performance studies to guide the railroad in future purchases of diesel motive power. At this time there remained a considerable number of F-7s, FP-7s, and F-3s on the roster and these would perhaps be up for retirement at an early date. In determining future motive power needs, it would be necessary to conclude how much work could be expected out of the fleet to be retained, in order to determine the nature and quantity of diesel power to completely modernize the fleet. This material is of considerable interest since it provides certain comparative data of use in understanding the more modern power on the railroad.

Study I calculated adhesion and speeds expected up the one percent with 5,500 trailing tons requiring 137,500 lbs. drawbar pull. Five GP-35s would require 11.8 percent adhesion to take such a train upgrade at 25.2 mph. Four GP-35s could be expected to make only 20.6 mph and would require 14.4 percent for this performance. Four GP-40s or the same number of U30Bs would about equal each other with the former requiring a 13.6 percent adhesion to enable 24.5 mph, and the latter tentatively expected to reach 24.4 mph with 13.1 percent adhesion required. It will be noted that adhesion was well below the normal maximum of 18 percent for bad rail and 20 percent for good rail, and that relatively equal performance on the one percent could be expected with four GP-40s, four U30Bs, or five GP-35s.

East of MP 784, GP-40 3525 followed by a mixed lashup of GP-35s and GP-40s, swings down the one percent grade toward Wendover, Utah, on the late morning of June 30, 1976. The east end of the system wasn't all flat, by any means.
Virgil Staff

Study II calculated adhesion and speeds expected up the 2.2 percent grade of the Inside Gateway with 4,200 trailing tons requiring 205,800 lbs. drawbar pull. With drag duty performance control, five GP-35s could make 15.7 mph with 18.2 percent adhesion required. This required adhesion equal to or less than the maximum of 18 percent for bad rail and 20 percent for good rail. Four GP-35s would theoretically fall down to 11.2 mph with a required adhesion of 22.2 percent. Since 22.2 percent adhesion would only rarely be available, four GP-35s could not possibly handle such a train. Four GP-40s could handle such a train at 11.2 mph assuming a 20.9 percent required adhesion, and the same number of U30Bs in power match should handle such tonnage at 15.9 mph with a required adhesion of 20.2 percent. Anderson called attention to these speeds as being very near the minimum continuous ratings for these locomotives, and such trains could be handled only on good rail. Very little, if any, extra tonnage could be tolerated and tonnage would need to be closely watched to avoid damage to traction motors.

Study III calculated adhesion and speeds expected up the 1.8 percent grade between Little Valley and Halls Flat westbound on the Inside Gateway, with 4,500 tons requiring

THE SEARCH FOR REPLACEMENT POWER   147

184,500 lbs. drawbar pull. With drag duty performance control, five GP-35s could make 18.2 mph with a required adhesion of 16.2 percent, or sufficient adhesion for bad rail in winter. Four GP-35s would require 19.7 percent adhesion to make 13 mph. The required adhesion here was greater than 18 percent for bad rail, and four GP-35s could not be expected to take 4,500 tons up the 1.8 percent under winter conditions. Four GP-40s would do only slightly better, and might attain a speed of 12.5 mph based on a 2,100-hp performance control with 18.7 percent adhesion required. Four U30Bs would handle such a train at 17.9 mph with a required adhesion of 18 percent. With power match cut in, U30B performance would be similar to the GP-40s with 2,100-hp performance control. It can be seen, based on this study, that four GP-40s would not equal the performance of four U30Bs, but that five GP-35s could handle the train very well at 16+ percent adhesion.

Study IV calculated adhesion and speeds expected up the 1.8 percent grade with 5,000 trailing tons requiring 205,000 lbs. drawbar pull. Five GP-35s should easily handle such a consist under winter conditions although four 3,000-hp locomotives probably would not. With power match cut in, the U30Bs' performance would be similar to the GP-40s' with performance control. However, the speeds in such a performance would be below the continuous rating of the U30Bs so that the units would be overloaded.

A careful perusal of these statistics may indicate possible operating advantages in specified uses of each of the two types of road power, and one may understand General Manager MacLeod's desire, under specified conditions, to employ the U30Bs wherever possible on the North Line. At the same time, and into 1969, Cuyler feared the WP's austere program for purchase of road and switching power would cause the railroad to lose ground in its costs of maintaining and operating its then-aging fleet of F units and Alco switch engines. "Eleven [new] yard units would permit us to considerably reduce the average age of the yard fleet and gain ground," he said.

In 1969-71, net ton miles were down from 1968, as were gross ton miles. Freight revenues per mile of road were up over previous years but so were operating expenses. The *California Zephyr's* continuing losses were hurting the Western Pacific, while many factions outside the railroad were attempting to force retention of a train that the railroad was unable to convince the public to ride.

Wisdom seemed to call for holding the line on expenses and terminating the passenger train. Christy worked on both. New switching power was not purchased, and GP-7s and GP-9s increasingly were found in switching service. Two secondhand switchers, to be numbered 607-608, were acquired from the ST&E in April 1970 as part of a trade in which the WP turned over two 660-hp switch engines Nos. 505 and 506. This gave the Western Pacific 1,080 additional horsepower for switching operations, and allowed the use of these two locomotives on jobs where 660-hp units were either too small, or completely inadequate.

In the torrid heat of a July afternoon in 1979, the 3069 West, along with units 3521, 3519 and 3515 wait at Wendover, Utah, for a chance to climb the hill west of town. The old diesel facility, and roadmaster headquarters, are in the background to the left, and what remains of the old Army Air Corps base is to the right. **Virgil Staff**

20

Getting a Move On

AS EARLY AS July 1958, the Great Northern had approached the Western Pacific about the possibility of adding a sixth unit to certain trains running south out of Bieber. The utilization of a sixth unit west out of Bieber would eliminate extra train miles from time to time, and when there was opportunity, it might be possible to consolidate the GWS and CAL into one train. Also, there was always the likelihood of eliminating some helper service between Keddie and Norvell.

The chief problem under discussion was the heavy grade and curvature on that line which raised some doubt about the feasibility of using six units. Five units normally handled the heavy tonnage trains on the fourth subdivision, and when the subject again arose in October 1958 it was agreed to postpone such tests because of rail conditions due to inclement weather.

The initial test of six units on a round trip between Oroville and Bieber was made over the Inside Gateway on May 23, 1960. At the same time, a plan was instituted to restore the west leg of the Keddie wye to expedite north-south movements. Five-unit trains over the railroad had preempted the booster units, and six-unit trains might require two or three cab units in a consist. The problem here was that when cab units were coupled nose to nose there was no extension of the control circuits. This was rectified between 1962 and 1967 by the application of control jumper receptacles in the nose of each cab unit to be so employed. Moreover, additional locking devices were applied between December 1967 and December 1968 to strengthen the nose doors of 29 cab units. In the meantime, on trains like the SWG or NCX, the power frequently operated out of Oroville on five units using a geep as either the cab or trailing unit and then adding the sixth unit or another geep to this train at Keddie. This could be done rather quickly but did restrict flexibility.

By August 1960, President Fred Whitman was thinking about handling larger trains on faster schedules with six, seven, or eight units. In July, the SWG had used six units on seven occasions and in each case this had saved a Keddie–Norvel helper turn. Southbound out of Bieber the six units returning permitted the handling of increased tonnage in some

Sunrise over the Great Salt Lake finds a fast westbound symbol east of Wendover, destined for points in California. These salt flats extend roughly from Knolls to Wendover, perhaps a bit less than 40 miles. This day, July 16, 1979, will be sizzling hot before the sun gets many degrees over the yardarm. **Virgil Staff**

Two units of U23B power and three of GP-40 snake an eastbound piggyback-container train around Antelope Hill in Nevada on June 30, 1974.
Virgil Staff

cases and gave better over-the-road time in all cases. Northbound, 80 or more cars were handled and as high as 4,400 tons, the typical train being 4,200 tons. This was compared with 2,800 tons with four units or 3,500 tons with five units on the SWG schedule.

The six units were used southbound on the CAL in each case but in a few instances these did not go through to Bieber, but were changed out on the road. Train CAL-20 handled 5,270 tons out of Bieber, making the run in five hours, 10 minutes, including some local work. The maximum that could have been handled with five units would have been 4,600 tons with a running time of about 20 minutes longer. CAL-19 had 131 cars and 7,325 tons with a two-unit GN helper to Halls Flat with running time of five hours, 15 minutes.

With five units and helper, the CAL-19 could not have handled over 6,400 tons and would have required about 20 minutes longer running time. A concomitant of five and six-unit operation was showing up in early 1962 in the effect this operation had on the extending of service life of material and component parts. Increased mileage resulting from five and six-unit operation shortened the interval for repairs, and as Cuyler said, "We are in need of repairs."

The tightening of schedules had been close to the heart of management almost from the beginning of the railroad. Terminal delays, connections with various locals, miscellaneous attempts to avoid lost motion of inspections, holding trains for cars, attempts to reduce detainment time of trains, and considerable revision of yards over the years to speed the servicing of trains, was a never-ending cycle.

The canyon was always a bottleneck, and it wasn't always a simple matter to keep out of the way of the passenger trains. The Western Pacific sometimes followed other railroads in improving its ratios, and at other times it set the pace. In the constant competitive enterprise that was railroading, the improvement of one ratio led to the decline in another. Competency and ingenuity and constant effort for improvement was what kept the WP on its feet.

President Whitman kept Munson on the trail of faster handling of trains through the terminals. This included the elimination of lost motion in train inspections and servicing of power, and will be discussed in detail in a future study. Faster schedules meant that all concerned had to understand their part in insuring that symbol trains could maintain their schedules. Hot box delays left little slack in the schedule for on-time arrival, and a hot journal often meant the missing of connections. The faster schedules of freight trains in 1958, both eastward and westward between the Bay Area and midwestern and eastern points, made on-time performance a joint enterprise, with final delivery time at the destination the only important goal.

In 1957-58, when comparing its placement with the considerable number of other railroads in the Central Western Region, the WP came out low in gross tons per train, and in second or third place in GTM per train hour, net tons per train, and train miles per train hour. Miles per locomotive day brought it up to first or second place, and the railroad was always first in net ton miles per car day, and car miles per car day.

Expediter and SWG schedules were tightened in 1958, and the new schedule of the Advanced CFS in February required dite the handling of trains through the yards. If trains were delivered late to the WP, there were more problems. As Munson once said, "We must do everything possible to avoid the finger of failure."

In 1958 the attempt was being made to better the competitive position, meet truck competition, and where possible to recover some of the business then moving on the highway. In August 1958, in order to make maximum speeds and a minimum time run, the Expediter was held to 2,100 tons with four units, 2,500 tons with five units, and a single unit helper was added out of Keddie with any tonnage greater than that. In September 1958, the schedule of the GGM was shortened to

It is late afternoon of August 27, 1977. A WP symbol with Burlington Northern pool power works throttle up the 1.50 percent out of Keddie. This is east of Tunnel 5 and can be seen from Indian Falls Road along the highway to Greenville.
Virgil Staff

extremely good handling on the part of all concerned to insure that this train arrived at Oakland at 4:00 P.M. or earlier. Freight train speeds frequently placed Western Pacific very high nationally, but the railroad suffered from transportation costs more than its neighbors, and manifests sometimes left Roper with not more than 1,400 tons.

Considerable emphasis had been placed on the longer, heavier trains, but Western Pacific always ran a considerable number of relatively light trains with sufficient power to meet the ever-tighter schedules. Fueling practices expedited train movements to every extent possible, and advantage was taken of every minute to condition the journals, and generally expe-

become more competitive with trucks, and 20 hours were cut from the running time between Oakland and Chicago.

When some trains failed to make their connection, special service trains were sometimes run since symbol trains tended to leave on time. Chief Engineer Frank Woolford once commented that "the running time on the main track is sufficient to adequately make this schedule if we can keep our trains out of the yards." New CFS and PC trains were established in October 1958 with fast, rigid schedules, and some perishable and merchandise traffic was placed on a fifth morning schedule from Oakland to Chicago.

In April 1960, the PBF schedule was changed to allow

24-hour running time on the Western Pacific. This and other faster schedules were requiring locomotives to operate at longer sustained speeds. Some difficulties were experienced on traction motors with high mileage around 300,000 that had been in slower service such as on locals and helpers. When this power was placed in faster service, there was a tendency for the insulation to break down and for brush troubles to develop. The normal change-out period for traction motors was 400,000 miles and the difficulty was not a serious one at the time although it was somewhat aggravated by the motors operating at higher voltages. Under these conditions, if there was any weakness in the insulation, a flashover might result which would not have occurred if the unit had been used in heavier low-speed service in which the system never reached the maximum voltage output of the generator.

At low speed and heavy tonnage the amperage is up and voltage is down; at high speed and lighter tonnage the reverse is true—amperage is down and voltage is up. The higher the voltage, the greater the tendency is for a flashover to occur if there is any weakness in the motor which includes insulation, grade of brush, and dust that collects in the motor. In order to overcome this to at least some extent, the grade of brushes was changed in the traction motors, and the insulation problem was largely overcome by placing later type traction motors under the units regularly assigned to fast service.

Additional speed restrictions were eased in 1960, but the men were not simply running fast trains since the engineering department and the superintendents were watching the speed tapes made on each run. On-time performance and the insistence on observing speed restrictions were not always compatible, especially when a train had been delivered late. The higher sustained speeds in 1960, compared with 1959, brought about changes in the electrical circuits, especially on the GP-9s in fast freight service.

The GP-9s operating, as has been noted, at higher voltages and lower amperages experienced surges brought about by wheel slips in high-voltage operation. These surges of voltage found the weaknesses in insulation and went through to ground causing flashovers. Western Pacific forces now found it necessary to refine their maintenance of electrical equipment on the freight units concerning insulation and condition of the commutators. Commutators were stoned on the traction

Frederick B. Whitman
He had larger trains on his mind.

H. C. Munson
On the trail of faster trains.

motors and the forces applied new epoxy-type insulation to the string bands to effect better insulation. This work started about May 1960 on the GP-9s, and these were placed back in the pool on the GGM and PBF runs to determine if this work would overcome the problem.

Cuyler had always been dubious about the wheel slip arrangement because the GP-9 had a higher generator output than the 1,500-hp units but still had the same type of wheel slip arrangement. There was no certainty that the wheel slips were causing the trouble but the GP-9s were placed back in the pool for 20 or 30 days on a test basis to learn how they would do with the 2001 Class of GP-20s which at that time were beginning to show certain defects of their own. More power was running through Oroville than was true for 1959, and a host of new engineers on the Eastern Division may have contributed to delays.

Longer trains at higher speeds required sufficient braking distances, and the signal department had been making studies to determine just how long trains could be allowed at given speeds on various districts. Trainmasters, dispatchers, and others watched carefully to assure that a consist did not deviate from the standard, and Munson cautioned Signal Department Engineer B.L. McNeill that "We are anxious to minimize our transportation costs as much as we can but with our primary objective remaining good performance."

Numerous tests were made of stopping distances on all districts, and a 25-30 percent safety margin was established in the braking charts. Train speeds varied but maximum freight train speed was 60 mph, and on fast trains the number of cars was restricted to 50 with total tonnage of 3,500 tons. Drag trains would be allowed 120 cars but their speed was restricted to 45 mph. Train length varied from 120 cars to 50 cars on through freights, and from 6,000 tons to 3,000 tons. By the end of 1963 certain speed restrictions were liberalized considerably, and the west leg of the Keddie wye was finally rehabilitated to allow a faster schedule on the Expediter.

The tightening of freight schedules was a never-ending challenge which has continued into the present. But the highest challenge in these years was when the railroad was attempting to work its way out of the cul-de-sac of steam days with its accompaniment of various labor agreements, terminal inspections, journal box waste, and multiplicity of crew change points. The speed governors on freight locomotives had been set for 65 mph but these could be set at a higher range. Concurrently, the trains would keep rolling, and the pressure would be continuous to get them to their ultimate terminals on time.

Crawling downgrade through Rattlesnake Gulch, at the western entrance to Arnold's Loop, is the 3524 and a new engineer. It is 11:40 a.m. on June 27, 1975, and Superintendent John Lusar, with a red flag, is around the bend to put the fear of this long hill in the hearts of the engine crew! Lusar himself is a little shaken after just having been buzzed by one of the crawling kinds of varmint.
Virgil Staff

GETTING A MOVE ON 153

21

TOFC and How to Drag

IN CONJUNCTION with the Great Northern and Santa Fe, piggyback operations were inaugurated via the Inside Gateway in 1954. The start was a slow one, but enabled the railroad to gather experience in the kind of facilities and operation that would be of most utility to its shippers. On March 17, 1959, piggyback service was inaugurated between Salt Lake City and the Bay Area for the handling of truck trailers of Pacific Intermountain Express, Interstate Motor Lines, and Garrett Freight Lines. And March 24, 1959, brought agreement between the railroad and Trailer Train Co. to participate in a pool of railroad flat cars bearing the mark "TTX."

Revenue trailers handled in piggyback service exceeded 5,300 in 1959 compared with approximately 750 in 1958. Operations were greatly expanded during 1960, and the railroad began moving automobiles in the long trilevel cars. Trailer-on-flatcar operations exceeded 7,600 in 1960, 8,764 in 1961, and 10,281 in 1962.

Increases in such movements continued year after year with many trains containing what seemed an unending line of piggyback and bilevel and trilevel rack cars. Containerization on the West Coast gained remarkable momentum in 1968 when steamship lines placed container ships into service from the Far East. The Western Pacific participated very heavily in this traffic, and is said to have been the first western road to establish an integrated Intermodal Services Department to efficiently coordinate the many functions related to both container and trailer-on-flat car traffic.

Seatrain Lines completed its marine cargo terminal at Oakland in 1969, and the company began moving third and fourth-

East of Sacramento the 3017 West waits in the hole at Del Paso for an eastbound hotshot. It is July 18, 1978. **Virgil Staff**

A westbound crew change at Winnemucca on the dismal, overcast afternoon of June 13, 1973. Piggyback traffic is in evidence on this train, headed by units 3004, 3064, 2251 and 2260.
Virgil Staff

class mail in daily trailer-on-flat service on September 27, 1970.

The TOFC cars had a length of from 50'0" to 105'3" and tended, especially on the curvatures of the Inside Gateway, to create their own enigmas. Consider a heavy tonnage train, traversing the heavy grades and curvatures of the North Line, with 9,000 hp on the head end. Upgrade, the train's mass tended to obey the laws of gravity and resistance. Place 9,000 hp on the point and one had the effect of an opposing force on either end of a coil spring. With sufficient force exerted at each end, the coil would tend to straighten and extend itself. When drawbar pull on an 85-foot car was directly across the curve on a long sub-chord, a heavily loaded flat might be forced hard against the low rail with sufficient force to turn it over, or if the car was too light, to climb the gage side of the inside rail.

Vice President and General Manager Harry C. Munson retired on February 29, 1964, after a distinguished career with the Western Pacific, and his place was filled by Myron Christy who functioned as executive vice president and general manager between March 1, 1964, and June 30, 1965. President Frederick B. Whitman, undoubtedly the most progressive chief up to that time, had come to the Western Pacific on October 1, 1948, and on June 30, 1965, he turned over the leadership of the Western Pacific to Christy. L.D. Michelson then took over the general manager's position from July 1, 1965, until December 1, 1969. All of these men were deeply concerned about the heavy lateral thrusts on rail curvatures, with the tendency of the longer cars to climb the rail or to roll it.

Cuyler, Shideler and others had often been trackside on the North Line to observe the long cars in operation, and it had been noticed that when the trucks on these cars came off a 10° curve onto tangent track, the trucks did not tend to straighten up until they had moved 400 or more feet over the tangent. On occasions, a slight rocking of cars had been observed which would, under certain conditions, facilitate climbing the inside rail on a curvature. This was especially noted on 100-ton covered hopper cars in early 1970, and CMO D.F. Pilkinton equipped all such system cars with truck spring snubbers in an effort to minimize the "rock-and-roll" characteristics.

Michelson had asked for a test of seven units on the north Line with 4,500-4,600 tons if Cuyler felt the drawbars would take it. This test apparently was accomplished in 1964 with the results unknown to this writer. Cuyler had been considering the possibility of training these 85', 86'9", and 89'4" cars on the rear, especially when empty, and an increasing number of reports from other railroads in late 1965 and early 1966 indicated the possible wisdom of such a move. Such instructions did not seem necessary on the east-west line, but might be of utility north out of Keddie.

Michelson believed in the ton-mile formula, and during periods when the power was in short supply, he sent out six units of the 913 Class with all the tonnage they could drag. Up the North Line they crawled, through Tunnel No. 6, coughing, gulping, sucking in their own exhaust, boiling out their water, bells ringing for miles, smoke trailing out the forward units, the sixth unit nearly dead. Into Spring Garden tunnel they roared with demonic passion, rear units kicking out two-thirds way through the tunnel, bells ringing all the way.

When the units shut down, the crews placed them back on the line when the train was outside the tunnel. When the units were not shut down, the men looked back to be sure they were not burning up the traction motors. With mixed power, you could never be sure just what was transpiring back in the consist.

You could smell the traction motors before they began to smoke, but you could never be certain a unit was not overloading unless you were on that unit. Especially would this be true of the GEs which went into the overload zone faster than the EMDs. Engineer James Boynton recalled the use of GP-20s in such service: turbos shut down, or backfiring through the air filters and shooting fire out the stacks. "When the ground relay would pop, it sounded like a cannon going off."

Another issue arising during these years was the tendency of heavy downgrade trains, with excessive dynamic braking from

The midmorning of April 23, 1966, finds the piggyback-laden eastbound GGM dropping down the east slope of Altamont Pass into Tunnel 3 at MP 57.67. To the right are the Southern Pacific tracks connecting Livermore with Tracy.
Virgil Staff

the head end, to jackknife and sometimes derail. Many of these trains had the retainers set up in addition to heavy automatic air applications sufficient to envelop much of the train in smoke. To overcome the problem of jackknifing, instructions were issued that no more than four units would be used in dynamic braking at one time, and this generally worked out well.

To cope with the problems of upgrade heavy tonnage trains, wherever possible the long cars were placed toward the rear of the train so they would not be subjected to the high tractive effort pull which increases thrust on the rail. Rocking of cars at speeds between 12 and 18 mph in areas of low rail joints, or where the track was unstable, was faced at least temporarily in early 1967 by establishing speed restrictions in these areas of not more than 10 mph or not less than 20 mph. These speeds tended to take trains out of the speed range where harmonics might cause cars to rock and derail.

Super-elevation changes on the High Line, and through the canyon after taking off the *California Zephyr,* tended to decrease this problem, and road foremen concentrated on working with new engineers to assure better control of slack action. This pertained to the proper operation of the dynamic brake in conjunction with air brakes, for good practice dictated that the train should be stretched at the proper time and should have all the slack gathered at the proper time; otherwise slack action could contribute considerably to derailment.

In May 1964, Michelson, Cuyler, and Lynch agreed that the maximum number of units to be coupled together in hauling a train could not be more than 10. This lashup would not be considered except in cases where it was necessary to make power moves to eliminate double heading or light movements. Whenever 913 or 801 Class units were coupled to multiple with higher-rated units, the maximum amperage that might be used in dynamic braking would be 600 amps, with not more than four units being in dynamic braking at one time. FT units would not be allowed in this kind of service although some nose plugs were being installed in 904 Class power to allow multiple-unit operation with others of similar class. Where possible, the same kind of units were kept together, sometimes mixing a big one with others, or an F-7 and a small geep. Also where possible, the older units were placed on the point in order to better control amperages.

The subject of switchers came up in May 1967 when General Manager Michelson began to consider the wisdom of replacing certain low-horsepower switching engines. The intent was to begin retiring the 504 Class with its high cost of maintenance due to heavy repair work that was becoming necessary. The 504 Class, because of light weight and small horsepower, were not being utilized to any great extent, and were considerd insufficiently strong to handle cuts of cars in a satisfactory manner.

The proposal was to downgrade the 701 Class of GP-7s to switch service and thereby eliminate a considerable number of yard engines that could be retired. This would increase the utilization by reason of reduction in the frequency of repairs, and produce a relatively low cost per mile. The date of this downgrading is uncertain, but the railroad began retiring the 504 Class in 1967. Enthusiasts around the railroad in the early 1970s certainly knew how dependent the company had become on its GP-7s in heavy terminal switching service.

Myron Christy
Curves were of concern.

L. D. Michelson
He believed in the ton-mile formula.
L.D. Michelson Collection

22

The Krauss-Maffei and Other Anachronisms

WESTERN PACIFIC management typically showed an interest in new or different forms of motive power. On October 31, 1949, Mechanical Engineer W.B. Wolverton and Cuyler inspected the new General Electric gas turbine locomotive, No. 50 of the Union Pacific, then being tested on that railroad. The two officials inspected the locomotive at Los Angeles and rode it to Barstow, a distance of 150 miles with a ruling grade of 2.2 percent.

Motive Power Chief E.E. Gleason was impressed by this attempt to perfect a new type of power for railroad use, but believed it had objectionable features which needed correction before such power would become practical. Some of these objections were: (1) high fuel consumption; (2) terrific noise; (3) high exhaust temperature; (4) improper balancing of horsepower and weight; (5) a gas turbine engine which could not be started inside the shop and had to be taken out in the yard for this purpose; (6) the need for one-hour preparatory time to start the gas turbine.

Cuyler calculated that the running repair costs would be extremely high, and was unfavorably impressed by the considerable slippage of drivers on tonnage that would have been handled without slipping by two 1,500-hp Electro–Motive units. In 1959, after considering and stating his additional objections to the 8,500-hp UP turbine type, he concluded that "here all of the eggs are in one basket for if a failure occurs it results in a total failure which would not occur if more units were in the consist of the locomotive."

At one time or another, Cuyler studied both the Milwaukee and Great Northern electrification, and at least theoretically toyed with the idea of electrification through the canyon. This never had much possibility, and calculations indicated that electric operation would be considerably more expensive than diesel. The initial expense of electrification would be staggering, to say nothing of the depreciation burden on such equipment, the cost of electric power, or operation and maintenance of substations, power lines, and electric locomotives. On the basis of ton miles moved, the cost of the electric locomotive would be perhaps twice that of the diesel.

In September 1961, Whitman indicated interest in tests to be conducted on the Southern Pacific and Rio Grande with Krauss–Maffei diesel-hydraulic engines built in Germany. Cuyler was asked to evaluate these hydraulics although he was never very impressed with their usefulness on American railroads. The six-wheel trucks were considered too rigid and could be expected to produce rapid flange wear. Wheel diameters must of necessity remain about the same, and on the WP one could expect rapid change-out of wheels. This would be a very time-consuming chore since gearboxes must be removed, drive shaft disconnected, and gearboxes disassembled.

The trucks were sprung much like steam locomotives, and it was expected that these would easily become unbalanced. In fact, there were so many modifications that would be required to make such units functional that these units were simply not considered practical. Maintenance costs could be expected to be very high and in general service, Cuyler assumed the units would be down most of the time awaiting repairs, and that it would be necessary to increase the number of units in order to take care of the out-of-service time.

Consideration was given in 1964 to the Alco 4,300-hp diesel-hydraulic locomotive but Cuyler concluded that numerous modifications again would be required before such a locomotive could be economical for a railroad the size of Western Pacific. In fact, it had been found to be more economical to standardize on one manufacturer's type of diesel-electric unit since it eliminated the necessity of having a dual store stock. And, having only one type of equipment on hand resulted in better maintenance.

In 1966 and 1967, Western Pacific management showed considerable interest in automatic train control systems produced by Westinghouse, Radiation Incorporated, and General Railway Signal Co. Cuyler and the management had been talking about the use of slave units since 1965, and in 1967 and 1968 he watched, with considerable interest, the experiments on the Norfolk & Western, and on the Pennsylvania Railroad. One potential problem with remote-control was that loss of radio continuity could be expected in the canyon between master and slave units and it was Cuyler's conclusion that such devices were in an experimental stage which the WP would be wise to avoid.

In 1955, the Western Pacific began application of spark arrestors as insurance against the likelihood that the diesels might set fires along the right-of-way. At one time or another, trespassers were to be found on or near the right-of-way, and itinerant occupants of freight trains sometimes tossed their cigarette butts of the moving trains. The diesels were likely to receive the blame for most right-of-way fires, and about August 1955 arrestors were ordered from Electro–Motive for two passenger units to observe their effectiveness.

This process of arrestor application was hastened in the following month by a fire along the right-of-way 10 poles west of milepost 221 which had been reported by a crew on train 56-1

Engine 2253, with BN 2524 and WP 3070, 3522 and 3052 prepare to take the siding at Greenville on August 27, 1977, for a meet with a heavy westbound symbol freight coming down the 2.2 percent out of Almanor. The westbound man was enveloped in fumes from smoking brake shoes, and upon clearing the east switch, there was a rest accompanied by the 2253 walking out of town with a mighty growl. Two decades previously the WP began applying spark arrestors to help prevent diesels from setting lineside fires. **Virgil Staff**

William B. Wolverton
An interest in the new and/or different.

Robert Mustard
Experiments in the Perlman-Flannery years.

NCX-1 from Berry Creek. Although there was no reason to believe this fire had been started by the diesels, the WP was as interested as anyone in helping to keep the canyon green.

Over the ensuing years, the railroad would experiment almost continually in the control of such emissions. Homemade arrestors were installed on the 501, 581, and 601 Classes, with Great Northern designs placed on the 701, 725, 801-805 Classes, and most likely on FTs and F-7s. All units received arrestor applications, and there was considerable experimentation with the arrestors of other railroads.

Homemade designs consisted of Draftac screens mounted directly to the top of the exhaust pipe. This arrestor used wire netting formed to cage in the exhaust pipe above the stack. In designing this cage, sufficient area had to be provided to eliminate the possibility of any back draft with consequent discomfort in the cab. The first of these possessed a mesh size which left too large an opening, but this was shortly corrected by application of screens with closer mesh. These usually possessed a #415 Draftac netting with openings of .130" x .750".

Less than 100 percent success was considered unsatisfactory. Potential difficulties were aggravated by the heavier fuel then being used which tended to leave heavy deposits of carbon in the exhaust channels. When the engine worked hard the carbon broke loose from being heated and was emitted from the exhaust stack. Conductor Burke, working the 56-Turn, had noticed that when small engines were used in the yard, they built up a deposit of carbon which was blown out when these engines pulled heavy tonnage out onto the Main.

By July 1956, the railroad had largely learned how to eliminate this action by using regular run diesel fuel at Stockton, Oakland and San Jose; by shutting the engines down at San Jose so as to cut their period of idling; and by changing out the locomotives every six or seven days so that they could be placed on the mainline under load to rid them of the carbon buildup in the exhaust channels.

Fuel additives had initially been found to be ineffective, although for a considerable period at a later time, the company successfully used a disbursing additive known as Burnzall which was said to eliminate the formation of carbons in the cylinder heads and exhaust channels. This conditioner was put in the fuel oil tank about two or three months before the dry season starting in 1958 to give the conditioner a chance to clean and prevent deposits of carbon in the exhaust channels. The Burnzall additive changed the makeup of the carbon so that instead of its being in hard flakes, it appeared in the exhaust manifold as a doughy mixture and did not fly out off the exhaust. August 1958 was said to be the dryest in California in 72 years, yet these engines set no right-of-way fires during the entire season.

In 1959 the mechanical forces began application of Far-Air cyclonic arrestors which directed the exhaust gases into a spinning action or uniform cyclonic manner, and pulled the hot carbon particles to the outer perimeter of the manifold where they rotated until burned out. This theoretically allowed only the spark-free gases in the center of the manifold to be emitted from the stack. These first cyclonic arrestors were welded and fitted into the exhaust manifolds then being used. These were not good applications; the manifold metal cracked and this resulted in continual maintenance costs. The most satisfactory idea was to replace the old manifold with new manifolds already equipped with the arrestor. These initially were applied to a considerable number of GP-7s and GP-9s.

Then in 1959, or the early half of 1960, a Shell Oil Co. research team, working with the railroad, concluded that the most effective means of dealing with the problem would be to regularly clean the venturi stacks by scraping and wire brushing. This was arranged to be done at monthly inspections, or more often, and from July 1960 all power regularly received this kind of care. Sometime prior to 1963 the railroad began using the Nalco additives which were applied to the fuel storage tanks for stabilization of the fuel to prevent heavy buildup of carbon inside the combustion chambers.

Additionally, in 1964 the brand of lube oil was changed to eliminate the use of any metallic soap detergents, and thus eliminate the presence of metal in the carbon flakes emitted from the stacks. Engineers were reminded not to pull the throttle out suddenly, since this might be the cause of emissions, until the engines had settled to their maximum rpm under full load.

The FT locomotives were considered to be the worst offenders by 1964, but these units would gradually be replaced by turbocharged power thus largely eliminating the problem. By the end of 1964, 11 GP-7s and GP-9s were equipped with cyclonic arrestors, and the railroad would shortly install Electro-Motive's new improved arrestors in units of the 913 Class. Unlike the earlier arrestors, these could be applied without removing the main hatch, so were not prohibitively expensive to install.

Western Pacific fuel was mostly a blend of distillates and residuals, and was generally of good quality considering the fuel that was available to railroads at that time. As has been noted, this fuel contained a stabilizing detergent, and the lube oil contained an organic-type detergent which was claimed to be ashless, and which should eliminate the metal in the carbon flakes.

In 1965 cyclonic arrestors were authorized for passenger units. By early 1966 the F-7s were beginning to receive them. But nothing remains static and by the middle of 1966 the F-unit exhaust systems were experiencing carbon buildup on the walls of the venturi portions of the systems, so that a constant program of scraping the venturi portions of the systems continued to be required.

Nevertheless, the railroad was essentially free from wayside fires. In 1968 WP locomotives used brake shoes with copper inserts which were supposed to prevent excessive sparking, and prior to 1970, and probably much earlier, spark shields were being installed on all wooden deck freight cars. New orders of covered hoppers were to be delivered with composition brake shoes. During the dry season, locomotive engineers were instructed to utilize dynamic brakes to the fullest, and additional units were employed if necessary to provide maximum dynamic braking.

Problems during the 1970s changed considerably with all the FTs off the roster, and most of the F-7s and F-3s on their way to being retired. All of the new road power was turbocharged with consequent pulverization of carbon emissions. The stacks of nonturbocharged power were inspected and cleaned regularly, and applications were made to GP-7s and GP-9s of Farr cyclonic arrestors possessing a trap to collect the emissions which had been separated out. The first cyclonic arrestors had had only a device which separated out the particles and then threw them out, but the new arrestors performed both functions.

Considerable emission experimentation took place under CMO R.W. Mustard throughout the Perlman-Flannery administrations, with installation of "low sac" injectors to Electro-Motive units, experiments with Hi-Dome pistons on Alco switchers, and a study of the uses of advanced speed schedules in General Electric units.

The Ford Fast, with its usual urgency, hastens through Battle Mountain, Nevada, on the afternoon of June 15, 1974. This is the paired trackage, and the symbol is holding the westbound main of the Southern Pacific.
Virgil Staff

23

Oroville, Sacramento or Stockton?

THE STORY BEHIND the proposal to use U30Bs on the *California Zephyr* dates to sometime in 1968 when Cuyler proposed that Shideler and Anderson investigate the operation of a single GE unit on that train. Patronage was at its usual low, and calculations indicated a single U30B, coupled in with a steam generator car, could handle an abbreviated train of 10 cars. The covered wagons in passenger service were old and expensive to maintain, and the steam generators on this equipment were in horrendous condition.

Cuyler did not choose to expend additional funds on these generators, and he suggested the purchase of three steam generator cars. A test was run out of Salt Lake on September 13, 1968, with WP754 on the point of Rio Grande generator car No. 250 and 10 cars, 1,023 tons. On September 15, train No. 18 went out with engine 754 on the point of 11 cars. Shideler was aboard these runs as a trouble-shooter, and spent most of his time attempting to keep the generator car on the line. These runs were considered substantially successful, although graphs of the eastbound run show the 754 lost 16 minutes on the run from Oroville to Salt Lake. Additional runs were later made with 751 Class power and GN generator cars purchased in 1968, and numbered 591-593.

Heavy freight power, such as this U30B, could have wound up on the *California Zephyr* under a rejected plan. Here, on October 8, 1977, Engineer Ted Wood handles a westbound grain train through the West Portal of Tunnel 37 into Sierra Valley.
Virgil Staff

These three generator cars, with two CFK-4225 steam generators each, possessed insufficient water capacity for eliminating water stops between Oakland and Salt Lake, and Anderson suggested to Cuyler that the standard *Zephyr* consist should include one U30B, one 804 Class cab unit, and a heater car. The 804 Class unit would be added to supply additional steam capacity and water capacity for winter operation, and to provide additional power in the summer when the train exceeded 10 cars. Furthermore, there would be need for one standard three-unit consist as backup in case of derailment or when power was tied up for federal inspection. The spare set of units would pay their way by performing shuttle service between Stockton and Oakland or San Jose, and would be available for passenger service when needed.

But it didn't happen. Time was running short for the *California Zephyr,* and with the railroad short on freight power, the U30Bs remained in freight service. Steam generator cars 591-593 found their place behind two units of 801 or 804 Class power which usually pulled the train after January 11, 1970. In these final months, the train usually ran nine or 10 cars, thus enabling fewer units on the front, and additional units for use in the freight pool.

Prior to retirement of President Christy on December 1, 1970, the hottest issue on the Western Pacific was the construction of the new diesel shops at Stockton. Since the beginning of dieselization, the chief shops for running repairs had been at the old Oroville roundhouse, with very heavy repairs at Sacramento after 1949. The plan had been to construct a diesel facility, and to retire the steam facility at Oroville. But economic conditions had always caused postponement.

Into sometime in 1959 the idea had been to build a minimum facility at Oroville to handle locomotive repairs. Since Oroville is at the foot of the hill, it would continue to function on the Western Pacific as Roseville does on the Southern Pacific. By the close of 1959 there was talk of building the shops at Stockton instead of Oroville, and by June 11, 1960, there seems to have been considerable agreement on the utility of such a move.

Behind the proposed movement of the shops to Stockton was a notion that during the previous three years, Western Pacific operations had changed enough to invalidate the reasons for continuance of maintenance facilities at Oroville. Expedited schedules both east and west required the use of heavy power west as well as east of Oroville if advantage was to be taken of relatively high-speed track. These schedules required that delays at intermediate terminals be held to a minimum.

In 1960, many trains were expedited by being mainlined at Oroville, and where possible both power and cabooses were run through to Stockton in both directions. Westbound trains were being preblocked at Roper (Salt Lake City) and Klamath Falls, and it was theoretically no longer necessary to switch all of these trains at Oroville.

Since Stockton was the actual point of origin and termination of most freight trains eastbound and westbound respectively, it was thought the elimination of Oroville as a point of power change would eliminate another terminal delay by running trains intact from Salt Lake City to Stockton westbound and from Stockton to Salt Lake City eastbound. On June 29, 1960, Cuyler wrote: "Competition has forced this railroad to eliminate all delays possible in order to retain what business we have, and it is for this reason that it has been decided the location of this shop will be at Stockton instead of Oroville."

In June 1963, though, Cuyler felt the railroad had done very well with its facilities at Oroville, the fruition of projects to remove the locomotive facilities to Stockton and essentially all car facilities to Sacramento would materially improve operating procedures and would provide a saving that would amount to approximately 17 percent on a discounted basis after taxes. Since 1960 the mechanical department had reduced 52 employees in the locomotive department, and additional employees would be released as a savings to this project. On June 17, 1963, Cuyler wrote Munson: "The reason why we are still able to make reductions is because of the tools that we have procured on our small tools budget, and because we have been able to receive the benefits of increased service life on improved materials from the manufacturer along with new methods and procedures that we have placed in effect."

An advantage to consolidating this work at Stockton would be the locating of the maintenance terminal at the end of the run where locomotives could be maintained during the layover period and would not have to be cut out at Oroville for maintenance. At that time the current arrangement resulted in locomotives being tied up at a terminal (Oroville) that did not have the force or the facilities to do this work.

The change would result in higher availability and would provide more time for maintenance. All of which would be the equivalent of providing at least four units more in utilization to the fleet. It was believed that the increased power flexibility and availability with the power pool at Stockton would improve WP ability to move tonnage either east or west, and to make up time, particularly on the first subdivision. Passenger power, then laying over at Oroville, could be used in freight service on a round trip between Oakland and Stockton. This usage in itself would be approximately the equivalent of adding three units to the diesel fleet with a value in excess of $600,000 a year.

In 1963 most eastbound power was cut out for maintenance and inspection at Oroville, and sometimes the power on westbound trains as well. The Oroville facility was an old 18-stall roundhouse, and power into the roundhouse had to be broken up and swung on the table for work in the stalls. This was time-consuming and expensive, and Cuyler calculated the movement of this facility to Stockton would eliminate a 10-minute to 1½-hour delay on all or any trains.

Consolidation of diesel store stock then at Oroville and Sacramento would allow reduction in stock at Oroville and an avoidance of expansion in the Sacramento store facility. Finally, the roundhouse was not fireproof.

Whitman was, however, concerned about the costs to the WP should it become necessary to indemnify the employees who lived in Oroville and Sacramento. All employees at Sacramento and Oroville were interviewed, and those at Sacramento, in a proportion of four to one, stated they would be willing to move to Stockton; at Oroville, the proportion willing to move was approximately six to one.

In October 1964, the question arose again as to the correct location for the diesel facility. Cuyler had originally supported construction at Oroville, but by 1960 had come around to supporting a facility for Stockton. In 1964, he again viewed the statistics and found that many of the savings expected at Stock-

Covered wagons dominate as power without assignment idles away the foggy hours at Stockton roundhouse on the chilly morning of January 2, 1965.
Virgil Staff

ton had by tight practices now been accomplished at Oroville. The construction of facilities at Oroville would cost less than if built at Stockton. However, if the facility were to be built at Oroville, the layover of power would still have to be at Stockton. The cutting in and out of power at Oroville was considered undesirable especially on westbound trains on tight schedules. Most of the power was therefore cut in and out of eastbound trains which shortened the time for maintenance.

In Cuyler's view, the maintenance point should be where the power laid over. On the other hand, it was costly to run unneeded heavy power on westbound trains through to Stockton considering fuel, maintenance cost per mile and enginemen's wages, in spite of this practice saving from 20 to 30 minutes on the schedule. Maintenance costs in 1964 ran to 15.50¢ per mile and it was felt any changes in shop location should show marked improvement in this area.

In early 1967 the board of directors had the opportunity to review a study recommending the construction of a consolidated locomotive maintenance facility at Stockton. At least twice in May, Christy stated his opinion that the company could no longer defer this project since it would shortly become necessary to completely refurbish and upgrade the Oroville roundhouse at a cost of $600,000.

Not only would such expenditures fail to be in the interest of efficient operations but the railroad would lose significant savings through an inability to eliminate many positions in the mechanical, stores, and operating departments.

Onetime savings of $2,182,000 were expected to be realized chiefly due to a reduction in size of the diesel fleet and non-replacement of those units retired. These savings would be partially offset by a onetime additional cost including severance payments to displaced personnel, and sums necessary to acquire the equities in homes of those employees to be transferred to Stockton. But careful marketing of these homes over a period of time would reduce the write-off losses of these equity acquisitions, and on May 15, Christy requested prompt approval of the project.

Steel for the proposed facility had been stored in the Stockton roundhouse for a number of years, and throughout 1968 and early 1969 these materials were erected into the shell of a diesel facility at Stockton. A storage tank of 160,000 gallons, and pumping facilities for the new fueling station were connected to five miles of four-inch pipe reaching to the Southern Pacific pipeline, and placed in service about December 31, 1969.

The pipeline would allow the reduction of the tank car fleet and would eliminate freight charges from other railroads into the Oakland facility. Oakland would continue to be furnished by tank truck and trailer, and all other points on the railroad would require tank car delivery with Stockton Yard as the loading point. This system did not become fully operative until approximately March 1970, at which time all points receiving tank cars of fuel were to discontinue adding Nalco 303 additive, as it would automatically be mixed with the fuel at the Stockton storage tank.

The new facility, constructed to absolutely minimal size, was intended to handle approximately 45 units daily. Stockton was the originating terminal for most symbol trains, and this location eliminated the necessity of hauling units dead to Sacramento for heavy overhauls, and eliminated the delay of changing power on symbol freight trains at Oroville. The existing 10-stall roundhouse and 50′ x 200′ store building at Stockton, both of which were of concrete construction, plus the 120-foot turntable, were retained. The Stockton store was located between the roundhouse and the diesel shop, enabling the material department to adequately serve both areas.

Overhead rolling doors on all sides allowed easy forklift access from any direction. Emphasis at the new store was on palletized handling of bulk material. Pallet rack layout with complete forklift accessibility was a great improvement over the old store arrangement and saved considerable labor.

Consolidation of diesel material at Stockton resulted in the closing of the store at Oroville, and relieved storage space at the Sacramento general store. The Sacramento store was then rearranged for improved material handling, with emphasis on designated marshaling areas to accumulate material for shipment via rail or truck over the entire system. Concurrently, the mechanical department continued to improve its computerized purchasing and inventory control system.

The 121 road freight locomotives received running maintenance in a new 76′ x 300′ repair bay with three tracks, while switch engines and local units received running maintenance in the roundhouse. The three-track running repair bay handled all maintenance up through annual inspection including wheel and traction motor changeouts and truck repairs. Two of these tracks were equipped with Whiting four-screw, 100-ton drop tables with the release track located in the heavy repair bay.

An underhung five-ton crane ran the length of the bay, and each locomotive spot was equipped with air, treated water, lube oil, and electrical reels which were retractable into the floor when not in use, thus resulting in a clear floor area. Dirty lube oil hoses were provided which occupied a trench along the outside of the rail, and this trench also allowed changing of pedestal liners at any location within the shop. Lube oil was stored in a 20,000-gallon tank located on the same spur. Both tanks were heated for easy pumping in winter months.

A 60′ x 325′ heavy repair bay was erected adjacent to the running maintenance shop. This portion of the new facility had one track of three-unit capacity, and was geared to provide heavy repairs on all WP and subsidiary locomotives with the exception of 16 locomotives which remained assigned to the old Sacramento Shops, 11 or so of which were of Sacramento Northern ownership.

This bay was equipped with a 30-ton P&H overhead traveling crane with a 7½-ton auxiliary hook. Most large machinery in this bay had been relocated from other terminals, which included engine lathes, the Niles wheel lathe, various hydraulic presses ranging from 25 to 100-ton capacity, pedestal grinders, drill presses up to 42-inch capacity, power hacksaws, and various other power machinery.

The new shop building was of steel-frame construction with overhead gas infrared heaters and mercury vapor lighting. Power exhaust ventilators operated in banks depending upon the amount of engine exhaust fumes present. Full-length pits were provided on all running repair tracks. Outside service facilities were available at two locations, and a 250-foot concrete pad provided for fuel, water and lube of 10 units simultaneously, as well as truck lubes in the same location. An 80-foot pit was located south of this area for traction motor inspection and gear lubes.

The climate in Stockton allowed substantial maintenance to be performed outdoors without breaking up consists to send them indoors. The sand tower was relocated from Elko. Engine

Sacramento Shops—the center for most heavy locomotive repairs in the 1950s. This was the schedule of annual and semi-annual inspections. Switch engines frequently received their cylinder work at Oakland or Stockton.
H. A. O'Rullian

blocks and other large parts were cleaned outdoors with Delta HWB high-pressure, hot-water machines located on a 100-foot-square concrete pad, and the heavy repair track ran across the slab enabling washdown of units awaiting engine and generator changes.

Moving notices were posted April 23, May 2, and May 18, 1969. On May 2, bids were called for to be received in the office of R.E. Schriefer not later than May 8, 1969, for positions to be transferred to Stockton. Beginning July 1, 1969, employees began working into the Stockton Shop. This movement of employees from other points was staggered over a period of time so as not to hamper the maintenance of diesel power. In August and September, additional employees moved into the facility from Sacramento and Oroville so that by the close of September the vast majority of heavy locomotive work and repairs formerly handled at three terminals was then consolidated at Stockton.

One foreman and one machinist remained at Oroville to maintain switch engines and service and inspect power to be turned at that point. Tracks 13 and 31, being the leads between the turntable and the yard, were retained with their sand, water, and fueling facilities, as was stub track 33 for fuel and sand unloading. Two stalls, with their platforms and deep pits, were retained for occasional servicing of power, and for flexibility at Oroville should this be required.

The Solano Railcar Co. leased the remainder of the facility for freight car repairs, and the turntable was to be used jointly. Service at Oakland Roundhouse was terminated on July 20, 1970, and Sacramento Shops shortly became the chief freight car repair shops, thus allowing the reduction of car repair forces at other points on the system. Oroville remained the point at which Big Hook No. 37 would be spotted, and No. 37 was converted to diesel power as of September 1972.

As the decade turned, Christy and those working with him found themselves fighting for the very existence of the railroad. *California Zephyr* expenses were exorbitant, and out-of-pocket operating losses for this train during 1969 were approximately $2,500,000. Storm damage in 1969, and a series of serious derailments between 1968 and 1970 reduced company profits to the vanishing point. The derricks reopened the line with ominous urgency, but the men continued to speak of the misfortunes of Ola, Beowawe, Tobin, and Tobar—Shafter, Clifside, Hammer Lane, and Floka. Total revenues for 1969 were 0.3 percent lower than 1968 levels, and wage rates and material prices were up considerably over the previous year. Railway operating income loss was at least $1,177,000.

On July 3, 1969, Cuyler wrote to his subordinates: "You are all aware of the present financial condition of the railroad because of the numerous accidents, derailments and storm damages. Something drastic must be done to curb expenses wherever possible, and I believe overtime is one of those areas where this possibility exists. Please get into this personally and do something about it."

But things didn't get any better, and on December 10, 1969, Christy wired to his superintendents: "Am sure you recognize that power problems complicated past several days by derail-

Steam locomotive 485 receives its final classified repairs at Sacramento in late 1950. It ran its last in October 1951, after which it was retired and sold to the Southern Pacific on January 23, 1953. An F-7 unit shares the bay, its star on the ascendancy.
H. A. O'Rullian

ment dislocations as well as units out of service. I have definite understanding with Mr. Cuyler's group about vital need to get situation under control and they are in process of reorganization and setting up specific program of action to do so. Suggest we give them benefit reasonable time to show improvement in the meantime working with them in every possible way to help with implementation of their solutions."

In the meantime, the movement of the shops to Stockton had created unanticipated problems almost capable of bringing the railroad to its knees. Quite a number of employees at Oroville decided they would not transfer to Stockton, and the railroad advertised throughout the nation for men to fill these jobs. Other employees went on the sick list. Some would not commit themselves as to whether or not they would move to Stockton. Some on the sick list would not state when they expected to be released by their doctor. Numerous employees laid off work, and others refused overtime.

The locomotive department was reorganized on November 16, 1969, and the department office was transferred to Stockton in March 1970. Long lines of dead power awaited repairs, and every locomotive that was operable was pressed into extra service. *California Zephyr* power into Oakland on No. 17 was immediately serviced and turned for a freight run to Stockton, and other passenger units were returned during the night for the morning run on No. 18.

There had always been a considerable number of highly placed individuals on the WP who believed the move to Stockton would be a monumental error. Now, they took little pleasure in what was transpiring, but the move had been accomplished and the company now had to live with its decision.

Prior to the final run of the *California Zephyr* on March 22, 1970, Christy must have spent a major portion of his time attempting to rid the railroad of this passenger-carrying millstone. In the final months, the train usually ran with two units since the relatively low patronage did not normally require the three units employed in earlier years. Two-unit power consists allowed substantial savings on the train, and made possible the use of the third unit for use in freight service during the period when power was in such great demand. The *Zephyr* looked remarkably good up to the final run. The author walked the interior of the train on dozens of occasions before departure time out of Oakland, and while in a few areas the carpets were somewhat worn, the interior of the train had essentially the same class that it had always possessed.

Surely, the equipment was growing tired, but a mechanical department decision in the 1960s had concluded there would be no downgrading of mechanical work that would in any slight respect detract from the safety of the equipment. The power was old, but well maintained, and if the train was frequently late into Oakland, this could be explained by late delivery at Salt Lake, unnecessary delays due to hot box detector activations, servicing delays at three or more locations, or to occasional waits for freight trains.

The *California Zephyr* was killing the Western Pacific; freight trains were its life blood. When a 90-car freight train came up the canyon, it was the *California Zephyr* which took the 74-car siding. The schedules for symbol freight trains were exceedingly tight, and it did not seem to follow that a symbol train should miss its Salt Lake connection because the *California Zephyr* happened to be in the canyon at the same time. Nos. 17 and 18 often made up considerable time, but over the years there had always been a careful perusal of speed recorder tapes. The priority was always safety.

Christy retired from the presidency on November 30, 1970, after serving in that capacity since June 30, 1965. Christy's service date with the company was January 16, 1949, and during the intervening years he consistently indicated a subtle comprehension of WP finances and operation. Freight revenues during 1970 increased 3.2 percent over 1969, but revenue ton miles were down 1.6 percent, and government traffic declined sharply. Numerous operating and nonoperating improvements were realized during 1970, but the balance sheets indicated total railway operating expenses of $68,673,000 in 1970, compared to $65,315,000 in 1969. The times were out of joint for the Western Pacific, and while the service to shippers and customers was maintained at maximum levels, the continued problems of existence in a world made to order for the chief competition, always made significant profits difficult to build and maintain.

The Western Pacific had been constructed as a means of enabling the Gould Empire to reach the Pacific. Its line had been superbly engineered by Gould surveyors to take advantage of a relatively snow-free route through the Sierra Nevada, and to require a minimal number of helper districts. But the major problem was the presence of a chief competitor which had earlier been given the birthright. This competition was largely a gift in perpetuity from the American people. Real competition was almost a farce in extensive areas where the

The brooding night engulfs the *Silver Feather* and the *Zephyr*'s passenger consist as it waits on the Oakland balloon track for a switcher to take it through the washer. It is March 19, 1970, and railroad officials and fans alike have likewise been brooding on the fate of this train. **Virgil Staff**

competitor had been given extensive land holdings not amenable to encroachment by anyone. This monopolistic position early led to influence in state legislatures, and when legal means had been insufficient to stop the construction of the Western Pacific, there are said to have been guns.

Based on reciprocity, big roads tended to exchange tonnage with other big roads, so that again the WP found itself in a seemingly impossible position. The idea of free enterprise was often believed in by the small businessman but used by the big one. To say there was never any real need for a road like the WP would be tantamount to asserting there was no need for competition even when competition was a practical impossibility. Nor would the inability to function be merely a temporary situation since the birthright had been given to another railroad before the appearance of the WP.

In fact, during construction, the WP found itself dealing with its chief competition in order to get through the Feather River Canyon. For any ordinary group of men, the construction and operation of the Western Pacific would have been considered to be an impossibility. But nothing seemed to be impossible with the WP, and through the years the employees of the company had confidence that their railroad would succeed and grow.

Had management, in the early years, been of lesser quality, the road would undoubtedly have totally collapsed of its own weight. A continued relationship with the older Gould roads, in addition to WP abilities and outside capital, kept the tonnage moving, and over the years the railroad did, in its own way, become a viable competitor.

An additional blow to railroads generally throughout the United States was the loss of business to truckers. The Woodrow Wilson administration had initiated the movement towards a modern highway system, and it could be expected that without government interference, a series of vested interests would arise to employ these highways in competition with the railroads. Since the highway system was largely financed by the public, there is no difficulty in understanding why the overcontrolled and restricted railroads should have found themselves at a competitive disadvantage with the truck lines they subsidized.

Continual reductions in size and scope were forced upon the railroads if they were to remain solvent. This was anarchy, but it was an anarchy established by governmental fiat subsidizing what otherwise could have existed only in a small way. Truck lines were responsible for a monumental destruction of tax-paying resources that could never be replaced, but every generation takes care of its own interests without much care for the future, and the railroads found themselves as helpless bystanders in a game of survival.

Government heavily taxed the railroads and subsidized the truck lines, so that the American railroads found themselves in a position where it was almost impossible to win. Railroad managements have frequently been accused of incompetency, but perhaps such is the opposite of reality. Western Pacific passenger trains might have been greater financial successes had the government been willing to give the company a share of the mail contracts. But those with the most received the most, and Western Pacific was left to its own devices. Considering the forces opposed to the existence of all but the biggest roads, the WP did magnificently.

Christy was caught in the traps already alluded to, and while the last years of the 1960s were increasingly bad ones for the WP, it can be seen that the intent was to create a situation capable of increasing the viability of the railroad. Termination of the *California Zephyr* and eventual consolidation of all repair facilities at Stockton and Sacramento were significant steps in that direction. Cuyler looked forward to the completion of these tasks, and for many years had spent considerable time in thinking through the angles to expedite the future consolidation of forces and maintenance work necessary to significant savings.

Unfortunately, these savings were not immediate from discontinuance of the passenger train, nor would they be immediately obvious, as has been noted, when repair facilities were moved to Stockton. It would be left to time and Alfred Perlman to again make the Western Pacific an assured and continuing member of the family of railroads.

24

Higher and Higher Horsepower

E.T. CUYLER retired as chief mechanical officer in April 1970, but continued as a consultant to the railroad until January 1, 1973. Over the years he had become increasingly impatient with locomotive builders who made big claims, but whose products failed to operate as advertised. Serious and expensive delays of symbol trains resulted when the "bugs" had not been worked out, and months of electrical modifications were often required.

Railroad managements desired increased horsepower, and the builders sought to provide such power to the best of their expertise at a given moment. The diesel-electric locomotive increasingly became a piece of sophisticated electrical and mechanical equipment, and the systems and components on one model became inadequate on those of a later vintage. Time and experience determined the extent to which a given component was adequate in a locomotive system, and each new model seemed to contain numerous problems seldom initially understood.

Excessive oil leakage, on the earlier power, always contributed to complaints of accumulation of oil on engine room floors. In general, reports over a period of 20 years indicate the floors and decks were regularly cleaned at the terminals, and that locomotives departed these terminals with floors clean and dry. But such conditions were not easy to control, and aging seals and gaskets materially contributed to the complaints of CMOs on numerous railroads.

A Keddie–Portola connection with GP-7 706 on the point climbs the .90 percent grade at MP 294 just west of Spring Garden loop, an instant before plunging into the tunnel. The main line follows a complete loop thus crossing above this point in its stretch toward Portola. **Joseph Ward**

A westbound drag with the 802-A and the 801-D, onetime *Zephyr* power, at about MP 210 on June 4, 1966. The track structure to the left is that of the Oroville Dam Railroad.
Virgil Staff

On the Western Pacific, the air compressor could be expected to leak oil from the back shaft seal housing, and the generator end speed increaser tended to leak oil from the top shaft seal—the oil running out over the floor. According to R.T. Ronan, diesel foreman at Oroville, the engine frame worked on the oil pan gasket under the cylinders, and leaked oil at all four corners of the FT engine. This working action was responsible for much of the back and front gear housing leaking oil. Where the bottom horizontal joint in the back gear housing worked on the gasket, oil was leaked where the generator fan draft blew the oil all over a wide area. Drains in the flywheel sumps sometimes became clogged, and it was a never-ending task to control oil leaks since even new engines leaked some oil when they became hot in service.

Some of the covers on the engines fitted more loose than they should, and at regular intervals the forces continued their program of tightening cap screws and bolts that secured the gasket seals. When tightening did not stop this leakage, the entire engine was changed out and replaced by an engine with a complete new set of gaskets. In 1962 there were numerous complaints of oil leakage on the floors, and the mechanical department stepped up its program of engine replacement to eliminate these problems. Traction motor gear cases on 1,350, 1,500, and 1,750-hp units also created significant problems of leakage and it became necessary to add grease to the cases at the end of each 10-day trip because most of the grease had leaked away.

The GP-7s were of considerable satisfaction to the railroad. These provided the company with impressive service, their chief problem in the early years being the upper and lower liner seals which more recently have been improved to put an end to most of the leakage earlier experienced. When the GP-9s were placed in fast east-west service with the GP-20s in early 1960, the D47B traction motors began flashing over causing severe damage to the motors and, in many cases, failed on the road. To overcome this problem, the GP-9s were taken out of service, commutators on the motors were stoned, and the string bands painted with epoxy coating to protect against flashovers. Some flashovers continued to occur but were fewer and of less severity than previously. Furthermore, an expensive change in the wheel slip arrangement, which would have ended the failures, was avoided. Ultimately, as with all modern power when traction motor changeouts were required, the GP-20s received D-77 motors.

The GP-20s, of which Western Pacific's were among the first, were a new milestone in Electro–Motive history in that they were the first 567 series engines to be equipped with a turbocharger. These turbochargers were installed to provide the additional air required to achieve 2,000 horsepower. Each time the locomotive's horsepower is increased, and the number of axles remains the same, the sophistication of the various control circuits must be increased to control that power.

One of the initial shortcomings of the GP-20 was the turbocharger. This turbo was a gear-driven and exhaust-driven compressor having a planetary gear train with a clutch mechanism allowing the diesel engine through the rear gear train to drive the compressor wheel at low throttle positions. In the range above throttle 6 or 7, the energy contained in the exhaust gases was sufficient to drive the compressor wheel off of the exhaust turbine wheel, so that in this mode of operation the clutch mechanism disengaged and the turbocharger was free-running. Early operations produced failures caused by faulty thrust bearings or foreign material damage to turbocharger blades, whereas later failures in 1962 involved slipping clutches.

An early gear ratio of the turbocharger was 20 to 1, meaning that the compressor speed was 20 times that of the crankshaft speed. Due to the relatively low horsepower of the engine compared to the air requirements of the engine, the exhaust energy was found to not always be sufficient to drive the turbocharger off the gear train and hence put it into a free-running mode. Prolonged operation of the turbocharger being driven through the gear train at high throttle position created excessive gear wear and chatter due to the carryover of the engine vibrations through the gear train into the turbocharger. Moreover, it was theorized at that time that one likely partial cause of such failures related to operating conditions which did not require that the engines be in full power position in order to meet the needs of the service. This would further aggravate the floating in-and-out movement of the clutch.

This problem was recognized by Electro–Motive, and the solution was largely accomplished by significant modifications including the change to a 18 to 1 gear ratio. Governors were modified, and as with the turbochargers, most of the work was performed without cost. But the company suffered delays from these and other sources, thus causing concern about making existing schedules.

In the months following delivery of the GP-20s, letters began to arrive from other railroads concerning ring breakage on this model. This was new to Cuyler since up to this time the only major problems with this power had concerned turbochargers, grounds in the wiring, and inadequacies in some of the newly designed relays. Cuyler answered these queries in the negative, and with affirmative statements on the excellent showing in the fast east-west runs.

Then, in early 1961, the mechanical forces at Oroville began to discover that the two top rings were showing signs of rapid wear. Cuyler believed this problem could be overcome with a slightly wider ring, although there were those outside the railroad who asserted the wear must be caused by an inadequate lubrication oil. Cuyler was reluctant to agree that the original quality of the oil was a significant factor since the company had been using Standard Oil RPM Delo 40 with complete satisfaction over the past 15 years.

Cuyler wrote: "It does seem to me that the fact that we were able to run one year where other railroads were only able to run three or four months before this trouble developed, would indicate the difficulty was on something other than oil." In the meantime, the forces replaced all the worn rings, modified injectors, governors, and timing degree, but did not change the brand of oil. Electro–Motive desired engine compression ring wear tests, and these were established under Project 870-96602-C, and Project 870-96602-D. Units 2007 and 2010 participated in this test, with the 2007 receiving the usual Standard Oil Delo RR-40, and engine 2010 receiving a high-quality competitive oil for the duration of the test.

Test rings and standard production rings differed chiefly in the depth of the groove in the chrome face, with the groove depth in the test rings being from .003 to .007 deep compared to the standard rings in which the groove depth extended to the depth of the chrome face. After one year, or 175,000 miles of service, test rings showed less gap increase and less radial wear than the standards, and the railroad concluded it could achieve satisfactory results with its stock oil following the other modifications.

In 1964 and early 1965, motor support bearings sometimes ran hot on the GP-20s and the mechanical department was initially puzzled by this situation since the bearings apparently had sufficient oil and the lubricating wicks were in good condition. Certain other railroads were experiencing similar difficulty, and it was Cuyler's impression that with the increased horsepower, the loading on the motor support bearings became more critical. This was considered to be a design problem since in the past the railroad had experienced very little trouble with these bearings. By March 1965, these problems had been largely erased by setting a limit of six micro inch finish on the axles and changing to a heavier type oil for lubrication.

The GP-20s were delivered with D47B traction motors. These were a great improvement over previous production models in that they possessed 33 square inches more bearing surface on each individual bearing, and in that oil consumption was greatly reduced by the motor support bearings returning oil to the oil reservoir instead of to the roadbed.

Western Pacific normally upgraded its traction motors when changed out, and most or all of the 2001 Class locomotives shortly received D57 motors. In early 1966, D57 motors shipped to Emeryville for rewinding were converted to D67s, but beginning about April 1966 all motors were rewound to D77 specifications for complete compatibility. Minimum continuous speed on the F-7s with their D27 motors was approximately 11.1 mph. The minimum continuous rating on the GP-20s was about 14 mph so that the difference in the continuous rating caused difficulty when these were involved with slow speed and drag tonnage.

With installation of D77 motors, the 2001 Class could operate in the 8th throttle notch at a minimum speed of 11.1 mph continuously without damage to the traction motors from overloading. Traction motors were ultimately replaced by D77s since the D57s were inadequate for the speeds at which the lower horsepower units were capable of operating. By 1968, the GP-20s, with D77 motors, were handling their assignments on train NCE very well in consists of four GP-20s and one GP-7 or GP-9 on the head and rear end.

Another shortcoming in the GP-20 lay in the wheel slip detection and correction system. This system was functionally similar to the through-cable wheel slip relay used in the GP-7 and GP-9 but it used the through-cable transductor system in which the traction motor current was passed through a transductor, and from two motors in opposite directions so that the magnetic flux produced by each cable canceled each other out thus enabling the transductor to possess no output.

When one axle would slip with relationship to the other, the traction motor currents would change and there would be a difference in magnetic flux. The AC transductor would produce a signal which was rectified through an AC to DC rectifying bridge and would activate a wheel slip or wheel creep relay or a combination of both. For high-speed wheel slip detection, the GP-20 was also equipped with a tube-type device known as a wheel slip sensitometer. This was actually the tube equivalent of a Zener diode in that at a certain voltage across the tube elements, which were two in series, the sensitometer would pass current and would recalibrate the wheel slip system to cause the circuit to become more sensitive. This device was never completely successful, and according to Superintendent of Locomotives Norman Anderson, it led to considerable high-speed unloading on the unit where the wheel slip circuit would pick up and drop out, and cause the units to load and unload and thus malfunction.

Over the years, the on-site problems, in their practical aspect, had been faced by General Diesel Supervisor John Francis Flynn, who retired on December 31, 1965, and by William F. Stevens who followed him as the second and final general diesel supervisor of the company. Stevens had been with the WP most of the time since May 24, 1944, and had been in charge of the diesel shop at Oakland when passenger power was maintained at that terminal. To Stevens, as to Anderson, each locomotive had its own personality, and if anyone on the WP knew each locomotive in the fleet, it was Bill Stevens.

The position of general diesel supervisor assumed a series of monumental tasks, and in April 1968, Norman Anderson joined the mechanical department at Sacramento to increase the depth of expertise, and together with Stevens, to improve performance on the diesel fleet. One of the first problems delegated to Anderson by Cuyler was the GP-20 and its multiple-unit performance in consists with units of various horsepower.

On the Western Pacific, the GP-20 had something of a bad name, although there was a general feeling that it was not a bad locomotive by itself, or in consist with other GP-20s. The experimental quality of the GP-20 undoubtedly had much to do with this attitude, and some of the problems have been noted. It is said that in one year, on 10 locomotives, the WP changed out 60 turbochargers. Couple a high-speed wheel slip problem, where the unit was loading and unloading, with a turbocharger blowing up, and one can understand why the GP-20 developed a bad reputation with the operating people.

Two other conditions on the GP-20 that were not faulty design but in later years reflected back on this locomotive, were the field loop dynamic braking circuit, and the pneumatic trainline sanding system. The field loop brake concept had been used by Electro–Motive from the early days of dynamic braking in 1,350-hp units. In this system, each unit was equipped with a separate three-pronged field loop recepta-

Eastbound train 62 steps along just west of MP 41 near Pleasanton, California, on the glorious morning of November 9, 1969. The 765 is clothed in its original livery, and its four-stroke cycle is a welcome addition to Western Pacific's more conventional turbocharged units.
Virgil Staff

A westbound visitor to Reno Junction on May 11, 1974, is a consist featuring the 2254, 3002 and 3010 on the curve east of Chilcoot Tunnel. Upon exiting the West Portal, there will be a fleeting presence in Sierra Valley followed by a crew change in Portola. **Virgil Staff**

cle connected by a jumper cable between each unit to hook the main generator battery fields in series. In dynamic braking, current from the batteries of the lead unit passed through the battery fields of each trailing unit, and then back through the other wire in the cable to the batteries of the lead unit.

Control of excitation was done by manipulating the amount of current through the field circuit, and this in turn controlled the dynamic braking effort. The design was a proven one, and the only major difference on GP-20s from that on older power was the presence of a load regulator commutator rheostat to control the amount of battery field current rather than a huge separate dynamic brake control rheostat in the control stand such as on the F-7s, GP-7s, and GP-9s. This was an improvement over previous models since the builder eliminated the cost of a duplicate commutator rheostat and used a micro-positioner relay to control the position of the load regulator, and therefore the amount of dynamic braking current.

A second condition of the GP-20 was the presence of a pneumatic sanding system in which the sanding function was trainlined from one unit to another in a consist. When the engineer in the lead unit turned on the sanding valve, air flowed into the sanding trainline pipe on each unit through a flexible hose coupling between each unit. The air pressure that existed in the trainline pipe then actuated a pneumatic control valve on each unit which in turn operated a sand control valve which applied sand to the rail through sand traps. All WP power up to and including the GP-20s possessed a pneumatic sand system. Sometime in the late 1950s or early 1960s, the builder had developed an electric trainline sanding system in which the trainlining of the actuating signal could be done electrically. Instead of using a pneumatic control valve in each locomotive, there was an electric control valve. A similar action was accomplished with electric trainlining available in the 27-pin MU receptacle.

The field loop dynamic braking circuit, and the pneumatic sanding system functioned properly on the GP-20s, but when the first GP-35s arrived, problems began to arise in these two systems. At the time of purchase, the GP-35s were to be compatible with WP locomotives of older vintage. This was the option taken rather than that of providing the GP-35s with the latest circuit innovations and retrofitting these systems on the GP-20s and on older power.

The dynamic braking system by 1963 had developed to the extent that the GP-35s possessed a potential trainline dynamic brake control. In contrast to the field loop braking in which each locomotive had a separate field loop receptacle which had to carry a maximum of 15 amperes, the potential wire system operated on the principle that the only trainline signal that was carried between units was a variable 0 to 74 volts to be carried between units on one of the spare 27 trainline circuits.

The voltage signal was carried to each unit on trainline 24 and each unit was equipped with the necessary control system to operate its dynamic brakes proportional to the voltage on this trainline. This system was very reliable and practical in that if the dynamic braking circuit failed on any of the trailing units, the unit could be cut out and would not affect the dynamic brakes on the remainder of the consist. To make the GP-35s compatible with older power, Electro–Motive included a field loop circuit which necessitated a motor-driven rheostat, and some extra transductors, capacitors, and rectifiers to produce a second dynamic braking system.

A typical situation arose with the placement of four GP-35s in a consist. There was a selector switch in the electrical cabinet that was set for potential wire. If a GP-20 was cut into the consist, the selector lever in each GP-35 had to be changed to field loop position, thus activating this additional equipment, and all of the units would operate in field loop braking. According to Anderson, when the GP-35s came to the prop-

HIGHER AND HIGHER HORSEPOWER   173

erty, the field loop system with which they were equipped was far from reliable, and there were problems with the motor-driven servomotor positioning this big faceplace commutator. So with the dual system, whenever a GP-20 found itself in the consist with GP-35s, a dynamic braking problem developed for which the GP-20 tended to receive the blame, but for which the GP-35 was the culprit since it was forced to use its own inadequate field loop braking system instead of the potential line brake control circuit.

A similar series of problems developed in the sanding system when the GP-35s were operated with the GP-20s or with older power. Electro-Motive had gone to electric sanding as basic with the GP-30s introduced in 1962. Western Pacific had none of these, but when the GP-35s were purchased in 1963, the company took the option of purchasing two sanding systems on the GP-35s to make them compatible with the GP-20s, GP-9s, GP-7s, and F-7s, rather than considering the option of upgrading older locomotives with pneumatic sanding to the newer, more reliable electric trainline system which had become basic on Electro-Motive power.

The electric system possessed an electric switch on the control stand which actuated the No. 23 wire trainlined to each unit. As a point of interest, Western Pacific was originally using trainline 11 as were a number of other railroads. This was changed over to No. 23 at the time of reworking the sand circuits to comply with the AAR standard and to permit universal pooling of power. When the No. 23 wire was actuated, this energized the electric control valve which applied the sand to the rail through the sand traps. On the pneumatic system there were pneumatic relay valves, control valves, trainline hoses and a multiplicity of other pneumatic equipment, in addition to the usual air leaks.

In order to make the GP-35s compatible with older power, Electro-Motive included both systems, in addition to two pressure switches to trainline or sense whenever the GP-35 was in a consist with pneumatic sanding arrangement. These pressure switches would, in trailing position, pick up the signal from the trainline hoses and would in turn actuate the electric sanding system. In leading position, the GP-35s needed two magnet valves to operate off the electric signal and apply air to the pneumatic trainline which would in turn actuate the sanding equipment on the trailing pneumatic sanding units. The chief problem here was that the two systems sometimes interacted with each other and caused problems in operation.

Anderson has explained that "the state of the art of rectifier designs had not come along with the rest of the locomotive and there were a number of rectifiers in the GP-35 sanding circuits that would have what is called 'leakage current.' A lot of times when the sanders would be turned on, the electric system would actuate the pneumatic system and the pneumatic system in turn would pick up the pressure switches and they would in turn duplicate what was being called for by the engineer. With certain diodes having leakage current through them, the whole system would keep itself turned on and when you tried to turn the sand off, it would just override your request and keep the sanders on and you would go down the railroad sanding continuously until you ran out of sand."

Another characteristic of the GP-20s related to the fact that they were Electro-Motive's first turbocharged engines. Matching the power applied to the engine and the turbocharger was an uncertain science, and the loading characteristics and other anomalies of the time were a new challenge. The result was an original design in a locomotive that was very slow loading. The load control pilot valve bushing in the governor which controlled the rate at which the load regulator moved from minimum field to maximum field position—which is the excitation in the power output—was exceedingly slow, and one could take a GP-20 and open the throttle from idle to run 1 and sit there for 20 to 25 seconds or more while nothing happened. Finally, the amperage would build up and the locomotive would begin to move.

This was not a characteristic of the GP-7 or GP-9 which possessed a gear-driven Roots blower providing sufficient air for the locomotive at any speed. Anderson assumed that with the GP-20 turbocharger design the builder had in mind that "when you opened the throttle—say you were starting a train out of the yard and they decided to wipe the throttle out to run 8 to get with it and get out of town, the engine and turbo would come up in speed together for awhile but once the turbo let go from the gear train, then it would be free-wheeling and would not necessarily produce air at sufficient rate to support the combustion of the amount of fuel that the governor was calling for. So to control this application of power, they built in this long time delay in the rate with which the load regulator could move from minimum field to maximum field, and tried to slow down the rate at which the power was increased."

This system worked well in road service, but in 1968 the number of road switcher and yard assignments with GP-7s and GP-9s had increased to the point that the railroad was running out of road switcher types of locomotives for locals and trains of this nature. The railroad had attempted to use GP-20s in this service but found them very unsuccessful because of the slow loading characteristics. When this power would arrive at an industry to spot cars, it just wouldn't load up fast enough for the men who were accustomed to GP-7s or GP-9s.

When Anderson came to the railroad in April 1968, the very first project he was asked to consider was the modification of loading characteristics on the GP-20s in order that they might be used in local service. The method developed was to install a road and switching selector switch on the control stand. In switching or local service, the circuit to the overriding solenoid was deenergized so that the load regulator remained in maximum field even with the throttle placed in idle.

So as not to produce too much excitation, a throttle response circuit was applied. This consisted of a group of resistors in the circuit between the battery fuse and the load regulator. This resistor assembly consisted of five resistors mounted in one bracket, and involved four contactors hooked up to the governor solenoid circuits. As the throttle was moved to each throttle position, a certain portion of these resistors were placed in the circuit to change the amount of maximum amperage available to the battery field.

When the load regulator was in maximum field with no battery field resistors in the circuit, there were 60 amps of battery field. But with the battery field resistor in the circuit, amperage was limited to approximately 10 times the throttle position. So that in throttle 1, the maximum amperage would only be 10 amps, whereas in throttle 6 the maximum of 60 amps would be reached. This would reflect itself on the load meter by giving about 300 amps in run 1, 600 amps in run 2, etc. This was when the locomotive was standing still. Combination of the throttle response circuit and the start selector switch gave the choice of the locomotive operating with faster or slower loading characteristics. This modification did not represent any correction of a problem but did allow the Western Pacific to use the GP-20s in local or switching service.

Incompatibility of earlier power with GP-35s, GP-40s, and U30Bs was a dual problem due to the field loop braking and pneumatic sanding systems in the GP-20s and prior power. All GP-35s possessed the dual system, as did the first 16 GP-40s and the first 19 U30Bs. Correcting the problem of incompatibility between the GP-20s and locomotives of newer design was a matter of removing the redundant systems on the newer designs after upgrading the GP-20s to the newest design circuits.

The GP-20s were first upgraded to potential line brake control for dynamic braking in what Anderson has called a "very cheap and dirty way" of trainlining the signal into the units, placing a few jumper wires on the right contactors, and hooking them up so they operated in potential. The pneumatic sanding system was converted to an electric system in a similarly "fast manner."

"It wasn't the correct total package of getting rid of all these pneumatic relay valves and control valves and going straight to electric magnet valves," said Anderson. "The reason these two 'improvements' were made to the GP-20s was so that they could be switched over to these systems in a hurry, and then when we started taking the field loop braking and the pneumatic sanding off the GP-35s, GP-40s, and U30Bs, there wouldn't be the problem of being unable to MU the units together. So that when the GP-20s were very quickly changed over to potential braking and electric sanding, we just stopped using the dual systems on the other units, and then as the GP-35s and GP-40s came through the shops for various work, the unnecessary systems were taken off and thrown away."

The reason for spending so little time in initially converting the GP-20s to the more modern system was the plan for a general upgrading program which had been considered for a number of years. Prior to 1969 the railroad had experienced failures with the GP-20s due to insulation failures of the neoprene-insulated wiring used in the high-voltage cabinet. After years of exposure to the heat of the cabinet and engine room, the insulation had become hard and brittle, and when the insulation finally cracked and broke off, sections of exposed wire created grounds and shorts and numerous problems and failures, including electrical fires.

This problem had come about because of the higher horsepower engine, and the naturally greater heat dissipated against the electrical cabinet located very close to the engine. The rail-

Singing downgrade in dynamic through Blairsden, California, on May 11, 1974, are 2254, 3002 and 3010. The grade is −0.85. By now the vibrations of the heavy train have surely engulfed the lonely section house.
Virgil Staff

road had gone in and spliced sections and thereby replaced considerable portions. Electro–Motive had recognized this problem shortly before the middle 1960s, and had developed cable form kits to rewire just the portion of the wiring in the cabinet. The area of greatest problem was in the upper area of the electrical cabinet which for some reason had been subjected to the most heat. Furthermore, the AC cooling fan contactors were located in an area directly above the main electrical cabinet and all the AC wiring to the contactors ran through the cabinet.

Over the years these three-phase fans had been a source of problems because if a cooling fan developed a frozen armature bearing, or if the fan single-phased because one of the wires burned off, the fan then drew excessive current, overheated the wires and often set the cabinet on fire. When Anderson first came to the WP it had been his intention to shop these GP-20s on a regular program basis and completely rebuild the electrical cabinets, replacing all the original rubber neoprene wire with the newer wire which possessed a silicon glass insulation and was heat resistant. At the same time he would re-analyze the entire wiring system, and bring it to the latest standards including the introduction of the latest wheel slip system (IDAC) as employed on the GP-40s from 3517 onward, and as retrofitted on all GP-35s and the first two orders of GP-40s.

One big benefit of the IDAC system was the absence of adjustments to be made, whereas the previous wheel slip device systems had all required considerable adjusting and calibration to make the systems operable within design specifications. Originally, when the mechanical department justified to management the application of IDAC to GP-35s and GP-40s, test runs had demonstrated that IDAC-equipped locomotives pulled trains better on heavy grades, and that the power had better control over wheel slippage so that the incidence of traction motor failures due to flashovers was reduced.

Anderson stated: "When this system for the GP-20s was approved in the latter part of 1969, we were originally going to change these and put in the IDAC, but after reviewing the deteriorated condition of the electrical cabinet, it would have been foolish to have gone in and made one small improvement and put in a lot of wiring associated with the IDAC system and

Running late, the eastbound CIX with the 3055 on the point, circumnavigates Williams Loop east of MP 294. This is one train, even though it may look like three railroads running on three different levels. The date is August 27, 1977. **Virgil Staff**

turn around later and strip it all out and rebuild the electrical cabinet."

Additionally there was the problem of AC contactors and cooling fan wiring starting electrical fires. To eliminate the source of this problem, the contactors for the No. 2 and No. 3 cooling fans were placed in a new cabinet to be mounted back on the equipment rack. The AC cabling for these fans and contactors was strung from the D14 alternator to this cabinet in a separate conduit entirely removed from the other locomotive wiring. The fan contactor for the No. 1 cooling fan could not conveniently be relocated, but to eliminate the chance of fire, a cabinet enclosure was built within the original contactor mounting area and the contactor inserted so that if the cable for the No. 1 cooling fan overheated, it would not burn out the electrical cabinet.

Concurrent with this work, the electric sanding magnet valves were installed and the entire sanding system rewired and converted to a straight electric system. The transition circuit was upgraded, and the GP-20s were converted from a three-relay transition to a two-relay transition which included the relay logic and circuit components very similar to a GP-38 using GP-40 components, and which brought considerable improvement in the reliability of the transition circuit.

Another improvement made on the GP-20s concerned the motor field shunting resistors involved in the transition circuit. When in use, they bypassed some of the current going to the traction motor fields causing the generator voltage to drop from what it had been, thus allowing an increase in the locomotive speed. These resistors were located outside the electrical cabinet under the walkway on the fireman's side of the unit just behind the cab. Since that portion of the locomotive is part of the underframe, and the hood in that area is removable, there was a gap between the hood and the steps or platform area.

In the winter, quite often water would run down between the hood and the platform portion of the underframe and leave moisture or water on the motor field shunting resistors. These would then ground out and cause a high-voltage ground when they were in the circuit causing the ground relay to trip. If the ground relay kept tripping, the unit was unloaded and could not be utilized until it was taken into the shop and the resistors removed, dried, and reinstalled.

During the course of the upgrading program, the metal brackets that held the motor field shunting resistors in place were cut out and so-called "standoff insulators" were installed to insulate the steel of the resistors from the steel of the carbody frame. Thus, any moisture reaching the resistors did not create an electrical path to the frame ground, and there was then no loss of units in wet weather to ground relay action caused by the motor field shunting resistors becoming wet.

Actually, these still became wet but the heat from the resistors evaporated the water, whereas previously when the resistors were cold and the moisture accumulated, the dust particles from the air and the oil or grease that might have accumulated around these would provide a path to allow current to the underframe of the locomotive and therefore cause ground relay action.

Finally, Western Pacific participated with Electro–Motive in testing a static dynamic brake regulator. Previous dynamic brake regulators were mechanical types. These regulators had an operating coil which sensed through resistor networks the amount of current through the grids of the dynamic brake circuit. Theoretically this operated through a system of mechanically operated fingers which would cause the regulator to control the excitation to prevent the grid current from exceeding 700 amps, and prevent the burning out of the dynamic brake grids. This was the theoretical function of the regulator although numerous times the finger interlocks would burn and quite often there would be a loss of regulator function so that the engineer would not know to turn down the dynamic brakes and the grids would burn out.

Furthermore, the mechanical operators were becoming prohibitively expensive, so that when in 1971 Electro–Motive came out with what Anderson called a "breadboard model" of the new design, the Western Pacific participated in a test by applying the new static dynamic brake regulators on locomotives 2007 and 2010. These static devices had no moving parts, and after the system had been proven, this improvement was incorporated into the GP-20 modernization program.

The Western Pacific received 22 GP-35s between 1963 and

1965. The GP-35 used a Model 567D3A turbocharged engine with 8½"-diameter pistons. It had a DC main generator with power coming off the armature through a commutator system, and distributed to the traction motors in two major connections. As all Electro–Motive locomotives had done since the beginning of time, it started off in series parallel. Two motors were in series, paralleled with two motors in series. The locomotives went through nine stages of motor field shunting and then transferred into parallel where all four traction motors were hooked in parallel with the main generator. Finally, it had five stages of shunting in parallel. The excitation system took AC power from the D14 alternator which controlled and converted to DC power for the main generator battery field through the magnetic amplifier and rectifier system.

The 2,500-hp GP-35, though a different model designation, was basically similar to the 2,250-hp GP-30 which was intended to be a revolutionary new direction in locomotive design. The GP-20 had effectively reached its full development since the DC excitation system had reached its capability and there were 74 volts on the battery and 1.2 ohms resistance in the battery field. Since it was impossible to shove any additional amps through this system, it was clear that additional horsepower would require additional excitation which the GP-20 system did not possess.

Electro–Motive then devised a system involving the D14 alternator as the power supply for the main generator excitation. In order to obtain this excitation, EMD had employed a magnetic amplifier system which was actually a system of controlling and converting the three-phase D14 AC power into DC power. Power was rectified and controlled at the same time.

The magnetic amplifier system brought with it numerous control problems that took many years to resolve. When the system failed, no one in the railroad industry apparently understood the basis of the problem; consequently no one knew how to make the repairs.

The GP-35 is also said to have been a difficult locomotive to keep going in that, in spite of its general sophistication, the design continued to include a DC generator. Horsepower range was so high that the differential between maximum voltage and maximum current narrowed to requiring 16 steps of traction motor field shunting or transition, and there was not sufficient space in the cabinet to include all the relay logic to function with straight relays. Consequently, Electro–Motive provided a motor-driven program switch which operated switches that in turn selected the shunting contactors to be picked up to provide the different percentages of traction motor field shunting. This system took considerable time to perfect, and in 1969 the WP continued to search out the transition circuit modifications necessary to make these locomotives reliable.

Transition conditions on the GP-35 often caused the wheel slip system to continue unloading because of an imbalance in the motor field shunting and traction motor currents. If the program switch failed to locate in the correct position at the right time, an out-of-phase situation would develop in which the transition circuit was "locked up." Commonly the program switch would become "hung-up" between positions so that it would not move either way, and the unit would remain unloaded.

Originally there were three transition relays on the GP-35, and one of these was eliminated and the system simplified. The power limit relay was eventually replaced by a static power limit switch which eliminated many problems said to have been experienced with the old relay. GP-35s early developed a wheel slip problem since they had a relay type wheel slip system similar to the GP-20s and the first 16 GP-40s. Unlike the GP-20s, they did not possess a wheel slip sensitometer, but were equipped with a high-speed recalibration of the wheel slip system.

Over the years the wheel slip system had apparently been one of Electro–Motive's biggest problems. The 1,350-hp FT locomotive had lurched badly during wheel slip correction, and later power sometimes possessed too much sensitivity in the system, often failed to correct when needed, and sometimes made corrections unnecessarily. This was somewhat dependent upon the reliability of shop personnel in setting the pickup and dropout valves of the wheel slip relays. Most of these problems were ended by installation of the IDAC system which produced a big difference in what the locomotive would pull.

The evolution of power contactor design was one familiar to the Western Pacific since from the beginning there had been many power contactor problems. Each time the locomotive went through the speed range of about 30 to 32 mph, with increase in locomotive speed, the unit would drop out its two series contactors, shift into parallel, and pick up the four parallel contactors. As the speed decreased to around 30-31 mph, the four parallel contactors would drop out and the two series contactors would pick up. In this manner the power contactors were operating all of the time in making and breaking the power circuit for transition. Since power contactors had a finite life, no matter how good the design, the point would ultimately be reached when the contactor would no longer open the circuit. Electro–Motive continued to improve its contactor design, and Western Pacific made the latest changes any time EMD developed an improved modification kit.

As with the GP-20s, the GP-35s had early trouble with their motor-support bearings running hot. In late 1964 and early 1965 the GP-35s were giving very unsatisfactory service because of the failure of relays to control excitation and loading of the engine, as well as the loading of grids in dynamic braking. Difficulty was experienced with governor settings and voltage regulators, but Electro–Motive was already aware of these problems and furnished the railroad with six modifications applicable to the wiring. Governors were changed out, and to save equipment such as turbochargers and braking grids, the mechanical forces temporarily reduced the horsepower output on all GP-35s to 2,000 hp until these changes could be instituted.

Flashovers were frequent, and the D67 traction motors are said to have been delivered with "uncured" green copper which necessitated the shop forces pulling the motors and stoning the commutators which were out of round. These problems had adverse effects on schedule performance and seriously affected the reliability of other units in the fleet because the shop forces were not always able to give them the proper attention due to power shortages caused by malfunction of the GP-35s. One knowledgeable individual stated: ". . . our difficulty with the GP-20 and GP-35 was the fact that they were not right when they left the factory and much of our time has been spent making modifications to correct the defects that were originally in them."

The year 1966 brought delivery of Western Pacific's first order of GP-40s. Demands for increased horsepower per unit now placed the GP-35 in a losing position because it appeared no longer possible to increase capabilities while using the same building blocks of earlier years. The GP-35 had a maximum voltage capability of approximately 1,000 volts. Its D32 main generator would not put out more than 2,400 amps continuously without burning up the copper inside. According to Anderson, "The GP-35 was a last go-around for the DC equipment. They just couldn't go any further with it, and that was the end of the state of the art on machinery of that physical size."

The new GP-40 came out with a 645E3 turbocharged engine which had an increased piston diameter of $9\frac{1}{16}$". Instead of possessing a DC main generator, the GP-40 used an AR-10 alternator with four banks of rectifying diodes, internal to the alternator, which produced DC power to the traction motors. The U30Bs also possessed an AC alternator, but conversion of AC power to DC was accomplished through rectifier panels mounted externally from the alternator. The DC power from the AR-10 alternator was connected to the traction motors in one mode, so that the motors remained in full parallel at all times.

Unlike the GP-35s which started out in series-parallel and transferred to parallel, the GP-40s operated in parallel at all times. The early GP-40s had either three or two stages of motor field shunting, but as rectifier development progressed, Electro–Motive was eventually able to eliminate the shunting altogether, and to develop a straight parallel full-field operation at all times. The numerous problems with transition circuitry in the GP-20s and GP-35s were not present on the GP-40s because they contained no transition functions.

The GP-40s, like most models that had come out on the market, initially brought with them numerous problems. The state of the art of heavy power diodes was not well developed, and there were perplexing problems in the beginning. The traction motor, which had been an area that needed constant upgrading as the horsepower of the locomotive was increased, suffered some manufacturing problems. In varnishing the armature to seal the coils, it is reported that an excess amount of varnish was reaching the commutator surface beyond the coils, and this led to flashover damage and commutator problems.

Western Pacific's first 16 GP-40s also had three stages of motor field shunting. Eventually the third stage of shunting was removed and this considerably improved traction motor commutation. When the 3517 Class was delivered in August and September of 1970, the AR-10 diode development had moved considerably further than had been possible with the earlier diodes, and Electro–Motive was able to increase the voltage rating of the machine from 1,000 volts DC on the first GP-40s to 1,300 volts DC on the 3517 Class which permitted the elimination of shunting altogether. The 3517 Class of GP-40s therefore became the first locomotives on the railroad to operate in full parallel motor connection with no shunting whatever.

Wheel slip problems on the first two orders of GP-40s were similar to those on GP-35s before the installation of IDAC.

But the GP-40s had eliminated all the series contactors and other items necessary to shift the locomotive from series-parallel to parallel, and even the first GP-40s were delivered with full parallel transition. Consequently, the chief function of the transition circuit on a GP-40 was, at the right speeds, to pick up the motor field shunting contactors to shunt the traction motor fields. The two series contactors were eliminated, and since transition shifting was not a regular occurrence, the power contactors dropped out only when the operator transferred from power to dynamic brake, or when he centered the reverser and spotted the locomotive.

It will be seen that the GP-40 was a greatly improved machine over the GP-35. GP-35s had reached their maximum capacity of 1,000 volts, and the D32 main generator of the GP-35 would not put out more than 2,400 amps continuously without burning itself out. The GP-40 had a capability of producing 1,300 volts and 4,200 amps, and in terms of horsepower, this engine had potential for considerable increases in the future should Electro–Motive care to move in that direction. Everyone on the railroad liked the GP-40s. The men in the shops spoke favorably of them, and the enginemen in their cabs had few evil words. If there was a high-horsepower locomotive that all the men preferred, it was the GP-40; easy riding, reliable, and relatively inexpensive and easy to maintain.

Western Pacific received 21 General Electric, 16-cylinder U30Bs between 1967 and 1971—the 760 Class being delivered in May 1969. Fifteen 12-cylinder U23Bs were received in June and July 1972. Both classes possessed turbocharged engines with nine-inch bore and 10½-inch stroke, and all were delivered with EMD trucks. The 2,250-hp U23Bs operated with 5GT581F1R main generators, whereas electrical transmission in the U30B involved a GTA9 or GTA11 traction alternator which converted mechanical energy into AC electrical power, with alternating current rectified to power the DC traction motors.

Direct current output of the GY-27 exciter energized the alternator rotor's field windings, which set up a rotating magnetic field causing AC to be induced in the alternator stator windings. The AC was then rectified by panel-mounted rectifiers which produced DC to drive the traction motors. All engines possessed a four-stroke cycle, and the turbochargers were exhaust driven. The U30Bs were Western Pacific's heaviest locomotives on four axles, and when operating they were said to "dig in and do very well."

Anderson delineated the most complete record of the 770-771 in *Pacific News* of July 1973. Anderson spent considerable time at the GE Erie plant but did not completely succeed in bringing about the modifications required for WP service. These units had not been rewired from their U36B days, and WP forces spent some two weeks attempting to revise the circuitry for dependable operation. Additional to numerous corrections of factory wiring, all axles had to be replaced since GE had furnished undersize axles not permitted on the WP. Traction motors were also replaced because of misapplication of pinion gears received on delivery.

Nothing will be noted concerning the problems posed by the U30Bs. However, post-delivery operation of the U23Bs immediately indicated the need for modifications, which included:

(1) C1 and FPC capacitors were vibrating out of their

About to leave Portola on the early afternoon of May 11, 1974, the eastbound CIX, with the 3532 on the point, awaits a highball. By this time Union Pacific pool power was becoming commonplace on the Western Pacific. **Virgil Staff**

clamps which only contacted the capacitor at top and bottom.

(2) In order not to overload the trainline circuit in dynamic braking, the positive feed to the exciter battery field was changed from the BG (21T) trainline circuit, to the local control positive.

(3) Control circuitry on GE units was established to set the unit dynamic braking whenever the reverser was centered and the engine was shut down. When the start button was pushed, the start field would be in the circuit. Should the engine be shut down with the control air drained, and should an electrician, working on the BKT, leave it in the motoring position instead of in the dynamic braking position, the starting field would be shorted out, and only the generator armature would be across the battery. Excessive current could then damage the battery as well as other components in the circuit. To avoid this possibility, a BKT interlock was made available by replacing it with a BR1 interlock. A BKT interlock was then installed in series with the starting contactors, and a BR1 interlock was accomplished by replacing the four-finger relay with a relay of five fingers.

(4) To minimize smoking, the cooling water thermostats were changed from 165° to 180°F., thus running the engines hotter.

(5) Undoubtedly the most serious problem concerned the physical location of the PR relay. These U23Bs are said to have been the first built by GE in some time that were equipped with DC main generators, and required motor field shunting. When the units were built, someone rerouted the cables to the motor field shunting resistors so that they passed through the cabinet near the PR relay. Whenever there was a current in the cables when operating in forward the PR relay would operate so as to energize the ORS and unload the unit. At 20 mph the locomotive would unload when operating in the normal forward direction, and would remain unloaded until it had made transition into parallel at 35 mph.

The credit for isolating this problem largely goes to Ron Brocious, the GE service engineer, since the Western Pacific did not want its locomotive superintendent out riding the power. Once the problem was isolated the solution was a simple one. The PR relay was physically moved to the front wall of the electrical cabinet away from the traction motor cables and motor field shunting resistor cables. These units were new, and Anderson was anxious that they perform to their best ability. A well-organized program was quickly mounted to rectify these problems, and in fact the correction was so immediate that most individuals outside the Stockton locomotive department never suspected what had transpired.

Finally, the U30Bs and U23Bs were always considered high-maintenance machines, and prolonged efforts were exerted during the administrations of Christy, Perlman, and Flannery to bring about improvements through experimental and research projects.

The Canyon

It is 10:35 a.m. on April 3, 1977, and the 3061 with units 2260, 3060 and 2010 trailing a piggyback consist work their way upgrade west of Virgilia. The shrill scream of flanges, the roar of the diesel engines and the rumble of the cars all combine to reverberate again and again as the Western Pacific fights to move tonnage through the Feather River Canyon. Yes, the Canyon is literally the symbol of the railroad—a part of its slogan and its emblem. We see it now as once the passengers of the lordly *California Zephyr* saw it, and as the train crews still see it—on this and the next few pages.

Virgil Staff

FT 909 leads the way out of Keddie on the main, headed for Oroville and points west via another 70 miles or so of Feather River Canyon. The railroad was built on a ledge high above the canyon floor; the wye is just out of view to the lower left. **Western Pacific, Virgil Staff Collection**

Spring Garden Loop is one of the most exciting locations in the Canyon. Here we watch the 3505, left, on the CIX crossing itself on its eastbound trek toward Salt Lake City on August 24, 1967. At lower left a Bieber-bound symbol crawls out of Tunnel 32, the west-to-north segment of the Keddie Wye. The date is August 9, 1969.
Both: Virgil Staff

From the comfort of a coach on No. 18, the photographer freezes a westbound cab unit, below.
Richard Steinheimer

THE CANYON 183

At 11:12 a.m. on April 3, 1977, an all-Burlington Northern consist composed of engines 2501, 6482, 2507, 2200 and 2087 breaks the stillness of the Canyon at MP 268.20. **Virgil Staff**

The WPE works its way up the Canyon east of Pulga in May of 1974 with the 3525 on the point and 10,000 horses. The Poe River Dam is to the right.
Virgil Staff

184 D-DAY ON THE WESTERN PACIFIC

About to die but proud to the last, the eastbound *California Zephyr* climbs the Canyon west of MP 268 on March 21, 1970—a symphony in steel comparable, in a way, to the majesty of the Canyon itself. **Virgil Staff**

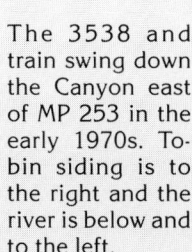

The 3538 and train swing down the Canyon east of MP 253 in the early 1970s. Tobin siding is to the right and the river is below and to the left.
Virgil Staff

THE CANYON 185

25

Some Comparisons

TO INCREASE the utility of road power for switching or local assignments, the GP-7s, GP-9s, GP-20s, the first two orders of GP-35s, and all U23Bs originally had dual controls. They also possessed footboards, as did the third order of GP-35s, and first two orders of GP-40s. The 3517 Class of GP-40s received a 43" plow, and all U30Bs came with 40" variety. At times, a considerable number of FTs, F-7s, GP-7s, or GP-20s possessed large snow plows for service out of Keddie or Portola, and at least in the early years, GP-7s were modified for application of plows and flangers. More recently, snow plow and ice flangers have been standard equipment on engines 913 and 2001.

FT locomotives were the only units not possessing contactors to break connections between the main generator and the traction motors. Each time the FT changed direction, the reverser handle in the cab had to be placed in the direction of movement and the throttle brought out to No. 1 position and then closed before the locomotive could be moved. When unattended, the reverser drum had to be placed on center and locked. Should the reverser not correspond to the direction of movement when the unit was being towed, the wheels would tend to lock and slide.

All 1,350-hp FT locomotives were equipped with 21-point receptacles, and all road power delivered after the FTs came with the 27-point variety. For this and other reasons, the FT power seldom operated with units of higher horsepower. All FTs operated in minimum field start, and toward the end of their existence on the WP, they were frequently coupled with the 801A, 801D, and 802A which operated in minimum field start as long as the FTs were around. As of about February 1965, all 27-point receptacle units operated in modified maximum field start with the exception of the three F-3s just noted. This loading remained too slow for GP-7s, GP-9s, and GP-20s, and all were modified to maximum field start, and in this order, prior to 1970.

All road power operated on Electro–Motive trucks, and all such units through the GP-35s possessed a similar axle with 6½" roller bearing journal. Because of the increased weight of the GP-40s, this model had a 6⅞" roller bearing journal, and a thinner inner race than that found on the axles of earlier units. The axles supporting GE power were somewhat heavier than those of EMD, and all U30Bs, compared to the EMDs with Hyatt roller bearings, had Timken bearings. About 1976 the WP began ordering GP-40 axles for all EMD road units, and in 1977 it began placing U23B axles, with their Hyatt bearings, beneath the U30Bs. U23B and GP-40 axles share the same design inner race.

Electro–Motive axles for road power had no dust collar but did have a water guard, as did also the U23B axles. The 6½x12" journals of the SW-1 and SW-9 axles were essentially similar except that there was no end collar on the SW-9. Alco switch engines, with the exception of the 563 Class, possessed a 7x14" friction bearing, while the latter class was delivered with the 6½x12" friction bearing. Baldwins rested on journals of similar diameter, and axles had end collars as did the first three orders of Alcos. Wheel sets on all diesel locomotives were of 40" diameter and of multiple wear wrought steel specification. All freight and passenger road power used the standard AAR tapered wheel tread, although *Claifornia Zephyr* equipment employed a special cylindrical wheel tread for higher speeds and an improved ride.

Prior to 1978 the standard air horn on road power had come to be the Nathan M5R24 with three bells forward and two

With its nose facing Chilcoot, the Reno Local assumes the tonnage of one of Western Pacific's most profitable branches. This is a relatively infrequently photographed line, and GP-7 707 is about to become a book celebrity. The date: November 26, 1971.
Joseph Ward

facing the rear. FT and F-7 cab units had had a pair of single tone Leslie Tyfon A-200-LPYA air horns with one forward and the second facing the rear. F-3 and FP-7 horns were similarly placed but identified as single tone Leslie Tyfon A-200-RR. In the early 1950s consideration was given to installing chime horns capable of simulating steam locomotive whistles. Nathan M-5 chimes were installed on locomotives 805A and 914D on September 19, 1951, and the 916D and the 805D received A-125-5D Leslie–Tyfons on October 18 and October 23, 1951, respectively.

In these tests, trainmen and enginemen considered the Nathan to be superior to the Leslie chime and single horn. The Nathan was believed to be more penetrating, and snowstorms did not interfere with the Nathan type. On December 18, 1951, the 805D received a Westinghouse E-2B Pneuphonic three-horn chime whistle to compare with the Nathan. Again all enginemen and trainmen preferred the Nathan. The Nathan was not so noisy in the cab and tonal and penetrating qualities were considered superior to the E-2B. Following this test the 803A, 804D, and 805A received M5R24 Nathan five-chime horns. The forward facing A-200-RR horns were removed but the passenger power continued to possess an A-200-RR facing the rear. The S5D five-chimes on the 804A and 805D were fully modulating, and could produce true modulation "from a melodious whisper to an arresting shout." For the remainder of its history, the 805D sported a S5D air chime generally considered to be the most beautiful horn on the Western Pacific.

The Western Pacific did its bit for the 1976 Bicentennial by painting GP-40 3540 red, white and blue and renumbering her 1776. It is seen here on a rainy April 10, 1976, at Sacramento Shops. On April 9, 1977, it was destroyed in a wreck at Hayward. **Virgil Staff**

The RDC cars were equipped with Westinghouse A-2 Pneuphonic air horns with a very shrill pitch. All classes of Alco switch engines were delivered with A-1 Westinghouse single chimes, and SW-1s always carried a single Typhon A125RR facing forward. Baldwins were delivered with a single horn, but about February 1949 these were replaced by Westinghouse double Pneuphonic horns of the AA-2 variety. Each SW-9 carried an M5R24, and similar air horns were ultimately placed on the 607 and 608.

All road power through the GP-9s had air-cooled (WXO) compressors, and power since that time was delivered with the water-cooled (WBO) models that circulated the engine cooling water through the compressor and intercooler for improved cooling. Some GP-7s, GP-9s, and at least one F-7 received WP applications of the WBO model. Traction motor gear ratios have been 62:15 on all Electro–Motive road-freight and switching power, 57:20 on all passenger units, and 81:22 on GE units, thus giving the GE power a slightly higher maximum continuous speed than that of the Electro–Motive freight units. The VO-1000s possessed a gear ratio of 68:14, and all Alcos were delivered with 75:16.

In the early years of the larger horsepower units, when there remained a large number of F-3s and F-7s on the roster, it was generally necessary to keep the older power on the point so as to remain within the amperage limitations of the traction motors and dynamic braking grids. Among the F-7s, only unit 922B early received a dynamic braking regulator which read the amperage and regulated the excitation to compensate for it, although by early 1978 all four operating F-7s had such regulators to enable these units to operate anywhere in a power consist. On 901 class units, the brake warning relay had picked up at 440 amps and dropped out at 430 amps, whereas on the F-3s, the relay contact was set to pull in at 560 amperes and drop out at 540 amperes. F-7 and GP-7 dynamic braking amperage capacity was 600 amps, while GP-9s, GP-20s, GP-35s, and GP-40s possessed a 700-ampere capacity, and U30Bs worked up to 740 amps. These were the maximum permissible grid current limits.

By 1978 all road units had received dynamic braking regulators, thus enabling them to be mixed without fear of burning up the grids in lower horsepower units trailing in a consist. GP-20s had been converted to potential line braking, in addition to the earlier established field loop braking, and all GP-35s, the 751-769, and the first two orders of GP-40s initially had dual systems of dynamic braking to allow their operation in consists with the field loop of earlier power. And by 1978 all field loop circuits had been removed except on the GP-7s which continued to have field loop braking but in which the potential braking signal had been trainlined to allow their presence in other power consists. GP-9s could be used anyplace in a consist, and if GP-7s were to be used in dynamic braking, they would be placed on the point. GP-35s were the first to come with potential line brake control, and older power was delivered with provision for field loop control to lead or trail.

Six types of brake equipment have been employed on WP

diesels. These have included the 14-EL on SW-1s, all Alcos, and the NW-2s. SW-9s had 6-BL equipment, and Baldwins the 6-DS. FT power possessed an 8-EL schedule with a KS-8-PB brake valve, and more recent road power through the GP-9s operated with the 24-RL. All later power including and following the GP-20s have had the 26-L schedule. In addition, *California Zephyr* power possessed Electro–Pneumatic equipment with a DSE-24-H brake valve and speed-governor control. This HSC system was a straight-air brake which admitted air into, or exhausted it from, the straight air pipe extending throughout the train. Speed governor control operated from a generator located on the axle, and providing voltage proportional to wheel speed. Electrical relays operated at generator voltage corresponding to certain speeds which caused the operation of an FS-1864 relay valve to provide the braking forces suitable for these speeds.

California Zephyr equipment operated with Model CF disc brakes, and on July 28, 1958, the WP disconnected the electro-pneumatic brakes by removing the 16:6 trainline jumper between each locomotive and the first car. The Burlington Railroad and the Pullman Co. are known to have begun removing the electro-pneumatic equipment from locomotives and/or cars in early 1959, and Western Pacific, against its better judgment, then began doing similarly.

The 24-RL brake schedule equipment on the WP came to consist of a Type II D24 brake valve, brake pipe cutout cock—sometimes known as the double heading cock, safety control cock, D-24-B feed valve, four-position K2A Rotair valve, and an S-40 independent brake valve. Since the 24-RL brake valve maintained pressure less adequately than the 26-L, the D24 brake valve was modified by the WP to use the first service position to provide the pressure-maintaining feature. On the Western Pacific, this schedule would MU only with 24 and 26 equipment.

The 26-L brake equipment included a 26C automatic brake valve, a three-position or two-position cutoff valve, regulating valve, MU2A valve or double-ported cutout cock, and an SA-26 independent brake valve. Because of the possibility of emergency use of freight power in passenger service, a three-position cutoff valve came installed on all GP-20s, GP-35s, the 751-769, and possibly on the 3501-3516. Power delivered following discontinuance of the passenger train came with a two-position cutoff. GP-20s, GP-35s, and the 751-769 possessed a MU2A valve about equal to the K2A Rotair valve on 24-RL equipment. The MU2A valve pilots the F-1 selector valve thus enabling the air brake equipment of one locomotive to be controlled by that of another unit. This is a three-position valve that will MU with 24, 26, or 6 brake equipment. GP-40s, the 770 Class, and all U23Bs have a double-ported cutout cock which performs about the same function but will MU only with 24 or 26 equipment.

All road power except the FTs initially came with automatic transition, and it has been noted that this was blocked off or disconnected on all F-3s, F-7s, and FP-7s. Later power always operated in automatic transition. All geeps through the 3516, and all U30Bs possessed a manual transition selector employed

The citizens of Elko, Nevada, participate in the excitement of June 24, 1975, with the temporary return of steam to the railroad. The Southern Pacific "Daylight" 4449 has arrived in front of Eastern Division headquarters and GP-40 3514 is spotted beside the old steamer as an object lesson in 20th-century progress. It is magnificently ignored by the crowd.
Virgil Staff

Inching its way westbound up the one percent of Antelope Hill in Nevada, is an all-Union Pacific power consist composed of 2835, 2820, 2864 and 3209. It is 12:05 p.m. of June 30, 1974, and there is another symbol not far behind. **Virgil Staff**

to shift for trailing covered wagons in a consist. Automatic transition equipment will not cause transition in entrained units not so equipped, since automatic transition is not a trainline function whereas manual transition must be. The engineer would shift manually for the covered wagons MU'd behind, even though the engineer's own unit would shift automatically. Three GP-20s had the selector removed during the modification program of this power. The U23Bs and the last two orders of GP-40s did not possess such a selector, and thus could not be used on the point of trailing F-3s, F-7s, or FP-7s.

The last two orders of GP-40s, units 3517-3544, were delivered with IDAC wheel slip devices. These had been applied by the WP, in 1968, on the first two orders, and were so effective that all GP-35s received them by July 1969, and the GP-20s shortly after. In 1970 or 1971 a traction motor cutout feature was applied to 15 locomotives in the first two orders of GP-40s. This eliminated the necessity for returning units dead-in-train to Stockton due to a single faulty traction motor. Locomotives 3517-3544 were delivered with this feature, but installations were never made on GP-20s or GP-35s. A program was instituted in 1966 to install ground protective automatic relay reset devices, and by the middle 1970s all road power possessed these with the exception of a few GP-7s and GP-9s. Sometime following delivery, power limit switches were removed from the GEs, as were the power match cutout switches.

The incompatibility of GE and EMD power came under early review. Electro–Motive power offered immediate throttle response, while GE units were longer in loading. Electro–Motive turbos always had a fixed amount of air exhaust since the turbo was gear driven. The GE turbo was a straight gas driven turbo which required time to get charging to apply the load, thus the load lag. Locomotives 3070-3071 and all U23Bs were delivered with an advanced speed schedule which overcame some of the slow acceleration of the diesel engine by operating it at notch 5 speed in throttle notches 1-5. Earlier U30Bs came with the "delayed" speed schedule. All these U30Bs were modified by WP forces to possess increased excitation to give a more rapid change in power, but none of them ever equaled the immediate loading of the EMDs.

Another characteristic of the GE units that complicated train operation was the tendency to drop the load following each change of throttle position. Consider a train crossing the desert doing 60 mph in No. 6 throttle position. A gradual rise in the track might influence the engineer to go into No. 7 throttle. However, the amps would drop off considerably, and engineers reported the amperage would not begin to build up for 30 or 40 seconds. It was sometimes thought better to operate in a lower notch from the beginning, since each time the throttle position was changed, the amps were dropped with only gradual recovery after a considerable period of time.

Concurrently, one might expect some run-in of the slack when the amps dropped, a situation that was conducive to breaking-in-two. But most consists included some EMD power, and the problem was less hazardous since the EMDs responded immediately. WP forces modified these GEs to reduce the dropping of their load, but could not provide sufficient excitation to completely obviate this problem without the concomitant problem of the power shutting down.

Finally, the problem of dynamic braking in consists of mixed power was always present. General Electric and Electro–Motive type of control differed in that the GEs possessed a grid current control, whereas the EMD system was one of tapered or field current control. To achieve full dynamic braking effort on a GE, it was necessary to be in full braking position. This was not true of the EMD. If the consist was mixed, the units were not always producing the same braking effort.

With a GE on the point, the rating was calculated on the GE unit which, had there not been automatic regulation on each trailing EMD unit, would have overexcited such units. If an EMD was on the point, the engineer went by the ammeter but he was not getting the full braking out of the trailing GEs. In such situations, it might be necessary to "widen out" on the dynamic braking lever to produce the equivalent of No. 8 throttle position on the GEs.

26

The Perlman-Flannery Years

ALFRED E. PERLMAN came to the presidency of the Western Pacific on December 1, 1970. Perlman was tough, civilized, and fascinating, and he provided connections and insights invaluable to a reestablishment of confidence. The books disclosed losses for the years 1969-1970, and Howard A. Newman, chairman of the board and principal executive officer since June 24, 1970, invited Perlman to rejuvenate the company and place it back among the paying railroads.

The slowing of the national economy, and related problems of the railroad, caused President Myron R. Christy to shuffle personnel toward the end of his era. Donald H. MacLeod had become vice president and general manager on January 6, 1970, and on April 15, David F. Pilkinton, chief mechanical officer of the M-K-T, became CMO of the WP with headquarters in Sacramento. One of MacLeod's virtues could be seen in his attempt to reduce the ton mileage, and to run shorter trains on schedule. But this was a time of bewildering insecurity for all personnel. The new general manager, best known over the system as "the ball of fire," expected action today and not tomorrow. Trainmasters and others came to expect the "chewing" for which they were seldom disappointed. MacLeod might appear at a roundhouse at 3:00 A.M. to determine if all hands were working, and he is said to have appeared, with field glasses, at the top of the Stockton Tower. This atmosphere of fear continued into the early part of the Perlman administration but tapered off by the close of 1971.

In partial defense of the latter activity at Stockton, it should be explained that the company was experiencing a "slowdown" among its switchmen, and among the forces of the new shops. The "bad order locomotive ratio" in March 1970 was 21.3 percent. Lines of units stood idle and out of service. Trains were ready to move but frequently lacked the power. It was at this time that William Gault, better known as "Scotty," was taken from the Oakland Roundhouse and placed in charge of the Stockton Shops. Whatever might be one's feelings toward events of the moment, calmer minds admitted that one of the functions of a railroad was to move tonnage, and one could expect management to take whatever steps necessary to assure that the company performed its function.

Perlman's entrance to the Western Pacific signaled a series of changes over the system seemingly breathtaking in its rapidity. Not that changes were new to the company. The years 1969-1970 brought changes so fast that long-term planning is said to have been impossible. William Stevens, onetime general diesel supervisor, stated it this way to the writer: "There are lots of new faces. Old-timers who have proven themselves now have to prove themselves again. For most, the opportunity will not arise again." Perlman needed a corps of individuals of distinguished executive talent upon whom he knew he could depend.

On January 1, 1971, Robert G. Flannery became executive vice president, with Robert C. Marquis becoming chief transportation officer on July 15. Flannery was ingenious, unruffled, and as some said, "terribly competent." His immediate background had been as vice president of the Penn Central Transportation Co. with prior service in an executive capacity with the New York Central System.

John Kelly, who exuded confidence, ability, and friendliness, was appointed director of public relations on June 21, and the nationally known Harry J. Bruce was elected vice president, marketing, on December 1. To look ahead, Perlman became chairman of the board and chief executive officer on January 1, 1973, at which time "Mike" Flannery took the presidency. Perlman retired on June 24, 1976, but assumed the title of chairman of the board, emeritus. In the meantime, Marquis became vice president, operation, on October 1, 1972.

When Perlman took over the presidency of the company, the Stockton Shops were completed, and the *California Zephyr*—

Alfred E. Perlman
A builder, not a wrecker.

Christy's chief millstone—was dead and buried. CMO E.T. Cuyler had expected a significant savings from relocation of the shops, and by this time there were only skeleton forces at any point other than Stockton and Sacramento. Some emergency diesel locomotive work was possible at Elko, Portola, Oroville, and Oakland but all services at Oakland Roundhouse had been discontinued on July 20, 1970, and the destruction of the old roundhouse began on July 13, 1971. All major locomotive work would take place at Stockton and most car department work at Sacramento.

Centralization of car department work at Sacramento allowed substantial reduction of forces, and Perlman took advantage of other opportunities by pulling most of the rail in and around the Oakland Roundhouse, and in sidings no longer required for passenger train run-bys. Yard trackage rearrangement was expedited at any terminal where significant savings could be expected, and shop machinery, excess buildings, obsolete rolling stock, and other miscellaneous items thought unnecessary, were dismantled.

The general reaction to these and other changes over the system tended to be disconsolate, and many old-timers concluded that the company could not bear such trauma—that it would lie down and never rise again. Some wondered if Perlman had been hired to wreck the company, and non-railroad personnel sometimes attempted to prove this thesis by reminding the listener that a major portion of the Yosemite Valley Railroad's locomotive roster had been scrapped shortly after sale to Perlman in September 1945. What none of these people understood was that Al Perlman was a professional railroad man who was not about to suffer the reputation of "railroad wrecker" in what would undoubtedly be his final venture. Moreover, the intent to wreck did not seem consistent with Perlman's past, or with his attempt to gather some of the finest railroad talent in the United States.

Management's chief contributions to a viable railroad did not primarily relate to motive power. What was accomplished included: (1) a reduction in the bad order car ratio from 9.6 percent of March 31, 1970, to 5.27 percent on May 31, 1971, and 2.3 percent in June 1973, enabling employment of additional rolling stock for revenue loadings; (2) programs to minimize car detention; (3) service improvements with tightening of schedules; (4) extension of sidings to eliminate train delays; (5) a continuing program of upgrading bridges to handle heavier loadings; (6) increased acquisition of specialized equipment to mechanize maintenance operations; (7) consolidation and centralization of offices which required smaller forces with concomitant tightening of departmental functions; (8) consolidation of yard and station personnel; (9) reductions in the work force; (10) installation of VHF transmitter and receiver stations, and increased use of portable and mobile radio communication between trackside crews and enginemen and dispatchers; (11) a tremendous increase in computer capabilities; (12) the programming of a total management system; (13) new unit and product cost controls; (14) an improved marketing organization; (15) a "sales sweep" program established in 1972 to spread the base of commercial business into the major market areas of the United States; (16) continuing emphasis on real estate sales for location of industries along the line; (17) expansion of intermodal facilities; (18) the inclusion in late 1972 and early 1973 of the Western Pacific Transport Co. to provide a trucking base supplemental to company rail operations, with less-than-carload shipments and door-to-door delivery.

Offices of the CMO were moved from Sacramento to San Francisco in January 1972, although the superintendent of locomotives, located at Stockton since the opening of the shops at that point, temporarily remained there into October 1972. Norman E. Anderson, who grew up along the Western Pacific, was superintendent of locomotives between October 1, 1971, and October 1972. Anderson could not conceive of leaving his locomotives for a desk job in San Francisco, and it was with keenest regret that he offered his resignation.

Ray E. Schriefer then filled the void in Stockton, with John Miller becoming superintendent of locomotives in San Francisco on November 1, 1972.

In the meantime, Perlman brought in Robert W. Mustard from the Penn Central to fill the position of CMO effective August 16, 1972. Mustard had been regional mechanical officer in New York and Cleveland, and from 1969 to 1972 filled the positions of regional mechanical officer with headquarters at Cleveland, and then at New Haven. The new CMO possessed a warm, likable personality, exerted very tight control, met with his San Francisco personnel the first thing each morning, regularly moved about his domain, and was considered by those who knew him best to be unquestionably competent.

Power acquisitions during the Perlman–Flannery years included General Electric demonstrators 303 and 304 rebuilt for the Western Pacific as U30Bs 770 and 771. These worked their way over the BN from Cicero, Illinois, and were received on the WP at Bieber on August 5, 1971. New GP-40 units 3527-3544 also worked their way over the BN and were received on the WP between July 24 and September 26, 1971. Fifteen U23Bs, numbered 2251-2265, were placed in service at Cicero between June 3 and July 7, 1972. These possessed 12-cylinder, 2,250-hp, turbocharged engines with 5GT581F1R DC main generators and the usual GE 752E8 traction motors. It was expected that these would be of considerable use in local service, and all included footboards and dual controls.

Three SW1500 non-turbocharged switching locomotives, numbered 1501-1503, were delivered on June 21-23, 1973. These possessed 12-645E engines, D32P main generators, and sported Nathan M5R24 horns similar to those on all geep road power on the Western Pacific. Finally, five GP-40-2 locomotives, with 645-E3B engines, were delivered on line at Bieber between July 19-29, 1979, and 10 additional locomotives of the same model arrived in the first half of 1980.

Cuyler had placed 50 locomotives and the self-propelled diesel car ferry on controlled maintenance about April 1967, and by his retirement most of the fleet was included. Procedures were established for a regular flow of lube oil samples between the WP and an outside chemical laboratory. The time involved in this procedure has earlier been noted, and when Perlman came to the railroad, a chemical laboratory was established at Stockton. Perlman had a long record of interest in the

Looking down Mission Street toward San Francisco Bay on the early Sunday morning of August 6, 1978. The general offices of the Western Pacific Railroad Co. can be seen in the first two buildings to the left beyond the structure under renovation. **Virgil Staff**

scientific study of lubrication oils, and the new laboratory enabled the continued use of such oils for as long as they possessed the necessary lubricating properties. Water leaks and diagnosis of other internal pathology were simplified, and the mechanical department could early show significant monetary savings in the maintenance and operation of its motive power.

The successive years of the Perlman–Flannery administrations provided perceptible shop improvements, continued experimental work on the General Electric locomotives, and a sophisticated long-term testing of lubrication oils. A proposal for testing was made by Standard Oil Co. of California's Chevron on March 25, 1974, with this research beginning in June and continuing at least into 1981. A program of prime mover overhaul was initiated in 1974 with 18 worked in that year, 20 in 1975, 30 in 1976, and 25 in 1977.

The previously employed system of progressive maintenance no longer seemed workable where trains were dependent on fewer units of higher horsepower. By the late 1960s Cuyler had been stripping out units "in place" or on the floor. Locomotives were now shopped based on a combination of mileage, lube oil analysis, and shop inspection. Schriefer considered any locomotive over 500,000 miles to be a candidate for shopping, although many units gave as high as 800,000 miles. Daily out-of-service percentage dropped from 7.8 percent in 1973 to 4.7 percent in the first half of 1977, with switch engines running as high as 7.5 percent in 1973 as compared with two percent in the first six months of 1977.

Between July 1971 and October 1972, 11 GP-7s and six GP-9s had their foot steps lowered from 18 to 14 inches above the top of the rail. Between 1973 and October 30, 1974, similar work was completed on the GP-20s. Finally, by the middle 1970s the railroad was removing front and rear footboards from all power in switching service built prior to April 1, 1975. Concerted attempts were made to derive improved use

of the men's time, and Superintendent of Locomotives John Miller informed the writer that "one of the first things we did when we got here was to move the material out of the storeroom where the men could get at it."

Average cost of maintenance per locomotive mile was .2105 in 1969, and .2134 in 1973. This figure increased to .2600 in 1974, and .3417, .4173, .4328, and .5850 in consecutively successive years. Locomotive miles declined in 1975 as compared to 1974, but the tremendous increase in costs after 1973 is said to have been largely due to increases in costs of locomotive materials—i.e., materials forwarded to GE and EMD for repair and return.

Firemen were taken off their runs between 1964 and 1968, and by the early 1970s there was increased need for the company to establish a training center for its engineers and other personnel. Controls from the left side of locomotive 3012 were removed on December 11, 1973, for inclusion in this center, and Schriefer wrote the manuals in the spring of 1974, and then taught the first class of new engineers. In June 1974, a new 1,000,000-gallon fuel tank was placed in operation at Stockton. This allowed the company to take advantage of the best market prices, and provided emergency supplies in times of general or local shortage.

A new system of fuel conservation had been tested on the Kansas City Southern Railway, consisting of a multiple-unit control panel allowing engineers to take one or more units off the line when tractive effort exceeded the power required. This "fuel-saver system," as it was called, was tested on the WP between March 1-10, 1977, using units 3536-3531-3511-3544 on two tests with the fuel savers, and two without. Runs were between Stockton and Salt Lake and return with fuel savers on train GGM-1 with 56-28-5924 tons, and SPBF-5 with 51-36-4795 tons. With the fuel savers not in use, the two runs took place with the GGM-4 with 68-23-6559 tons, and

The salt flats sometimes function as a huge drumhead to create an unbelievable crashing of sharp, pounding sounds. Here, the dull thudding of drums at sunrise contributes innuendo to this westbound manifest hastening across the flats for California. It is 6:10 a.m. of June 25, 1978, and the golden fingers of the sun are casting a pinkish glow that grows brighter with the morn.   **Virgil Staff**

the B/PBF-2 with 47-21-4307 tons. On one run for which the statistics are known, the savings are said to have averaged 10.23 percent. Application of fuel savers was begun on February 25, 1977, and the remaining turbocharged road power, with exception of some of the GP-20s and all of the GP-40-2 model, received applications shortly thereafter.

Concurrently, four of the five remaining F-7s had their automatic transition activated since the manual transition circuit used trainline 18-19 to be used for the fuel savers on their first application to the turbocharged units. The four F-7s were partially rewired, and received dynamic brake regulators, recabled grid circuits, a new wheel slip protection circuit for dynamic braking, and potential wire braking to enable them to lead or trail with other power. Engines 913 and 921 were rebuilt at Morrison-Knudsen at Boise, and the 917 and 918 received their modifications at Stockton.

Early in the Perlman-Flannery administrations all locomotives were being maintained at Stockton, with some heavy work, such as accident damage or an occasional engine change, still being done at Sacramento. There was no particular assignment of motive power, although the GP-35s and GP-40s were generally used on symbol trains between Stockton and Salt Lake City. F-3s and F-7s were used for drag service over the entire system, although in later years the remaining F-7s were mostly to be found running into Oakland or on a San Jose turn. The U30Bs generally ran from Stockton to Bieber or beyond, Stockton to Oakland, and on occasion could be found running into Salt Lake. The GP-7s, GP-9s, and GP-20s were used on a system basis, but generally in local or yard service, and sometimes mixed with F-7s and used on the High Line or elsewhere as needed. They were seldom MU'd with big power on symbol trains, but if so, then usually on the point. In late 1977 and early 1978, most of the GP-40s appeared to be over on the Union Pacific working off their hours, and power was probably as short as it had ever been during the era of dieselization.

In spite of recession and nervous months during the oil squeeze, the Perlman-Flannery years have generally been tolerable ones for the Western Pacific, with an average per year of 3,904,662,000 ton miles of revenue freight in road service between 1972 and the close of 1979, and 77,221,000 ton miles in nonrevenue freight during the same years. Locomotive unit miles for the same period averaged 10,143,267 in road service and 677,017 in yard switching service. Railway operating revenues increased for each year excepting 1975, but operating expenses were not far behind, and railway operating income was disappointing.

Revenue freight tonnage, at its highest levels during 1972-1974, began to drop significantly in 1975 and only gradually increased after that year. The Western Pacific was a lean railroad, and profits were exacted only following the most stringent controls and innovative management. Nonetheless, the railroad produced a profit each year, and management reduced the operating ratio from 96.5 percent in 1975 to 93.8 percent in 1977. This was approximately similar to the ratio for other Western class 1 railroads and an improvement over all U.S. class 1 railroads with their deterioration in ratios of slightly

F-7 915-A leads the way up the one percent of Wendover Hill west of Arnolds Loop on the afternoon of April 11, 1967. The Toana Range is in the background and the potent aroma of sage is everywhere.

Richard E. Shideler

It is 11:55 a.m. on June 20, 1977, and the westbound 3525 carries its own breeze as it highballs along the southern edge of the Great Salt Lake, at Lakepoint, east of MP 906. **Virgil Staff**

less than 96.4 percent in 1975 to 96.7 percent in 1977.

Western Pacific commenced running its power through to Klamath Falls, Oregon, on the evening of May 31, 1953, and in August 1956 the power began operating into Bend, Oregon, and points north. Effective March 20, 1971, a WP-BN pooling agreement was initiated with BN power regularly running into Oroville or Stockton, or to points such as Pulga, Twain, or Paxton where it could be exchanged with WP power coming up the canyon. About May 1971, Union Pacific power started appearing regularly on the Western Pacific, and in July the WP began operating regularly over the Union Pacific.

Power consists might not be solidly foreign power but were frequently indiscriminately mixed with that of the Western Pacific. This created interesting problems. For example, when the BN and WP began pooling in 1971, the minimum continuous speed of BN units was 14 mph as compared with 11.5 mph for units of the Western Pacific. This difference in minimum continuous speed had to be kept in mind when operating BN locomotives since these must not be operated continuously at a speed lower than 14 mph. When operating BN units with WP U30B power, the power match cutout switch on the WP units had to be placed in the "mixed consist" position to enable all units to share the train tonnage equally. Due to gear ratio difference, BN units indicated a higher traction motor amperage than WP units, and the transition speeds were slightly higher on the BN units than on those of the WP.

With the *California Zephyr* no longer running the canyon, the superelevation had been reestablished for slower freight service, and speed restrictions increased by five to 10 miles per hour. During the blustering storms that blasted through the canyon, broncos (pilot cars) preceded every train east or west, north or south, and radio communication enabled most trains to traverse the canyon in relative safety. The Western Pacific had never believed in more than six units for power. Additional units, when employed, were to increase the horsepower for speed. Tonnage was normally not added beyond the capabilities of six units since this frequently resulted in break-in-two. Additional units might be in the consist but these were to be isolated. Cuyler and the superintendents had developed these general rules by the early 1960s, the major change in policy relating to dynamic braking.

In 1963, dynamic braking was theoretically permitted on only the first four units, but by December 1970 operative dynamic braking was allowed in consists of five GP-type units, six F-type units, or five units if the consist was a mixture of the two types. When it became necessary to use more than the above number of units in a consist under power, the dynamic brakes had to be cut out on the excess trailing units. In January 1973, CMO Mustard ordered that the power on the head end should usually be limited to five units, and that in dynamic braking units should not exceed any combination totaling more than 24 axles. Timetable No. 3, effective July 28, 1974, brought the limitations up to date with locomotive consists not to exceed six operative units, and operative dynamic brakes on the head end not to exceed four six-axle units, six four-axle units, or any combination totaling 24 axles. Going down the hill called for considerable sophistication since excessive units in dynamic braking tended to destroy the track, and to cause the lighter trailing equipment to climb the rail.

Some very heavy trains, such as the 10,000-ton-unit grain trains, have traversed the canyon westbound, but over the years it generally came to be believed that eastbound trains should normally possess tonnage commensurate with what was known about the likelihood of drawbar failure. Very heavy trains had run the High Line in steam days with 150 cars or more. In the early 1950s, High Line trains not infrequently received six articulated or Mikado steam locomotives, with four on the front end spaced 10 cars apart, and two on the rear with one just ahead of the caboose and the other 10 cars forward.

In diesel times, and for many years, North Line trains were generally restricted to 3,800 tons eastbound in the winter from Greenville to Almanor, and 4,500 tons westbound from Bieber to Halls Flat. In the summer, eastward trains were given up to 4,000 tons, and 4,800 tons westbound from Bieber to Halls Flat. Undoubtedly the greatest limitations in the diesel age were the curvatures. Heavy trains straightened the curves, and rolling stock climbed the rails. With the power tugging from the head end, and helpers pushing from the rear, the cars sometimes went on the ground.

The concept of derailment dynamics is not completely understood, and there are those who believe that very long

Robert G. Flannery
He kept the railroad intact.

trains, even possessing only head-end power, may tend to go on the ground in areas where reverse curvatures and consequent varied friction levels may be established between the wheels and the rails. It has taken time and experience to learn what is possible, and in this age front-end power limitations are generally established and helper locomotives are no longer employed. Burlington Northern trains generally have a limit of between 4,200-4,800 tons, and cars 65 feet or longer are not to be in the first 20 cars of the train. Although helpers are in the past, it is interesting that at least as late as July 1972 helper engines behind occupied steel cabooses were limited to not more than two units or 3,600 horsepower.

In the middle and late 1970s, Flannery and Marquis relentlessly continued to push for data system changes and online information systems more sensitive to management needs. As of 1979, the railroad operated four main-frame computers and a number of mini-computers, and was well on the way to the completion of its cathode ray tube installations in major rail yards. The rebuilding of freight cars for specialized service continued apace, and emphasis over the period could be seen in grade crossing signal improvements, installation of flash flood detectors, hot box detectors, and more modern equipment for roadway gangs.

An average of the 10-year period between 1970 and 1979 indicates that the railroad, each year: (1) placed 6.6 miles of rail in new industrial, switching, and running tracks; (2) laid

62.9 miles of rail in replacement; (3) laid 97,547 ties; (4) put down 79,588 cubic yards of ballast; (5) and surfaced 340.9 miles of track. Railroad facilities were "neat as a pin" and one could hardly conjecture why the road had once been known as the "Wobbly."

In addition to pooling of power and cabooses with the Union Pacific and the Burlington Northern, new interdivisional runs theoretically enabled the expediting of schedules on the WP proper. Among these were the running through Wendover of freight service crews effective June 9, 1972, and the inclusion of enginemen on December 29 of the same year. The running through Keddie, between Oroville and Bieber, and between Portola and Bieber, became effective for conductors and trainmen on August 16, 1974, and similar interdivisional service became effective for enginemen on May 1, 1978.

It will be recalled that since commencement of railroad operations, tonnage to San Francisco had been ferried from Oakland via San Francisco Bay. This was an expensive operation and conducive to delays should enough westbound tonnage arrive in Oakland for transshipment to San Francisco. On November 8, 1978, the *Las Plumas,* Western Pacific's only means of transshipment over its own rail system, was officially taken out of service, although it is known that this car-ferry made two or more runs following that date.

Even prior to November 8, the railroad had started an emergency detour via the Southern Pacific at Newark. The *Las Plumas* had been operating on 12-hour shifts, but more and more it was down for maintenance, and the WP had been running certain of its grain trains over the Southern Pacific to San Francisco. After November 1978, this marine veteran of better than 21 years rested in its berth at the 25th Street slip in San Francisco.

In 1977 Newman announced a plan to sell the assets and business of the Western Pacific Railroad Co. (a California corporation), to a new company formed by the railroad's operating management. To accomplish this, Newman transformed the name of the California corporation, and certain of its subsidiaries, to Old West Rail Co., Old Sacno Co., Old Tide Co., and Old Stan Co., all of which he sold to Newrail Co. on April 4, 1979. Delta Finance Co., and W.P. Transport Co., both subsidiaries of Old Stan Co., did not change their names since their stocks would ultimately be transferred to Newrail. Newrail Co., Inc. (a Delaware corporation), had been incorporated on February 13, 1978, and on the following day Flannery incorporated, in California, the New Sacno Co., New Tide Co., and New Stan Co., with intent that these become wholly-owned subsidiaries of the company upon Newrail's investment in their stock.

On February 16, 1978, the Western Pacific Railroad Co. (a

An eastbound freight headed by unit 3524 works its way toward Elko, Nevada, at 12:15 p.m. on June 16, 1974. The westbound Southern Pacific main can be seen on the far side of the Humboldt River; this is paired trackage territory for the two railroads. **Virgil Staff**

California corporation and subsidiary of WPI) entered into an agreement with the railroad's operating management to sell the railroad's assets and business for approximately $14 million cash. Flannery raised this cash by the sale of the new companies' equity securities, and the purchase became effective April 4, 1979. Newrail Co., Inc., then became the Western Pacific Railroad Co., and its three subsidiaries changed their names to Sacramento Northern Railway, Tidewater Southern Railway, and Standard Realty and Development Co. By this means, Flannery and six directors acquired control of the company, and saved it from possible predators. Newman's WPI received something less than $14 million in cash, and recorded an approximately $71 million loss after tax benefits of approximately $45 million. Newman had never accepted any of the railroad's liabilities, and these were now passed on to Newrail and the new Western Pacific Railroad Co.

Flannery thus maintained the railroad intact. It possessed a new incorporation date of February 13, 1978, as compared with the previous one of June 16, 1916, and it was alive and healthy. As of December 31, 1979, it owned and operated 1,150 miles of single track and 182 miles of branch, with total mileage of 1,482. Of the 146 diesel units in service, 38 were built prior to December 31, 1959, and 108 since January 1, 1960. Ten GP-40-2 locomotives were acquired early in 1980 bringing the grand total in early 1980 to 156 locomotives. As of December 31, 1979, the company operated 249 service cars, 53 cabooses, 5,957 freight cars in revenue service, and 217 units of highway revenue equipment.

Heraclitus believed that the world was not static, but rather in a state of flux. The Interstate Commerce Commission's recent attitude towards consolidations seems to indicate a similar belief. Of great surprise to those who viewed it was the presence on Western Pacific rails, in December 1979, of two cabooses and the railroad's business-observation car No. 1 tugged by locomotives 3548 and 3549. On board were J.C. Kenefick, president of the Union Pacific, and R.G. "Mike" Flannery of the Western Pacific. Few knew of Kenefick's presence on the railroad, and there was no advertising. The mystery was of only short duration, for on January 8, 1980, the Union Pacific announced its intent to merge with the Missouri Pacific, and on January 21 came the announcement of merger with Western Pacific. Prior to this time Union Pacific had purchased 9.9 percent ownership in the Western Pacific and as of December 31, 1979, owned 139,800 shares of common stock out of a total number of 1,410,000.

In the agreement between the two railroads, Pacific Subsidiary, Inc., a subsidiary of Union Pacific, offered to purchase Class A common stock at $20 a share, with shares purchased through this offer being placed in a voting trust until the ICC could come to a decision. The intent was to gain 100 percent control of the railroad and integrate it into the Union Pacific system.

The merger movement of the 1970s had threatened to engulf the Western Pacific in a series of events in which it would either merge or be trapped. Decades earlier, George Gould had envisioned in the WP a western terminus and connection for his Rio Grande and Missouri Pacific railroads. The story of Gould's failure is well known, although the historic struggle of the little Western Pacific has never been chronicled. What became clear towards the end of the 1970s was the unlikelihood that the railroad could maintain its solvency or even its existence in a coming world of rail giants. Flannery had held the railroad together since 1972, and in spite of recessionary developments and bounding inflation, managed to maintain solvency.

But time was running out for the Western Pacific. Railroad facilities and right-of-way were attractive and well-maintained, and the long time-freights rolled in increasing numbers. But rate increases were hardly sufficient to cover wage increases and the rising cost of materials. Inflation was despoiling the railroad, and the consolidation movement throughout the United States was outlawing its existence. Flannery had early let it be known that the railroad was "open" to merger. He certainly would not give it to anyone but rather would play the part of diplomat in serving what were hoped to be the best short-term and long-term interests of the system.

Futurity will occasion the testimony of corporate dependency recast to varying logos and the rubric of undisputed possession. And while the ledgers of Wall Street fail to encompass the ancestral heritage of those ribbons of steel, there will always be men who will remember. For nothing forever remains the same, and institutions and the handiwork of men pass in parade as do their devisors. Should the bystander, on some morrow, find himself amidst the ruins of old *Trego,* and sense the stride of an approaching time-freight in the song of its impending arrival against the remote antipodes of the timberless mountain, then let him awaken to the stirring of the past, and perhaps there will be remembrance of the men and women who called this the Western Pacific.

George Gould's fancy would have been tickled by the cast of modernity existent across the tristate span of the transportation system he sired. Conceived in a world of giants hungering to extinguish his dream, the Western Pacific Railway Co.'s system had been turned over to the operating department in a fabric beset with crises. Untreated ties and timbers everywhere, collapsing tunnels, a sinking and washed-out Main across the lake and over the Salt Flats, the sinking of fill and cribbing throughout the canyon, slides and floods all bred the travail of a system tottering to its ruin. Ballast was primarily mud and dirt, and by the 1920s one could lift the spikes from their pockets, if one could locate the main line among the weeds.

Engine and train crews took their trains through the canyon never knowing whether they would make it home for days or even weeks. With the Feather River raging below and seemingly miles of cliffs and rocks hanging above them, the men carried their bottles and expected the worst. Although Western Pacific's engineering department was always considered to be superb, when the maintenance of way forces completed one job, there were several others claiming attention. It was a gutsy railroad, and here the men lived and died with an evangelical confidence that someday this would all be different.

When the diesel came, there wasn't an articulated on the railroad that couldn't have rolled it up the canyon with its wheels turning westbound. But management believed it recognized the benefits of the new machines, and should the reader sometime find himself west of Proctor, or on Antelope Hill, or deep in the Feather River Canyon, undoubtedly he will receive that sense of exhilaration that comes from watching the big turbocharged power go up the hill.

All-Time Roster of Western Pacific Diesel Power

The vagaries of compiling numbering changes adversely complicate any systematic delineation to support a simplified and easily comprehensive roster. The four-unit 1,350-hp FT power consists were delivered in configurations of O-A-B-C with "O" and "C" designating cabs, and "A" and "B" denoting boosters. For example, the four-unit consist of Engine 901 could be read as 901, 901A, 901B and 901C with the 901 and the 901C being cabs. Ultimately, with the railroad in possession of cabs and boosters for F-3s, FP-7s and F-7s all cabs were given "A" or "D" designation, and all boosters received a letter "B" or "C".

The 801 Class was composed of three-unit consists in an A-B-B configuration with cabs taking the unit number only, and boosters taking a "B" or "C" designation. This ultimately placed cabs inconsistently lettered with the cabs of other classes, and F-3 cabs came to carry the unit designation accompanied by the letter "A".

The 804 Class of FP-7 and their F-7 boosters were delivered in an A-B-A configuration and lettered A-B-C. This caused the second cab to be lettered similar to F-3 boosters, and to FT boosters in the second designation. When the "C" lettered cab was relettered to "D", all covered wagons, including the four-unit F-7s, were lettered as most of them were to remain.

In this roster, it should be understood that locomotive weights are not necessarily calculated with maximum supplies carried, although weights in working order, satisfactory to the carrier, are generally listed for the 501 Class through the 725 Class. From the 801 Class through the 922 Class, weights per class are based on lists acceptable to the carrier in 1959. Unit weights were averaged, within each given class, to arrive at a figure satisfactory for that class. This is total weight on the rail in working order and generally includes a full crew and completely full complement of other supplies. All other locomotive classes from the 1501 and 2001 classes onward are an average computed from the specification sheets of the builder. Within the categories of a given class, the actual weights, at a given time, may be slightly excessive or light.

The determination of tractive effort entails problems assuring that tractive effort, as here listed, will never be precisely correct. Actual effective tractive effort depends upon horsepower, traction motor and generator capability, gear ratio, weight on drivers, and condition of rail. In simplifying a generally complex task, the Western Pacific has shown only the starting tractive effort, which in general is approximately 25 percent of the total locomotive weight. Western Pacific's figures have been accepted for given classes with the exception of the 901, 904, 907, 913 and 922 classes whose TE was initially calculated per four-unit consist.

In order not to complicate the situation, TE per unit has been figured by taking the total purported TE of a four-unit consist, and dividing this by four. In comparing TE with that of other units, it should be noted that adhesion will be fractionally different since FT boosters tended to weigh less than FT cabs. Moreover, FT power always ran in multiples of two since standard couplers were never applied between cabs and boosters. Concerning F-7s, booster units were always heavier than cabs. In the final years for the F-3s and FP-7s, TE was equalized on paper for units within a given class. Adhesion would theoretically be somewhat dissimilar since F-3 boosters were heavier than cabs, and FP-7 cabs were heavier than the F-7 boosters that might accompany them.

Although not included in this roster, all derricks and cranes have been dieselized. Finally, construction dates for the last two orders of GP-40s have been taken from the date of shipment since specification sheets on these classes tend to indicate a construction date following the date of shipment.

Retirement data is taken from ICC Form 1-A, or from FRA 6180 which became effective with the first inspection in October 1972, or not later than October 31. Renumberings are usually taken from the same forms, or from other manuscript evidence.

On the Western Pacific, the SW-1, like all switchers up to and including the Baldwins, was delivered in black, with white striping. Starting TE at 25% adhesion was 50,000 pounds but the SW-1 could only produce such TE up to about 2¾ mph after which it dropped off rapidly. In spite of the WP's early enthusiasm for this model, it proved to be too small for many jobs and was quickly replaced by 1,000-hp units when they became available. Oakland, Aug. 23, 1941. (For a photo of an S-1 switcher, see page 24.)
Guy L. Dunscomb

SW1 — EMC — 600-HP — 50,000 POUNDS T.E. — 199,000 POUNDS WEIGHT

LAST NO.	PREVIOUS NO.	ORIGINAL NO.	DATE BUILT	SERIAL NO.	DATE VACATED	DISPOSITION	NOTE
501			8/17/39	906	11/17/66	SN RY 401	
502			12/6/39	988	3/4/66	SN RY 402	
503			12/6/39	989	2/29/72	Assoc. Metals, Sacto.	

S1 — ALCO — 660-HP — 50,000 POUNDS T.E. — 202,000 POUNDS WEIGHT

LAST NO.	PREVIOUS NO.	ORIGINAL NO.	DATE BUILT	SERIAL NO.	DATE VACATED	DISPOSITION	NOTE
504			4/29/42	69685	12/27/67	SN RY 405	1
505			4/29/42	69686	10/22/68	ST&E 505	2
506			5/6/42	69687	10/22/68	ST&E 506	3
507			5/6/42	69688	8/27/70	Chrome Crankshaft Co., Bell Gardens, Ca.	
508			5/21/42	69689	12/4/71	Associated Metals, Sacramento.	
509			5/21/42	69690	12/29/67	GE	4
510			5/21/42	69691	9/5/72	ST&E	
511			6/8/42	69692	11/21/67	GE	5

S2 — ALCO — 1000-HP — 57,500 POUNDS T.E. — 230,000 POUNDS WEIGHT

LAST NO.	PREVIOUS NO.	ORIGINAL NO.	DATE BUILT	SERIAL NO.	DATE VACATED	DISPOSITION	NOTE
551			9/22/43	70206	10/17/68	GE	
552			9/22/43	70207	2/12/70	TS 745(2)	6
553			11/16/43	70952	2/15/73	Associated Metals, Sacto	
554			11/16/43	70953	6/12/69	TS 744(2)	7
555			12/15/43	71287	12/4/71	Associated Metals, Sacto	
556			12/15/43	71288	11/3/70	Chrome Crankshaft	
557			12/17/43	71289	12/31/76	ST&E 557	
558			12/17/43	71290	8/27/70	Chrome Crankshaft	

S2 — ALCO — 1000-HP — 57,500 POUNDS T.E. — 231,000 POUNDS WEIGHT

LAST NO.	PREVIOUS NO.	ORIGINAL NO.	DATE BUILT	SERIAL NO.	DATE VACATED	DISPOSITION	NOTE
559			2/3/50	76905	10/17/68	GE	
560			2/13/50	77018	12/31/76	ST&E 560	
561			2/13/50	77019	12/31/76	ST&E 561	
562			2/13/50	77020	7/29/70	SN 406	8

S2 — ALCO — 1000-HP — 57,600 POUNDS T.E. — 230,400 POUNDS WEIGHT

LAST NO.	PREVIOUS NO.	ORIGINAL NO.	DATE BUILT	SERIAL NO.	DATE VACATED	DISPOSITION	NOTE
552(2)			1949	76774	11/3/70	Chrome Crankshaft	131

S2 — ALCO — 1000-HP — 57,500 POUNDS T.E. — 230,000 POUNDS WEIGHT

LAST NO.	PREVIOUS NO.	ORIGINAL NO.	DATE BUILT	SERIAL NO.	DATE VACATED	DISPOSITION	NOTE
554(2)			1948	75659	2/15/71	Chrome Crankshaft	132

S4 — ALCO — 1000-HP — 57,500 POUNDS T.E. — 231,000 POUNDS WEIGHT

LAST NO.	PREVIOUS NO.	ORIGINAL NO.	DATE BUILT	SERIAL NO.	DATE VACATED	DISPOSITION	NOTE
563			5/26/51	78777	10/24/73	CCT 50	9
564			5/26/51	78778	12/31/76	ST&E 564	

VO-1000 — BALDWIN — 1000-HP — 60,000 POUNDS T.E. — 245,400 POUNDS WEIGHT

LAST NO.	PREVIOUS NO.	ORIGINAL NO.	DATE BUILT	SERIAL NO.	DATE VACATED	DISPOSITION	NOTE
581			9/14/45	71528	9/10/73	Purdy Co.	10
582			9/14/45	71529	8/27/70	Chrome Crankshaft	
583			10/11/45	71542	9/10/73	Purdy Co.	11
584			10/11/45	71543	7/17/70	SN 407	12
585			10/12/45	71544	11/21/70	Chrome Crankshaft	

The 551 class of S-57, S-2 switchers (like all Alcos) rumbled, banged and clanked as if they would shake themselves apart, but they performed yeoman service. Continuous traction motor rating was 830 amps. Like the later Alcos, these were turbocharged to produce 1,000 bhp. Here, the 553 wears the new orange, aluminum and black livery. Sacramento, Nov. 13, 1952.
H. A. O'Rullian

The 559 class, Type 404DL 1,000-hp standard switcher, was essentially like the 551 class of S-2 but was delivered with diagonal number boxes and MU control for road service. Stockton, May 24, 1952.
Guy Dunscomb

Alco's 563 class of S-4 was delivered with MU control, AAR trucks, automatic shutter control, two 45-degree number boxes in place of the standard, and special handhold and step arrangements. Unit 563 wears the prevalent orange. Oakland, April 12, 1968.
Don Hansen

Fresh out of the Sacramento Shops is the S-60, VO-1000 No. 583 in its new paint scheme of orange and black. The Baldwins spent their later years in and around Stockton, but in earlier times roamed the main line. Units did not possess transition in the traction motor connections but had them series wound thus providing a constant drawbar tension. Continuous rating was 1,060 amps for five minutes. Tonnage rating up the Third Subdivision was 1,150 tons, similar to that of the Alco S-57. Sacramento, Aug. 11, 1966.
Richard Shideler

SW9 — EMD — 1200-HP — 62,000 POUNDS T.E. — 247,800 POUNDS WEIGHT

LAST NO.	PREVIOUS NO.	ORIGINAL NO.	DATE BUILT	SERIAL NO.	DATE VACATED	DISPOSITION	NOTE
601			5/20/52	16636			
602			5/20/52	16637			
603			6/25/52	16638			
604			6/26/52	16639			
605			6/26/52	16679			
606			7/15/52	16680			

NW2 — EMC — 1200-HP — 62,000 POUNDS T.E. — 248,000 POUNDS WEIGHT

LAST NO.	PREVIOUS NO.	ORIGINAL NO.	DATE BUILT	SERIAL NO.	DATE VACATED	DISPOSITION	NOTE
607			10/10/39	889	5/11/73	SN 607	13
608			5/10/40	1000			14

SW1500 — EMD — 1500-HP — 63,096 POUNDS T.E. — 258,800 POUNDS WEIGHT

LAST NO.	PREVIOUS NO.	ORIGINAL NO.	DATE BUILT	SERIAL NO.	DATE VACATED	DISPOSITION	NOTE
1501			5/31/73	72692-1			
1502			5/31/73	72692-2			
1503			5/31/73	72692-3			

The SW-9 class of S-62 switchers possessed rigid trucks which proved detrimental to track alignment when run above 30 mph. One of this type normally worked Portola since this was the only engine capable of the job without difficulty. It was the only switcher class to be delivered in orange, aluminum and black. Sacramento, Jan. 2, 1965. **Virgil Staff**

This NW-2 in orange is an early EMC 1,000-hp model, now with a 567B engine, and classified by the WP as an S-62. Most paint jobs from early 1966 through the end of the 1960s were essentially solid orange; the WP wanted to eliminate the aluminum lacquer which deteriorated rapidly because there was no primer that could be used over the lacquer. Sacramento, June 29, 1969. **Richard Shideler**

GP7 — EMD — 1500-HP — 62,100 POUNDS T.E. — 251,700 POUNDS WEIGHT

LAST NO.	PREVIOUS NO.	ORIGINAL NO.	DATE BUILT	SERIAL NO.	DATE VACATED	DISPOSITION	NOTE
701			10/8/52	17025			
702			10/8/52	17026	7/1/81		
703			10/9/52	17027			
704			10/10/52	17028			
705			10/10/52	17029			
706			10/13/52	17030			
707			10/13/52	17031			
708			10/14/52	17056			
709			10/14/52	17057			

GP7 — EMD — 1500-HP — 61,700 POUNDS T.E. — 246,800 POUNDS WEIGHT

LAST NO.	PREVIOUS NO.	ORIGINAL NO.	DATE BUILT	SERIAL NO.	DATE VACATED	DISPOSITION	NOTE
710			3/30/53	18166			
711			4/1/53	18167	7/30/71	SN 711	15
712			4/2/53	18168	7/16/71	SN 712	16
713			4/4/53	18169			

GP9 — EMD — 1750-HP — 61,900 POUNDS T.E. — 247,600 POUNDS WEIGHT

LAST NO.	PREVIOUS NO.	ORIGINAL NO.	DATE BUILT	SERIAL NO.	DATE VACATED	DISPOSITION	NOTE
725			9/6/55	20696			
726			9/9/55	20697	7/17/70	EMD	17
727			9/9/55	20698			
728			9/6/55	20699			
729			9/9/55	20700			
730			9/9/55	20701	8/17/64	EMD	18
731			9/14/55	20754			
732			9/9/55	20755			

F3A — EMD — 1500-HP — 60,000 POUNDS T.E. — 240,390 POUNDS WEIGHT

LAST NO.	PREVIOUS NO.	ORIGINAL NO.	DATE BUILT	SERIAL NO.	DATE VACATED	DISPOSITION	NOTE
925A	801A	801	6/21/47	3925	9/4/71	EMD	19
925D	802A	802	6/23/47	3926	2/16/71	GE	20
803A	803		6/24/47	3927	9/23/71	EMD	21

F3A — EMD — 1500-HP — 59,000 POUNDS T.E. — 236,500 POUNDS WEIGHT

LAST NO.	PREVIOUS NO.	ORIGINAL NO.	DATE BUILT	SERIAL NO.	DATE VACATED	DISPOSITION	NOTE
926A	801D		3/15/48	3148	7/27/70	EMD	22

F3B — EMD — 1500-HP — 60,000 POUNDS T.E. — 246,423 POUNDS WEIGHT

LAST NO.	PREVIOUS NO.	ORIGINAL NO.	DATE BUILT	SERIAL NO.	DATE VACATED	DISPOSITION	NOTE
801B			6/21/47	3928	7/7/70	EMD	
801C			6/21/47	3929	9/4/71	EMD	
802B			6/23/47	3930	11/18/67	GE	23
802C			6/23/47	3931	10/11/71	EMD	
803B			6/24/47	3932	9/23/71	EMD	
803C			6/24/47	3933	7/8/70	EMD	

The three SW-1500 switchers normally worked Oakland and San Francisco, but here we see the 1502 at Stockton on September 2, 1978. **Virgil Staff**

GP-7, RS-62 unit 709 is fresh out of the paint shop. This livery remained on the GP-7s into the early 1970s after which they began to appear in green. The company herald under the cab window began to disappear about 1971 in order that a large unit number could be put there. Note the Pyle National ashcan headlight, typical of WP for years. **H. A. O'Rullian**

GP-9, RS-62 No. 728 at Stockton in the late 1970s. This dark green is almost black, and front end stripes are in dark green and orange. Tonnage ratings were equal to the GP-7s and either would take 1,500 tons up the Third Subdivision. **Virgil Staff**

FP7 — EMD — 1500-HP — 61,000 POUNDS T.E. — 252,750 POUNDS WEIGHT

LAST NO.	PREVIOUS NO.	ORIGINAL NO.	DATE BUILT	SERIAL NO.	DATE VACATED	DISPOSITION	NOTE
915A(2)	804A		1/20/50	9002	9/1/72	GE	24
916D(2)	804D	804C	1/20/50	9003	8/24/72	GE	25
805A			1/25/50	9004	8/24/72	GE	
805D	805C		1/25/50	9005	10/11/71	EMD	26

WESTERN PACIFIC ROSTER 205

F7 (Psgr) — EMD — 1500-HP — 61,000 POUNDS T.E. — 248,025 POUNDS WEIGHT

LAST NO.	PREVIOUS NO.	ORIGINAL NO.	DATE BUILT	SERIAL NO.	DATE VACATED	DISPOSITION	NOTE
804B			1/20/50	9006	3/10/72	GE	
915C(2)	805B		1/25/50	9007	6/5/72	GE	27

FTA — EMC — 1350-HP — 56,250 POUNDS T.E. — 230,298 POUNDS WEIGHT

LAST NO.	PREVIOUS NO.	ORIGINAL NO.	DATE BUILT	SERIAL NO.	DATE VACATED	DISPOSITION	NOTE
902A(2)	901A	901	11/29/41	1410	4/23/64	EMD	28
901D	901C		11/29/41	1411	5/31/60	EMD	29
901A(2)	902A	902	12/20/41	1412	5/31/60	EMD	30
902D	902C		12/20/41	1413	4/23/64	EMD	31
903A	903		1/10/42	1414	12/16/63	EMD	32
903D	903C		1/10/42	1415	12/16/63	EMD	33

FTA — EMD — 1350-HP — 56,250 POUNDS T.E. — 235,146 POUNDS WEIGHT

LAST NO.	PREVIOUS NO.	ORIGINAL NO.	DATE BUILT	SERIAL NO.	DATE VACATED	DISPOSITION	NOTE
904A	904		6/28/43	2096	11/25/64	EMD	34
904D	904C		6/28/43	2097	4/14/65	EMD	35
905A	905		7/7/43	2098	11/25/64	EMD	36
905D	905C		7/7/43	2099	3/29/67	EMD	37
906A	906		9/22/43	2100	5/29/66	EMD	38
906D	906C		9/22/43	2101	5/21/66	EMD	39

FTA — EMD — 1350-HP — 56,250 POUNDS T.E. — 234,321 POUNDS WEIGHT

LAST NO.	PREVIOUS NO.	ORIGINAL NO.	DATE BUILT	SERIAL NO.	DATE VACATED	DISPOSITION	NOTE
907A	907		7/14/44	2783	10/24/63	EMD	40
907D	907C		7/14/44	2784	10/24/63	EMD	41
908A	908		7/18/44	2785	3/29/67	EMD	42
908D	908C		7/18/44	2786	5/21/66	EMD	43
909A	909		7/20/44	2787	4/5/65	EMD	44
909D	909C		7/20/44	2788	3/29/67	EMD	45
910A	910		8/21/44	2789	12/16/63	EMD	46
910D	910C		8/21/44	2790	5/29/66	EMD	47
911A	911		8/23/44	2791	4/5/65	EMD	48
911D	911C		8/23/44	2792	5/21/66	EMD	49
912A	912		11/9/44	2793	11/25/64	EMD	50
912D	912C		11/9/44	2794	4/14/65	EMD	51

FTB — EMC — 1350-HP — 56,250 POUNDS T.E. — 224,206 POUNDS WEIGHT

LAST NO.	PREVIOUS NO.	ORIGINAL NO.	DATE BUILT	SERIAL NO.	DATE VACATED	DISPOSITION	NOTE
902B(2)	901B	901A	11/29/41	1416	4/23/64	EMD	52
901C	901B		11/29/41	1417	5/31/60	EMD	53
901B(2)	902B	902A	12/20/41	1418	5/31/60	EMD	54
902C	902B		12/20/41	1419	4/23/64	EMD	55
903B	903A		1/10/42	1420	12/16/63	EMD	56
903C	903B		1/10/42	1421	12/16/63	EMD	57

FTB — EMD — 1350-HP — 56,250 POUNDS T.E. — 226,133 POUNDS WEIGHT

LAST NO.	PREVIOUS NO.	ORIGINAL NO.	DATE BUILT	SERIAL NO.	DATE VACATED	DISPOSITION	NOTE
904B	904A		6/28/43	2102	11/25/64	EMD	58
904C	904B		6/28/43	2103	4/14/65	EMD	59
905B	905A		7/7/43	2104	11/25/64	EMD	60
911C(2)	905C	905B	7/7/43	2105	5/21/66	EMD	61
906B	906A		9/22/43	2106	5/29/66	EMD	62
906C	906B		9/22/43	2107	5/21/66	EMD	63

The FTs went through numerous paint scheme modifications, and this photo shows the third and final scheme in orange and black, and aluminum or simulated stainless steel upper and lower panels. Some FTs continued to be seen in the early 1960s with the zebra-striped pilot. Here is a 904 class, D-225, FT at Portola, March 27, 1960. **Don Hansen**

Booster unit 911B of the 907 class in the garden at Oroville on Dec. 28, 1963. Cab units had medallions on the nose, and each booster had one on the side, one side of unit only. **Norman E. Anderson**

Here is F-3 802-A in freight service in orange, black and aluminum with stainless steel lower side panels. By early 1950, the Western Pacific was attempting to mimic this scheme on freight units with paint that simulated the stainless steel effect. Oakland, Feb. 26, 1966. **Virgil Staff**

Unit 801-B, F-3, shows middle side panels of DuPont Orange 254-8273, with portions above the middle panels painted aluminum as were the trucks, underframe, pilot and sometimes the roof. Unlike FT and F-7 freight boosters, these passenger boosters had medallions on both sides. Oakland, Feb. 8, 1970. **Virgil Staff**

Prior to Sept. 15, 1955, all cab and booster units had 6⅝" lettering, then changed to 14". The flying wings were in DuPont Red Duco 254-9089R with white lines. Towards the end of the *California Zephyr*, the wings were applied when the unit was painted at Oakland, but not when painted at Sacramento. FP-7 804-A at Oakland in March 1970. **Virgil Staff**

No. 18 was derailed by a slide at Blinzig on May 18, 1957. Here we see the 804B, which had been badly damaged, fresh out of the Sacramento Shops. Note the black roof, and a 22⁹⁄₁₆" by 26¹⁄₁₆" company medallion, one on each side. **Richard Shideler**

Unlike the passenger units, this 922 Class F-7 has lower side panels in smudge-resistant gray, not stainless steel. The roof and trucks were in black, and F-7s never received the flying wings. A four-unit F-7 consist was classified as D-239, and one unit would lug 1,375 tons up the Third Subdivision, or 280 tons more than the equivalent of one unit of FT. Oakland, March 16, 1968. **Virgil Staff**

The 916C at Oakland on Dec. 29, 1967. The 14" letters were produced by Demp Nock stencils. **Virgil Staff**

FTB — EMD — 1350-HP — 56,250 POUNDS T.E. — 229,330 POUNDS WEIGHT

LAST NO.	PREVIOUS NO.	ORIGINAL NO.	DATE BUILT	SERIAL NO.	DATE VACATED	DISPOSITION	NOTE
907B	907A		7/14/44	2795	10/24/63	EMD	64
907C	907B		7/14/44	2796	10/24/63	EMD	65
908B	908A		7/18/44	2797	3/29/67	EMD	66
908C	908B		7/18/44	2798	5/21/66	EMD	67
909B	909A		7/20/44	2799	4/5/65	EMD	68
909C	909B		7/20/44	2800	3/29/67	EMD	69
910B	910A		8/21/44	2801	12/16/63	EMD	70
910C	910B		8/21/44	2802	5/29/66	EMD	71
911B	911A		8/23/44	2803	4/5/65	EMD	72
905C(2)	911C	911B	8/23/44	2804	3/29/67	EMD	73
912B	912A		11/9/44	2805	11/25/64	EMD	74
912C	912B		11/9/44	2806	4/15/65	EMD	75

F7A — EMD — 1500-HP — 59,750 POUNDS T.E. — 232,065 POUNDS WEIGHT

LAST NO.	PREVIOUS NO.	ORIGINAL NO.	DATE BUILT	SERIAL NO.	DATE VACATED	DISPOSITION	NOTE
913	913A(2)	920A	1/27/50	8976	5/5/81	Cal State RR Museum	76
913D			1/19/50	8963	7/3/69	GE	
914A			1/23/50	8964	10/21/75	Purdy	77
914D			1/23/50	8965	10/22/71	EMD	
804A(2)	915A		1/24/50	8966	6/3/70	EMD	78
915	915D		1/24/50	8967			79
916A			1/25/50	8968	3/24/65	EMD	80
804D(2)	916D		1/25/50	8969	7/1/70	EMD	81
917A			1/26/50	8970	10/25/67	Bechtal	82
917	917D		1/26/50	8971			83
922A(2)	918A		1/26/50	8972	9/71	EMD	84
918	918D		1/26/50	8973	1/20/82	Pacific Locomotive Assoc.	85
919A			1/27/50	8974	6/26/69	GE	
919D			1/27/50	8975	7/12/71	EMD	
920A(2)	913A		1/19/50	8962	10/22/71	EMD	86
920D			1/27/50	8977	3/20/72	GE	87
921A			1/30/50	8978	7/12/71	EMD	
921	921D		1/30/50	8979			88

F7A — EMD — 1500-HP — 59,750 POUNDS T.E. — 230,725 POUNDS WEIGHT

LAST NO.	PREVIOUS NO.	ORIGINAL NO.	DATE BUILT	SERIAL NO.	DATE VACATED	DISPOSITION	NOTE
918A(2)	922A		6/11/51	10803	9/1/72	GE	89
922D			6/11/51	10804	11/18/67	GE	
923A			6/12/51	10805	10/25/67	Bechtal	90
923D			6/12/51	10806	7/21/71	EMD	
924A			6/12/51	10807	6/18/69	GE	
924D			6/12/51	10808	3/24/65	EMD	91

F7B — EMD — 1500-HP — 59,750 POUNDS T.E. — 243,801 POUNDS WEIGHT

LAST NO.	PREVIOUS NO.	ORIGINAL NO.	DATE BUILT	SERIAL NO.	DATE VACATED	DISPOSITION	NOTE
922B			6/11/51	10809	6/18/71	EMD	
922C			6/11/51	10810	7/12/71	EMD	
923B			6/12/51	10811	7/3/69	GE	
923C			6/12/51	10812	6/5/72	GE	
924B			6/12/51	10813	3/10/72	GE	
924C			6/12/51	10814	3/20/72	GE	

F7B — EMD — 1500-HP — 59,750 POUNDS T.E. — 244,220 POUNDS WEIGHT

LAST NO.	PREVIOUS NO.	ORIGINAL NO.	DATE BUILT	SERIAL NO.	DATE VACATED	DISPOSITION	NOTE
913B			1/19/50	8980	9/3/71	EMD	
913C			1/19/50	8981	11/18/67	GE	
914B			1/23/50	8982	2/16/71	GE	
914C			1/23/50	8983	9/1/72	GE	
915B			1/24/50	8984	6/18/69	GE	
805B(2)	915C		1/24/50	8985	6/3/70	EMD	92
916B			1/25/50	8986	3/10/72	GE	
916C			1/25/50	8987	6/18/69	GE	
917B			1/26/50	8988	10/11/68	GE	
917C			1/26/50	8989	6/26/69	GE	
918B			1/26/50	8990	6/18/71	EMD	
918C			1/26/50	8991	9/1/72	GE	
919B			1/27/50	8992	6/26/69	GE	
919C			1/27/50	8993	6/18/69	GE	
920B	806B	920B	1/27/50	8994	3/10/72	GE	93
920C			1/27/50	8995	6/26/69	GE	
921B			1/30/50	8996	5/30/72	GE	
921C			1/30/50	8997	7/18/68	GE	94

GP20 — EMD — 2000-HP — 64,100 POUNDS T.E. — 257,000 POUNDS WEIGHT

LAST NO.	PREVIOUS NO.	ORIGINAL NO.	DATE BUILT	SERIAL NO.	DATE VACATED	DISPOSITION	NOTE
2001			12/1/59	25623			
2002			11/25/59	25624			
2003			11/24/59	25625	8/17/64	EMD	95
2004			11/27/59	25626			
2005			11/21/59	25627			
2006			11/25/59	25628			

This was the first paint scheme in green (939-AL-365) and came to be known as "Southern Green" or "MacLeod Green." Here is GP-20 RS64 No. 2010; one of these would take 1,750 tons up the Third Subdivision or 250 more tons than a GP-9. Elko, July 8, 1972.
Virgil Staff

Here is GP-35 RS65 unit 3018 in its original paint at Elko in 1972. Only a smudge appears where the company herald, or medallion, appeared under the cab window; a large black number will appear under the window. In 1980 all remaining GP-35s and 15 GP-40s of the first two classes were remanufactured at Morrison-Knudsen in Boise, Idaho. At that time each received a dual white oscillating light on the nose, air conditioning and upgraded equipment.
Virgil Staff

GP20 — EMD — 2000-HP — 64,100 POUNDS T.E. — 257,000 POUNDS WEIGHT

LAST NO.	PREVIOUS NO.	ORIGINAL NO.	DATE BUILT	SERIAL NO.	DATE VACATED	DISPOSITION	NOTE
2007			7/30/60	26041			
2008			7/30/60	26042			
2009			7/30/60	26043			
2010			7/30/60	26044			

U23B — GE — 2250-HP — 65,560 POUNDS T.E. — 262,230 POUNDS WEIGHT

LAST NO.	PREVIOUS NO.	ORIGINAL NO.	DATE BUILT	SERIAL NO.	DATE VACATED	DISPOSITION	NOTE
2251			5/25/72	38397			
2252			5/25/72	38398			
2253			5/25/72	38399			
2254			6/8/72	38400			
2255			6/8/72	38401			
2256			6/8/72	38402	5/6/80	UP	96
2257			6/8/72	38403			
2258			6/8/72	38404			
2259			6/14/72	38405	10/6/81		97
2260			6/21/72	38406			
2261			6/14/72	38407			
2262			6/21/72	38408			
2263			6/23/72	38409			
2264			6/29/72	38410			
2265			6/29/72	38411			

GP35 — EMD — 2500-HP — 65,000 POUNDS T.E. — 258,600 POUNDS WEIGHT

LAST NO.	PREVIOUS NO.	ORIGINAL NO.	DATE BUILT	SERIAL NO.	DATE VACATED	DISPOSITION	NOTE
3001			11/22/63	28398			
3002			11/22/63	28399			
3003			11/23/63	28400			
3004			12/4/63	28401			
3005			12/4/63	28402			
3006			11/23/63	28403			
3007			12/4/63	28404		(Cf. Note 98.)	98
3008			12/4/63	28405			
3009			12/4/63	28406			
3010			12/4/63	28407			

GP35 — EMD — 2500-HP — 65,000 POUNDS T.E. — 258,600 POUNDS WEIGHT

LAST NO.	PREVIOUS NO.	ORIGINAL NO.	DATE BUILT	SERIAL NO.	DATE VACATED	DISPOSITION	NOTE
3011			11/20/64	29030	7/13/70	EMD	99
3012			11/27/64	29031			100

GP35 — EMD — 2500-HP — 65,000 POUNDS T.E. — 259,000 POUNDS WEIGHT

LAST NO.	PREVIOUS NO.	ORIGINAL NO.	DATE BUILT	SERIAL NO.	DATE VACATED	DISPOSITION	NOTE
3013			3/31/65	30217			
3014			3/31/65	30218			
3015			3/31/65	30219			
3016			3/31/65	30220	7/13/70	EMD	101
3017			3/31/65	30221			
3018			4/2/65	30222	10/6/81		102
3019			4/6/65	30223			
3020			4/6/65	30224			
3021			4/10/65	30225	11/12/71	BN	103
3022			4/10/65	30226			

U30B — GE — 3000-HP — 72,000 POUNDS T.E. — 287,000 POUNDS WEIGHT

LAST NO.	PREVIOUS NO.	ORIGINAL NO.	DATE BUILT	SERIAL NO.	DATE VACATED	DISPOSITION	NOTE
3051	751		9/15/67	36451			104
3052	752		9/18/67	36452			105
3053	753		9/19/67	36453			106
3054	754		9/21/67	36454			107
3055	755		9/21/67	36455			108

U30B — GE — 3000-HP — 72,000 POUNDS T.E. — 289,000 POUNDS WEIGHT

LAST NO.	PREVIOUS NO.	ORIGINAL NO.	DATE BUILT	SERIAL NO.	DATE VACATED	DISPOSITION	NOTE
3056	756		9/10/68	36833			109
3057	757		9/11/68	36834			110
3058	758		9/18/68	36835			111
3059	759		9/18/68	36836			112

U30B — GE — 3000-HP — 72,000 POUNDS T.E. — 285,000 POUNDS WEIGHT

LAST NO.	PREVIOUS NO.	ORIGINAL NO.	DATE BUILT	SERIAL NO.	DATE VACATED	DISPOSITION	NOTE
3060	760		4/21/69	36998			113
3061	761		4/21/69	36999			114
3062	762		4/22/69	37000			115
3063	763		4/23/69	37001			116
3064	764		4/24/69	37002			117
	765		4/29/69	37003	6/15/72	Schnitzer	118
3066	766		4/30/69	37004			119
3067	767		5/6/69	37005			120
3068	768		5/6/69	37006			121
3069	769		5/7/69	37007			122

U30B — GE — 3000-HP — 72,000 POUNDS T.E. — 286,275 POUNDS WEIGHT

LAST NO.	PREVIOUS NO.	ORIGINAL NO.	DATE BUILT	SERIAL NO.	DATE VACATED	DISPOSITION	NOTE
3070	770		7/23/71	35935	3/3/81	Assoc. Metals, Sacramento	123
3071	771		7/16/71	35936	3/3/81	Assoc. Metals, Sacramento	124

GP40 — EMD — 3000-HP — 69,250 POUNDS T.E. — 277,000 POUNDS WEIGHT

LAST NO.	PREVIOUS NO.	ORIGINAL NO.	DATE BUILT	SERIAL NO.	DATE VACATED	DISPOSITION	NOTE
3501			5/18/66	31662			
3502			5/20/66	31663			
3503			5/19/66	31664			
3504			5/20/66	31665			
3505			5/17/66	31666	7/1/70	EMD	125
3506			5/66	31667			
3507			5/25/66	31668			
3508			5/24/66	31669			
3509			5/26/66	31670			
3510			5/21/66	31671			

GP-40 No. 3503 awaits a call at Oakland about 1971. Morrison-Knudsen's remanufacturing of 15 GP-40s included GV and GX cards, a performance control panel, and the elimination of traction motor field shunting. **Virgil Staff**

GP-40-2 unit 3550 is spotted at Stockton on May 24, 1980. Both classes have module control cards and motor-driven switchgear, but the dual white oscillating light on the nose is found only on the 3550 class. This is the current (1982) paint scheme and dates from early 1979 when the 2251 and the 3541 received this livery as a test.
Virgil Staff

GP40 — EMD — 3000-HP — 69,250 POUNDS T.E. — 277,000 POUNDS WEIGHT

LAST NO.	PREVIOUS NO.	ORIGINAL NO.	DATE BUILT	SERIAL NO.	DATE VACATED	DISPOSITION	NOTE
3511			3/16/67	33056			
3512			3/17/67	33057			
3513			3/17/67	33058			
3514			3/16/67	33059			
3515			3/18/67	33060			
3516			3/18/67	33061			

GP40 — EMD — 3000-HP — 69,250 POUNDS T.E. — 277,000 POUNDS WEIGHT

LAST NO.	PREVIOUS NO.	ORIGINAL NO.	DATE BUILT	SERIAL NO.	DATE VACATED	DISPOSITION	NOTE
3517			8/21/70	36824			
3518			8/21/70	36825			
3519			8/21/70	36826			
3520			8/21/70	36827			
3521			8/21/70	36828			
3522			8/22/70	36783			
3523			8/21/70	36784			
3524			8/28/70	36785			
3525			8/28/70	36786			
3526			8/27/70	36787			

GP40 — EMD — 3000-HP — 69,250 POUNDS T.E. — 277,000 POUNDS WEIGHT

LAST NO.	PREVIOUS NO.	ORIGINAL NO.	DATE BUILT	SERIAL NO.	DATE VACATED	DISPOSITION	NOTE
3527			8/13/71	37838	5/12/80	Assoc. Metals, Sacramento	126
3528			8/13/71	37839			
3529			8/13/71	37840			
3530			8/14/71	37841			
3531			8/13/71	37842			
3532			8/14/71	37843			
3533			8/13/71	37844			
3534			8/13/71	37845			
3535			8/14/71	37846			
3536			8/13/71	37847			
3537			8/14/71	37848			
3538			9/15/71	37849			
3539			9/14/71	37850			
3540	1776	3540	9/16/71	37851	5/12/80	Assoc. Metals, Sacramento	127
3541	1976	3541	9/16/71	37852			128
3542			9/17/71	37853			
3543			9/19/71	37854			
3544			9/20/71	37855			

GP40-2 — EMD — 3000-HP — 69,250 POUNDS T.E. — 277,000 POUNDS WEIGHT

LAST NO.	PREVIOUS NO.	ORIGINAL NO.	DATE BUILT	SERIAL NO.	DATE VACATED	DISPOSITION	NOTE
3545			7/8/79	786220-1			
3546			7/16/79	786220-2			
3547			7/11/79	786220-3			
3548			7/10/79	786220-4			
3549			7/14/79	786220-5			

GP40-2 — EMD — 3000-HP — 69,250 POUNDS T.E. — 277,000 POUNDS WEIGHT

LAST NO.	PREVIOUS NO.	ORIGINAL NO.	DATE BUILT	SERIAL NO.	DATE VACATED	DISPOSITION	NOTE
3550			4/19/80	786277-1			
3551			4/8/80	786277-2			
3552			4/8/80	786277-3			
3553			4/11/80	786277-4			
3554			4/12/80	786277-5			
3555			4/16/80	786277-6			
3556			4/19/80	786277-7			
3557			4/12/80	786277-8			
3558			4/15/80	786277-9			
3559			4/19/80	786277-10			

RDC2 — BUDD — 516-HP — 8,100 POUNDS T.E. — 112,500 POUNDS WEIGHT

LAST NO.	PREVIOUS NO.	ORIGINAL NO.	DATE BUILT	SERIAL NO.	DATE VACATED	DISPOSITION	NOTE
375			5/15/50	5008	4/27/62	Northern Pacific Railway	129
376			6/26/50	5010	4/27/62	Northern Pacific Railway	130

HEATER CARS — ST. LOUIS CAR CO. — 165,700 POUNDS WEIGHT

LAST NO.	PREVIOUS NO.	ORIGINAL NO.	DATE BUILT	SERIAL NO.	DATE VACATED	DISPOSITION	NOTE
591			1928		4/7/71	Great Western Enterprises	133
592			1928		2/17/72	OP&E	134

HEATER CARS — AMERICAN CAR & FOUNDRY — 170,000 POUNDS WEIGHT

LAST NO.	PREVIOUS NO.	ORIGINAL NO.	DATE BUILT	SERIAL NO.	DATE VACATED	DISPOSITION	NOTE
593			1913		2/17/72	OP&E	135

U23B engine 2259 sits at Sacramento in the late 1970s. The original paint scheme was in 939-534-738 green, with orange stripes to nose and rear, and painted backwards. Numbers were 1" apart instead of the standard 3". In late 1972 some units began receiving a large "WP" on the nose, which became standard for road power until 1979 when the 3541 and 2251 were painted in the present solid orange nose. **Virgil Staff**

A slight change in greens was made in 1971. Here, U30B unit 3060 appears in its original paint at Wendover on June 18, 1974. The WP went to "MacLeod Green" as standard in 1970, and to a slightly lighter green (939-54-738) known as "Perlman Green" in 1971. The U23Bs and other locomotives received their Perlman Green in 1972. The green became lighter still about April 1973, when Sterling Polyurethane green became standard. **Virgil Staff**

Vessel

LAS PLUMAS Albina Engine & Machine Works, Portland, Oregon.
(July 1957)

Official Number: 274346
Decked Barge Type Diesel Motor Vessel, Steel, Welded.
Western Pacific Railroad Car Ferry
Register Length: 362.4'
Register Breadth: 59.1'
Overall Length: 375.0'
Register Depth: 15.1'
Highest Fixed Point Above Water When Light: 57.2', masthead light.
Net Register Tonnage: 1533 tons
Gross Tons: 2255
Horsepower: 2100
Draft: Loaded: 10.0'. Light: 6.0'

ROSTER NOTES:
WESTERN PACIFIC RAILROAD COMPANY

NOTE
1. Retired 12/27/67 and renumbered to SN No. 405. No. 405 sold to Quincy RR by S/O 8973 dated April 9, 1973.
2. Retired 10/22/68 to ST&E account trade to ST&E for ST&E No. 1001 which then renumbered to WP No. 608. Originally UP No. 1001.
3. Retired on 10/22/68 in trade to ST&E for ST&E No. 1000 which became WP No. 607. Originally EMC demonstrator No. 889 and then UP No. 1000 prior to purchase by ST&E. WP No. 506 actually turned over to ST&E on 4/24/69.
4. Sold to GE for delivery to Pacific States Steel, Union City, Calif.
5. Sold to GE c/o Pacific States Steel of Union City, Calif. Unit moved out of Oakland 11/27/67.
6. Retired to TS and renumbered to TS No. 745(2) circa 2/12/70. Retired by TS to ST&E on 12/31/76. (WP No. 552[1] had been traded to the TS in return for the 745(1) which became the WP No. 552[2] retired 11/3/70.)
7. WP No. 554(1) retired to TS and renumbered as TS No. 744(2) on 6/12/69. Traded to Oakland Terminal Ry on 2/25/70 in exchange for ex-Spokane International No. 1216 becoming TS No. 747 on same date. WP then received TS No. 744(1) which it retired as 554(2).
8. Retired to SN along with WP No. 584 in exchange for the WP No. 926A (SN No. 303). Renumbered to SN No. 406 on 7/29/70. Retired to Levin Metals Co. and departed the property on 4/3/74.
9. Sold to CCT becoming CCT No. 50. No. 50 retired to TS on 12/31/76 in exchange for TS No. 746 which became CCT No. 80 on same date. TS No. 50, ex-CCT No. 50 (never included on TS roster), retired 1/10/77 and sold to Foster Farms, Livingston, Calif., by SO 179/76 dated 12/27/76.
10. WP Nos. 581 and 583 sold to Purdy Co. by SO 119/73. Purdy sold to Joseph Simon & Son of Tacoma, Wash., who sold units to Auto Train Co., Sanford, Fla. Units officially retired 9/10/73.
11. Cf. Engine No. 581.
12. Retired to SN along with WP No. 562 in exchange for WP No. 926A (SN No. 303). Renumbered to SN No. 407 on 7/17/70. Retired 2/15/73. Sold to Associated Metals, Sacramento.
13. Ex-EMC demonstrator No. 889; then UP No. 1000; then ST&E No. 1000. Ex-ST&E No. 1000 exchanged with WP No. 506 on 10/22/68 with No. 1000 becoming WP No. 607. Retired by WP in 5/73 after SN sold No. 405 to Quincy RR, and renumbered to SN No. 607.
14. Ex-UP No. 1001; then ST&E No. 1001. ST&E No. 1001 exchanged with WP No. 505 on 10/22/68. Renumbered to WP No. 608 on 2/7/69 and placed in service 2/12/69.
15. Traded with WP No. 712 in exchange for SN No. 301A and No. 301D acquired for sale in 5/71 and "retired" on 6/18/71 and 9/3/71 respectively. No. 711 retired by WP and renumbered to SN 711 on 7/30/71. WP Nos. 301A and 301D never placed on WP roster.
16. Traded with WP No. 711 in exchange for SN Nos. 301A and 301D acquired for sale in 5/71 and "retired" on 6/18/71 and 9/3/71 respectively. No. 712 retired by WP and renumbered to SN 712 on 7/16/71.
17. Damaged at Keddie on 5/20/70.
18. Damaged in derailment at Beowawe with Nos. 2003, 924D, and 916A on 9/21/63.
19. Renumbered to 925A on 7/12/68.
20. Renumbered to 925D on 7/5/68.
21. F3 cab units given suffix letters sometime between 1950 and April 1951.
22. Ex-NYO&W No. 503. Acquired by SN in 1957 to become SN No. 303 although it was never so numbered except on paper. Leased to WP on 8/2/57 becoming WP No. 801D. Renumbered to WP No. 926A on 8/10/68. Lease canceled with WP on 6/30/70 and unit ownership transferred to WP in 7/70 in exchange for WP No. 562 and No. 584.
23. Sold to GE care of Precision Engineering Co., Mt. Vernon, Ill.
24. Renumbered to 915A(2) on 4/21/70. Destroyed at Pollock on 5/19/72.
25. Renumbered from 804C to 804D on 6/7/51. 804D renumbered to 916D(2) on 4/14/70.
26. Renumbered from 805C to 805D on 4/11/51.
27. Renumbered from 805B in April 1970.
28. 901 renumbered to 901A on 1/11/50 and to 902A(2) on 5/5/60.
29. Renumbered from 901C on 1/11/50.
30. 902 renumbered to 902A on 12/29/50 and to 901A(2) on 5/5/60.
31. Renumbered from 902C on 12/29/50.
32. Renumbered from 903 on 12/23/49.
33. Renumbered from 903C on 12/23/49.
34. Renumbered from 904 in Dec. 1949.
35. Renumbered from 904C in Dec. 1949.
36. Renumbered from 905 on 1/5/50.
37. Renumbered from 905C on 1/5/50.
38. Renumbered from 906 on 1/6/50.
39. Renumbered from 906C on 1/20/50.
40. Renumbered from 907 on 1/12/50.
41. Renumbered from 907C on 1/12/50.
42. Renumbered from 908 on 1/7/50.
43. Renumbered from 908C on 1/7/50.
44. Renumbered from 909 on 1/21/50.
45. Renumbered from 909C on 1/21/50.
46. Renumbered from 910 on 12/24/49.
47. Renumbered from 910C on 12/24/49.
48. Renumbered from 911 on 1/27/50.
49. Renumbered from 911C on 2/15/50.
50. Renumbered from 912 on 1/2/50.
51. Renumbered from 912C on 1/2/50.
52. 901A renumbered to 901B on 1/11/50 and to 902B(2) on 5/5/60.
53. Renumbered from 901B on 1/11/50.
54. 902A renumbered to 902B on 12/29/50 and to 901B(2) on 5/5/60.
55. Renumbered from 902B on 12/29/50.
56. Renumbered from 903A on 12/23/49.
57. Renumbered from 903B on 12/23/49.
58. Renumbered from 904A in Dec. 1949.
59. Renumbered from 904B in Dec. 1949.
60. Renumbered from 905A on 1/5/50.
61. 905B renumbered to 905C on 1/5/50 and to 911C(2) on 5/17/66.
62. Renumbered from 906A on 1/6/50.
63. Renumbered from 906B on 1/20/50.
64. Renumbered from 907A on 1/12/50.
65. Renumbered from 907B on 1/12/50.
66. Renumbered from 908A on 1/7/50.
67. Renumbered from 908B on 1/7/50.
68. Renumbered from 909A on 1/21/50.
69. Renumbered from 909B on 1/21/50.
70. Renumbered from 910A on 12/24/49.
71. Renumbered from 910B on 12/24/49.
72. Renumbered from 911A on 1/27/50.
73. 911B renumbered to 911C on 2/15/50 and to 905C(2) on 5/17/66.
74. Renumbered from 912A on 1/2/50.
75. Renumbered from 912B on 1/2/50.
76. 920A(1) renumbered to 913A(2) in Oct. 1971. Renumbered to 913 on 7/1/75. Retired and donated to Cal State RR Museum, Sacramento, 5/5/81.
77. Consigned to Chehalis Industrial Tract, Chehalis, Wash.
78. 915A(1) renumbered to 804A(2) on 4/21/70.
79. Renumbered from 915D on 7/1/75.
80. Damaged in derailment at Beowawe, 9/21/63.
81. Renumbered 4/14/70.
82. Consigned to Mount Newman Mining Co., Australia.
83. Renumbered from 917D on 7/1/75. Unit possesses a "C" engine and functions at about 1750 horsepower.
84. Renumbered from 918A in Sept. 1971.
85. Renumbered from 918D on 7/1/75.
86. Renumbered from 913A(1) in Oct. 1971.
87. "C" engine installed in 1970 but unit rated for 1500 horsepower. Damaged beyond economical repair at Westwood, 11/7/71.
88. Renumbered from 921D on 7/1/75.
89. Renumbered from 922A in Sept. 1971.
90. Consigned to Mount Newman Mining Co., Australia.
91. Damaged in derailment at Beowawe, 9/21/63.
92. Renumbered from 915C(1) in April 1970.
93. Renumbered to 806B on 6/14/67 and renumbered back to 920B on 9/30/70.
94. Consigned to W.A. & G. R.R.
95. Destroyed in derailment at Beowawe, 9/21/63.
96. Destroyed on U.P. at Devils Creek, 11/17/79.
97. Destroyed at Deeth, Nevada, with 3018 on 9/12/81. Scrapped on site.
98. Destroyed on BN in October 1977. Not retired by FRA.
99. Destroyed in derailment at Floka, 3/28/70. WP No. 3011 had earlier been substituted for the 2003 which destroyed in 1963.
100. WP No. 3012 substituted for No. 730 destroyed in derailment in 1963.

101	Destroyed at Floka, 3/28/70.	
102	Destroyed at Deeth, Nev., along with 2259 on 9/12/81. Scrapped on site.	
103	Destroyed on BN, 7/16/71. Sold to BN.	
104	Renumbered from 751 on 5/15/72.	
105	Renumbered from 752 on 7/24/72.	
106	Renumbered from 753 on 7/24/72.	
107	Renumbered from 754 on 7/19/72.	
108	Renumbered from 755 on 5/10/72.	
109	Renumbered from 756 on 6/17/72.	
110	Renumbered from 757 on 6/19/72.	
111	Renumbered from 758 on 5/17/72.	
112	Renumbered from 759 at Morrison–Knudsen.	
113	Renumbered from 760 on 5/24/72.	
114	Renumbered from 761 on 5/22/72.	
115	Renumbered from 762 off the property on 12/8/72.	
116	Renumbered from 763 on 5/24/72.	
117	Renumbered from 764 on 6/27/72.	
118	Damaged beyond repair on the BN, July 1971.	
119	Renumbered from 766 on 5/31/72.	
120	Renumbered from 767 on 5/9/72.	
121	Renumbered from 768 on 5/15/72.	
122	Renumbered from 769 on 7/1/72.	
123	Ex-GE demo. No. 303; rebuilt for WP as No. 770 and renumbered to 3070 on 4/19/72.	
124	Ex-GE demo No. 304; rebuilt for WP as No. 771 and renumbered to 3071 on 10/4/72.	
125	Destroyed at Floka, Nev., 3/28/70.	
126	Destroyed at Hayward, Calif., on 4/9/80.	
127	Orig. 3540. Renumbered for Bicentennial, 3/22/76. Returned to service as 3540 on 12/2/79. Destroyed at Hayward on 4/9/80.	
128	Renumbered for Bicentennial, 5/6/76. Renumbered back to 3541 on 2/21/79 and placed in service on 4/27/79.	
129	Became NP No. B-31 and said to have been operated, along with the B-32, from Fargo, N. Dak., to Winnipeg, Manitoba, Canada, between July 1962 through May 1969. Subsequently stored in Seattle and sold to Amtrak by BN on 8/1/72.	
130	Became NP No. B-32. Cf. Note 129. Stored at Great Falls, Mont., prior to sale to Amtrak, 8/1/72.	
131	Ex-MP No. 1047; ex-TS No. 745(1). Traded to WP for WP No. 552(1) and renumbered to 552(2) circa 2/20/70. Retired 11/3/70 and sold to Chrome Crankshaft Co.	
132	Ex-MP No. 1058; ex-TS No. 744(1). Traded to WP for WP No. 554(1) which became TS No. 744(2). TS No. 744(1) renumbered to 554(2) and retired on 2/15/71.	
133	Ex-G.N. Ry. Heater Car No. 1 purchased from GN in 1968. Equipment installed by G.N. in 1928 and re-equipped in 1946. Equipped with two CFK-4225 Vapor–Clarkson steam generators producing 2250 lbs./hr. each. Boiler water capacity: 3570 gals. Fuel oil capacity: 1100 gals. Length over buffers: 43'–8 1/8".	
134	Ex-G.N. Ry. Heater Car No. 2. Equipment installed by G.N. in 1928 and re-equipped in 1946. Same specs as for Heater Car No. 1.	
135	Ex-G.N. Ry. Heater Car. Converted by G.N. in 1943 and diesel generator applied in 1952. Equipped with two CFK-4225 Vapor–Clarkson steam generators producing 2250 lbs./hr. each. Boiler water capacity: 4860 gals. Fuel oil capacity: 1180 gals. Length over buffers: 44'–2 1/2".	

LOCOMOTIVE ROSTER BY CLASSES

CLASS	CLASS BY TE	INCLUSIVE UNITS
501	S-50	501-503
504	S-50	504-511
551	S-57	551-558
559	S-57	559-562
563	S-57	563-564
581	S-60	581-585
601	S-62	601-606
607	S-62	607-608
701	RS-62	701-709
710	RS-62	710-713
725	RS-62	725-732
801	D-176	801-803
801D	—	801D
804	D-176	804-805
901	D-225	901-903
904	D-225	904-906
907	D-225	907-912
913	D-239	913-921
922	D-239	922-924
1501	—	1501-1503
2001	RS-64	2001-2006
2007	RS-64	2007-2010
2251	—	2251-2265
3001	RS-65	3001-3010
3011	RS-65	3011-3012
3013	RS-65	3013-3022
3051	RS-72	3051-3055
3056	RS-72	3056-3059
3060	RS-72	3060-3069
3070	—	3070-3071
3501	RS-68	3501-3510
3511	RS-68	3511-3516
3517	RS-68	3517-3526
3527	—	3527-3544
3545	—	3545-3549
3550	—	3550-3559
375	—	375-376

*552(2) and 554(2) were never given a class designation on the WP.

LOCOMOTIVES CURRENTLY ON THE W.P. ROSTER AS OF NOV. 1981

SW9	601-606
NW2	608
GP7	701, 703-710, 713
GP9	725, 727-729, 731-732
F7	915, 917, 918, 921
SW1500	1501-1503
GP20	2001-2002, 2004-2010
U23B	2251-2255, 2257-2258, 2260-2265.
GP35	3001-3006, 3008-3010, 3012-3015, 3017, 3019-3020, 3022
U30B	3051-3064, 3066-3069
GP40	3501-3504, 3506-3526, 3528-3539, 3541-3544
GP40-2	3545-3559

WP Subsidiary Companies

DIESEL ROSTER OF THE TIDEWATER SOUTHERN RAILWAY

CLASS	ROAD NO.	BUILDER	SERIAL NO.	DATE BUILT	WEIGHT	T.E.	MODEL	NOTES
735	735	GE	28337	11/46	88,000	26,400	44-ton	TS-1
741	741	GE	29468	1/48	138,000	41,300	70-ton	TS-2
741	742	GE	29470	1/48	138,000	41,300	70-ton	TS-3
741	743	GE	31726	6/53	138,000	41,300	70-ton	TS-4
744	744(1)	Alco	75659	3/48	230,000	57,500	S2	TS-5
	744(2)	Alco	70953	11/43	230,000	57,500	S2	TS-6
744	745(1)	Alco	76774	5/49	230,400	57,600	S2	TS-7
	745(2)	Alco	70207	8/43	230,000	57,500	S2	TS-8
746	746	Alco	77840	12/49	247,400	61,800	RS1	TS-9
746	747	Alco	77171	10/49	247,400	61,800	RS1	TS-10

NOTES:

TS-1—Renumbered from TS No. 135 in March 1952. Sold to Pickering Lumber Corp., Standard, Calif., on Apr. 8, 1967.
TS-2—Renumbered from TS No. 141 on Dec. 11, 1951. Retired Nov. 7, 1966, and sold to Preston W. Duffy & Son, Columbus, Ohio.
TS-3—Renumbered from TS No. 142 on May 22, 1951. Retired Feb. 8, 1968, and sold to Preston W. Duffy & Son.
TS-4—Retired August 16, 1968, and sold to Preston W. Duffy & Son.
TS-5—Renumbered to WP No. 554(2) on July 7, 1969, in trade for WP No. 554(1) which became TS No. 744(2). TS No. 744(1) originally MP No. 1058 acquired in 1967 and retired as WP No. 554(2) on Feb. 15, 1971.
TS-6—Renumbered from WP No. 554(1) on June 12, 1969. Assigned to Oakland Terminal Ry. on Feb. 25, 1970, in exchange for ex-Spokane International No. 1216 becoming TS No. 747 on same date.
TS-7—Ex-MP No. 1047 purchased from Preston W. Duffy & Son in 1967 and renumbered to TS No. 745(1). Traded to WP for WP No. 552(1) and renumbered to WP No. 552(2) circa Feb. 20, 1970. WP No. 552(1) became TS No. 745(2) in interval between Feb. 12-20, 1970. WP No. 552(1) retired Nov. 3, 1970, and sold to Chrome Crankshaft Co., Bell Gardens, Calif.
TS-8—Renumbered from WP No. 552(1) in Feb., 1970. WP traded its 552(1) to the TS for the 745(1). TS No. 745(2) retired to ST&E, Dec. 31, 1976.
TS-9—Ex-Spokane International No. 1218 renumbered TS No. 746 on Feb. 2, 1970, to replace TS No. 745(1) retired and traded for WP No. 552(1) which then became TS No. 745(2). TS No. 746 traded to CCT Dec. 31, 1976, in exchange for CCT No. 50 which, although never placed on the TS roster, became TS No. 563 on the same date. TS No. 746 then became CCT No. 80 and departed WP property on Jan. 13, 1977. TS No. 563 "retired" Jan. 10, 1977, and sold to Foster Farms, Livingston, Calif., by SO 179/76 dated Dec. 27, 1976.
TS-10—Ex-Spokane International No. 1216 exchanged from the Oakland Terminal Ry. with the TS No. 744(2) on Feb. 25, 1970, and became TS No. 747 on same date. Sold to Purdy Co., Ewing, Calif., in August 1975.

DIESEL ROSTER OF THE SACRAMENTO NORTHERN RAILWAY

CLASS	ROAD NO.	BUILDER	SERIAL NO.	DATE BUILT	WEIGHT	T.E.	MODEL	NOTES
141	141	GE	15121	4/42	88,000	26,400	44-ton	SN-1
142	142	GE	28331	11/46	88,000	26,400	44-ton	SN-2
142	143	GE	28332	11/46	88,000	26,400	44-ton	SN-3
142	144	GE	28334	11/46	88,000	26,400	44-ton	SN-4
142	145	GE	28335	11/46	88,000	26,400	44-ton	SN-5
142	146	GE	28336	11/46	88,000	26,400	44-ton	SN-6
142	147	GE	15120	4/42	88,000	26,400	44-ton	SN-7
201	201	GE	32297	6/55	139,000	41,300	70-ton	SN-8
201	202	GE	32595	7/56	139,000	41,300	70-ton	SN-9
301	301A	EMD	3146	1/13/48	236,500	59,000	F-3	SN-10
301	301D	EMD	3147	2/25/48	236,500	59,000	F-3	SN-11
301	303	EMD	3148	3/15/48	236,500	59,000	F-3	SN-12
401	401	EMC	906	8/17/39	201,000	50,000	SW-1	SN-13
401	402	EMC	988	12/6/39	201,000	50,000	SW-1	SN-14
403	403	Alco	74343	10/45	230,000	57,500	S-2	SN-15
403	404	Alco	76775	5/49	230,000	57,500	S-2	SN-16
405	405	Alco	69685	4/29/42	202,000	50,000	S-1	SN-17
	406	Alco	77020	2/13/50	231,000	57,500	S-2	SN-18
	407	Baldwin	71543	10/11/45	245,400	60,000	VO	SN-19
	711	EMD	18167	4/1/53	246,800	61,700	GP7	SN-20
	712	EMD	18168	4/2/53	246,800	61,700	GP7	SN-21
	607	EMC	889	10/10/39	248,000	62,000	NW2	SN-22

NOTES:

SN-1— Old No. 40 of SFNV. Renumbered to SN141 after acquisition by SN. Retired to GE on June 20, 1956.
SN-2— Retired Nov. 20, 1970. Sold to Chrome Crankshaft Co., Bell Gardens, Calif. Shipped to Anaconda, Montana.
SN-3— Retired March 7, 1969. Sold to Associated Metals, Benicia, Calif.
SN-4— Retired July 30, 1971. Sold to Chrome Crankshaft Co.
SN-5— Retired July 30, 1971. Sold to Chrome Crankshaft Co.
SN-6— Retired September 21, 1971. Sold to Chrome Crankshaft Co.
SN-7— Ex-SFNV No. 30; SFNV No. 30 originally jointly owned by WP & SFNV. SFNV No. 30 taken over by WP and purchased by SN in 1956. Retired by SN as SN No. 147 on Dec. 4, 1970. Sold to Chrome Crankshaft and shipped to Anaconda, Montana.
SN-8— Retired Feb. 9, 1968. Sold to Preston W. Duffy & Son, Columbus, Ohio.

SN-9— Retired June 26, 1967. Sold to Prescott & Northwestern R.R. via Preston W. Duffy.
SN-10— Ex-O&W No. 501 sold to SN by Hyman-Michaels Co. in July 1957 and numbered to SN No. 301. Renumbered to 301A on Mar. 10, 1960. Acquired by WP in May 1971 and retired to EMD on June 18, 1971.
SN-11— Ex-O&W No. 502 sold to SN by Hyman-Michaels Co. in July 1957 and numbered to SN No. 302. Renumbered to 301-D on Mar. 10, 1960. Acquired by WP in May 1971 and retired to EMD, Sept. 3, 1971.
SN-12— Ex-O&W No. 503 sold to SN by Hyman-Michaels Co. in July 1957. Unit carried No. 303 only on paper and was leased to the WP on Aug. 2, 1957, and renumbered to WP 801D. Renumbered to 926A on Aug. 10, 1968. Lease canceled June 30, 1970, and traded to WP in July 1970. Retired to EMD July 27, 1970.
SN-13— Ex-WP No. 501 retired to SN, Jan. 17, 1966. With SN No. 402 dieselized the SN. Sold to Corn Products Co., Stockton, Jan. 9, 1981. Retired Jan. 15, 1981.
SN-14— Ex-WP No. 502 retired to SN, March 4, 1966. With SN No. 401 dieselized the SN. Finally retired, but not yet sold, July 1, 1981.
SN-15— Ex-MP No. 1053 purchased from Preston W. Duffy & Son in 1967. Summer 1971 Chico Air Line Bridge strengthened and no longer required the lighter GEs on that line. Retired Feb. 2, 1972, and sold to Associated Metals, Sacramento.
SN-16— Ex-MP No. 1048 purchased from Preston W. Duffy & Son in 1967. Renumbered to SN No. 404 on May 29, 1967. Retired July 18, 1973, and sold to Purdy Co., Sacramento.
SN-17— Ex-WP No. 504 to SN on Dec. 27, 1967. SN sold No. 405 to Quincy RR by S/O 8973 dtd. April 9, 1973. SN then needed additional power, and received WP No. 607, May 8, 1973.
SN-18— Ex-WP No. 562 to SN on July 29, 1970. Traded to SN with WP No. 584 in exchange for WP No. 926A (SN No. 303). Retired by WP on April 3, 1974, and sold to Levin, Richmond, Calif.
SN-19— Ex-WP No. 584 to SN on July 17, 1970. Traded to SN with WP No. 562 in exchange for WP No. 926A (SN No. 303). Retired by WP on Feb. 15, 1973, and sold to Associated Metals, Sacramento.
SN-20— Ex-WP No. 711 renumbered to SN No. 711 on July 30, 1971. Acquired in trade with the WP No. 712 for SN No. 301A and 301D.
SN-21— Ex-WP No. 712 acquired and renumbered to SN No. 712 on July 16, 1971. Acquired in trade with the WP No. 711 for SN No. 301A and 301D.
SN-22— Retired from WP to SN in May 1973 after SN sold No. 405 to Quincy R.R. SN No. 607 operating on SN effective May 11, 1973. (No. 607 had been received by the WP from ST&E, No. 1000, on Oct. 22, 1968, and ST&E received WP No. 506 in trade on Oct. 22, 1968.)

Selective Bibliography of Company Files

Since the mass of material in this study is taken from primary sources, the detailed development of footnotes and bibliography would be prohibitive to the extent that such documentation would entail dozens of additional pages. However, an abbreviated list of significant files, most of which have undergone destruction, is here included.

007	Weather Reports	417.05	Watering, Fueling, Water and Oil Tanks
023	Fuel	417.1	Main Engine; Pistons, Heads, Cylinders
200.44	Cost of Operating Diesel Locomotives	417.11	Traction Motors
200.46	Condition of Engines	417.2	Supply of Wheels, Diesel Locomotives
200.47	Operating Statistics of Diesel Locomotives	417.22	Air Brakes, Dynamic Brakes....
200.48	Operating Statistics of Steam Locomotives	417.6	Safety Appliances, Handholds, Grab Irons, Steps....
200.49	Selected Train Service and Locomotive Costs	417.62	Piping Diesel Locomotives
221.51	Accounts, Additions and Betterments (AFE's)	417.66	Whistles, Bells, Horns, Headlights, Back Up Lights
353	Fuel Oil Stations and Facilities	420.	Floating or Marine Equipment
353.2	Water Stations and Water Treatment	420.5	Las Plumas
401.1	Lubrication Schedule	430.	Dieselization at Various Terminals
401.12	Diesel Fuel Oil	430.14	Shop and MM Orders
401.3	Lubrication, General	431.01	Lettering, Numbering, Painting
410.23	Air Brake Equipment, Locomotives	520.01	Instructions to Train and Engine Crews
411.04	Condition of Locomotives	520.3	Running of Trains
411.14	Spark Arrestors	520.31	Train Schedules and Speed of Trains
412.001.1	*California Zephyr* Trains	522.2	Movement and Performance of Freight Trains
415.		522.21	Delay of Freight Trains
415.001	RDC, Construction, Changes, etc.	530.	Utilization of Locomotives
417.	Diesel Circulars	530.01	Locomotive Power Situation
417.001	Purchase of Diesel Locomotives; Construction, Dimensions, Design, Weight, Building and Purchasing, Performance, Test Runs....	530.2	Assignment and Transfer of Locomotives
		531.	Tonnage Rating of Locomotives
		532.	Doubleheading Locomotives; Length of Locomotive Runs
417.001.1	*California Zephyr* Diesels	MBR	Morning Business Report
417.003	Change in Construction	—	Transportation Department *Bulletins*
417.01	Assignment of Newly Acquired Diesels	—	Transportation Department *Notices*
417.02	Boilers or Steam Generators	—	System *Timetables* since 1939
417.03	Wiring; Batteries, Diesel Locomotives	—	Operating Department *Rules* for 1952, 1961, 1971
417.03.1	Electrical Control Circuits and Components	—	*Freight Schedule and Train Blocking Instructions*, 1976
417.043	Repairs and Servicing of Diesels		

INDEX

A
Accounts, store 61, 62
Airlines, freezing of 86, 91
Alazon 10
Alco defects 24
Alco, S-1 .... 23, **24**, 26
Alco, S-2 .... 26, 44, 46, **202**
Alco, S-4 .... 47, 48, **202**
Allen, Grant 82, 127, 128
Almanor **89**, 97
Antelope Hill 79, 82, **150**, **190**
Altamont **31, 35, 45, 47, 53, 54, 64, 72, 93,** 130, **156**
Anderson, Norman 146, 147, 162, 172, 174-176, 179, 192
Arrestors, spark 159-161
Assignment of Power 11, 12, 21, 23, 24-26, 46, 48, 52, 55, 56, 63, 64, 72, 96, 111-113, 127-132, 148, 195
Availability 54-59, 63, 64, 76, 114, 163
Axles 186

B
Baldwin, VO-1000 .... 26, 49, 50, **202**
Battle Mountain **161**
Bieber 10, 49, **105**, 128
Blackout shields 24
Blairsden **175**
BN, minimum continuous speed 196
Brake equipment 188, 189
Brakes, FT dynamic 73, 74
Braking amperage, dynamic 73, 188, 190
Braking, dynamic 26, 53, 155-157, 161, 173, 175, 178, 188, 190, 195, 197
Braking limits, dynamic 157, 197
Break-in-twos 21, 22, 88, 130, 190
Broncos 197

C
California Zephyr **33,** 37, 39, 43, 98-100, 118, 162, 163, 166-168
    Baggage car tanks 89, 91, 98, 99, 100
    Generator cars 162, 163
Chestnut Junction 10
Chilcoot **162**
Christy, Myron 104, 123, 146, 148, 155, **157**, 163, 164, 166-168, 191
Clinton Jct. 10
Clio **99, 103**
Competition 10, 151, 167, 168
Compressors 188
Consists, power 37, 171
Contri, Larry 52, 111, 114, 127, 131
Control Case 138
Control circuits 149, 157
Controls, dual 52, 186, 194
Cooper-Bessemer engine 141
Crew qualification 21, 62, 63
Curtis, Glen 23, 52, 111, 112, 122, 123, 128
Curvatures 10
Cuyler, E.T. 21, **22**, 38, 42, 43, 46, 51, 52, 55, 57-61, 64, 75, 78, 81-83, 87, 91, 102, 104, 107, 108, 114, 127, 128, 131, 138, 140, 144, 146, 148, 150, 153, 155, 157-159, 162, 163, 166-169, 171, 192, 193, 194
Cylinder heads, liners, seals 75, 76, 88, 89, 91, 99, 170

D
Decks, dirty 169, 170
Delays 62, 63, 150, 163

Del Paso **154**
Derrick 37 166
Diesel advantages 12, 17, 104
Diesel retirement 138, 141, 142, 144, 157
Dieselization 26, 27, 43, 44, 46, 47, 49, 53, 54, 109, 111-113, 127
Dieselization, percentage 41, 44, 46-49, 53, 54, 61, 62
Dieselization Plan A 44, 46-49, 52-54, 109, 111
Dieselization Plan B 43, 44, 49, 54, 109, 111-114, 127, 128
Division, Eastern 44, 79
Duggan, John 21, 23, 64, 72, 100, 109

E
Electrification 158
Elko 49, 53, 55, 83, 96, 97, 100, 102, 107, 165, **187**
Elsey, Charles 10, **11,** 13, 23
EMD (Electro-Motive Division, General Motors):
    FT assignments 21, 26, 63, 64, 72, 89
    FT cooling system 59, 91
    FT(WP) 20, 21, 25, 26, 39, 74, 200, **207**
    F-3 .... 37, 39, 40, 43, 44, 49, 200, **207**
    F-7 .... 44, 48, 49, 79, 80, 200, **208**
    FP-7 .... 46, 48, 99, 109, 200, **208**
    GP-7 .... 52, 54, 113, 170, 174, **205**
    GP-9 .... 88, 89, 129, 152, 170, 174, **205**
    GP-20 .... 138, 141, 153, 170, 178, **210**
    GP-35 .... 141, 142, 173-175, 177, 178, **210**
    GP-40 .... 142, 144, 175, 179, 193, **213**
    GP-40-2 .... 193, 199, 213
    NW-2 .... 148, **203**
    Studies 43
    SW-1 .... 11, 12, **200**
    SW-9 .... 53, 113, 129, **203**
    SW1500 .... 193, **205**
    Two unit combinations 91, 93, 94, 109, 113, 127
Engines, comparison 567 with 201A 12
Engines, four cycle 141, 142
Englebright, E.W. 10
Ex Parte 174 85
Exposition Flyer 39-41, 43, 44, 109

F
Feather River Canyon 16, 21, 77, 78, 83, 91, 106, 129, 130, 150
Firemen 11, 12, 62, 194
Flangers 186
Flannery, R.G. 108, 191, **197**, 198, 199
Flynn, John 59, 172
Footboards 186, 194
Forces 43, 49, 56-60, 83, 114, 163, 166, 192
Fuel consumption and tests 11, 18, 19, 48, 62, 88, 89, 96, 101, 102, 128, 144
Fuel quality 76, 104, 105
Fuel saver system 194, 195
Fuel statistics 11, 12, 48, 62, 127
Fuel tank enlargement 100
Fuel tanks 103
Fueling and watering 13, 21, 23, 26, 49, 56, 96-103, 117, 142, 164, 194

G
General Electric–EMD incompatibility 146, 190
GE, U23B 179, 180, 190, 193, **215**
GE, U30B 144, 146, 175, 179, 180, 190, 193, **215**
Gear ratio 80, 188
Generators, steam 38, 41, 88, 89, 91, 98, 162, 163

Gerlach 55, 99
Gleason, E.E. 38, 47, **49,** 51, 52, 81, 100, 104, 112, 123, 127, 158
General Motors GM-103. . . . . 13-18, **19**
General Motors Train of Tomorrow **38**
Gould empire 167, 199
Grades. 10, 82
Greenville **159**

H

Headlights and indicators 9, 24, 92-95, 205, 210, 213
Helpers, diesel 52, 81, 111, 113, 127-129, 131, 149, 197
Hercules **123, 125, 126**
Horns 21, 187, 188
Horsepower and problems 146, 170-180, 188
Hot boxes 150
Humaconna **123, 125, 126**
Hydraulic, Alco 158
Hydraulic, Krauss-Maffei 158

I

Idling. 88, 89, 106
Injectors, sticking 96
Interdivisional runs 198

K

Keddie 21, **28,** 47, 49, 55, **57, 81,** 83, 96, 97, 111, 127, **134, 151,**
182, 183, 198
Keddie wye 149, 153
Korean War 49
Knolls **145**

L

Lakepoint **196**
Lights, ground 93
Line, gradient 7, 62
Locomotives, Superintendent of 192
Loftus, D.L. 132, 141
Lubrication and lubrication schedules 106-108, 193, 194
Lubrication laboratory **106,** 108, 194
Lynch, Jim 82, 91, 92, 103, 129, 157

M

M-601 . . . . **132**
MacLeod, Donald. 148, 191
Maintenance, controlled 193
Maintenance costs 47, 49, 57, 61, 83, 141, 164, 194
Maintenance, progressive. 56, 59, 60, 193, 194
Maintenance schedules. 21, 43, 56, 57, 64, 150, 163, 194
Marquis, R.G. 191, 197
Marysville. **22, 34**
Mason **136**
Mason, E.W. 10, **11,** 20, 23, 76
Medallions 205, 207, 208, 210
Michelson, L.D. 143, 144, 146, 155, **157**
Midway 54
Miller, Jack **108,** 192, 194
Mitchell, Harry 43
Moccasin **131**
Modifications 83-88, 96, 99, 117, 118, 149, 169-180, 190
Morrison-Knudsen 195, 210, 213
Muhl, Karl 12
Munson, H.C. 47, 48, 53, 54, 82, 99, 100, 105, 111, 112, 124, 129,
141, 150-153, 155
Mustard, R.F. 89, 155, **160,** 192, 197
M.V. Las Plumas 10, 122-126, 198

N

NCE 10, 46, 47, 49, 77, 149, 155, 197
Newman, Howard 191, 198, 199

Newrail 198
Niles Canyon **32, 41, 110,** 112
Niles tower **140**
Nosing. 53, 113, 129

O

Oakland 10, 39, **42,** 43, 49, 55, **60, 70,** 83, 97, 98, 100, 121
Odermatt, C.W. 12
Oil disposal and reclamation 107, 108
O'Neill, William 10, 13, 15, 20, 23, **38,** 39, 47, 51, 55, 75, 76, 86, 91
Oroville 21, 26, 43, 44, 55, 56, 58-60, 64, **66,** 72, 76, 83, **84,** 91, 94,
96-98, 100, 107, 114, 127, 149, 153, 163, 164, 166, 167, 170
Oroville line change **36**

P

Paint:
    Alco 24, 29, 200, **202**
    Baldwin **200, 202**
    FT **20,** 26, **63, 74,** 207
    F-3 . . . . 37, **207**
    F-7 . . . . 46, **208**
    FP-7 . . . . 46, **208**
    GP-7 . . . . 53, 205
    GP-9 . . . . **205**
    GP-35 . . . . **210**
    GP-40-2 . . . . **9, 213**
    MacLeod green 210, 215
    Perlman green 215
    Solid orange 203
    Sterling Polyurethane **215**
    SW-1 . . . . 12, **200**
    SW-9 . . . . 53, **203**
    U23B. 215
    U30B **172,** 215
Paired trackage 10
Palisade canyon. **198**
Paxton **9, 17, 31, 95**
Performance studies 146-148
Perlman, A.E. 108, 168, 191, **192**
Perlman-Flannery contributions 192-194, 197, 199
Pilkinton, D.F. 108, 155, 191
Pleasanton **43, 172**
Piggyback and container 154
Plows 186
Pool, Great Northern 113, 114, 128, 149, 196
Pool, Union Pacific 196
Portola 49, 54, 55, **58, 62, 78,** 83, 91, 94, 97, 99, 100, 101, 103,
137, 180, 203
Power, location on train 89, 188, 190
Preblocking 163
Proctor **107**
Pulga. **86, 101, 184**

Q

Quigley, J.P. 11, 23
Quincy Junction **61**

R

Ratings, drag 77-79, 82
Ratings, north line 77-81
Ratings, tonnage 15, 16, 18, 25, 27, 77-81, 109, 202, 205, 208, 210
Ratio, bad order 191, 192, 194
Ratio, operating 195
Ratio, transportation 127-132
Receptacles 186
Reciprocity 168
Relay, ground protective 190
Reno branch 46, 49-51, **173,** 188
Reorganization, locomotive department 167
Repairs 12, 26, 27, 83, 150, 157

Repairs, running	60, 62
Rich Bar	**139**
Rings	76
Ring breakage, GP20	171
Rio Grande, power exchange	132
Road foremen	21, 62, 63, 78
Roadside improvements	197-199
Rolling stock, quantity	199
Ronan, R.T.	59, 170
Roster, total	10, 27
Roundhouses	43, 49, 55, 57-60, 66, 67, 164, 192
Rowley	**111**
Royal Gorge and RDC	44, 48, 49, 91, 109, 110, 115-118

S

Sacramento	49, 55, **68, 70**, 83, 96, 97, **121**, 163, 165, **166**, 168, 192, 195
Sacramento Northern	44, 46, 52, 85, 198, 199
Salduro	**114**
Sale of Western Pacific	198, 199
Salt flats	**149, 194**
Salt Lake City	55, 96, 97, 99, 100, 101, **130**, 132
San Francisco	10, 55, **92**, 97, **193**
San Francisco, general offices	10
San Francisco, Chief Mechanical Officer move to	192
San Jose	83, 97
Schedules	99, 100-103, 127, 129-131, 138, 142, 150-153, 163, 164
School, training	194
Schriefer, R.E.	60, 138, 192, 194
Shideler, Richard	108, 146, 155, 162
Shutters	48, 59, 91, 92
Slaves	158, 159
Smith, Edward	10, 13
Speed, minimum continuous	39, 79, 111, 171
Speeds, train	26, 128, 131, 152, 153, 167, 197
Spring Garden	**169, 176**
Stapp, Henry	21
Statistics, operating	10, 20, 24-26, 44, 46-48, 58, 61, 72, 148, 150, 151, 157, 166, 167, 191, 193-195
Steam:	
C-43	51, 77, **109, 112**
Costs	54, 83, 111
Steam–diesel comparison	11, 12-19, 23, 26, 41, 48, 83
Flying Scotsman	**124**
GS-6	**25**, 41, 77, **166**
Steam helpers	17, 47, 78, 79, 81, 111
M-80	**18**, 19, 46, 47, 77, 79
M-100	**15, 16**, 20
M-137/151	**15**, 16-18, 46, 77
MK-60	16, 49, 77, **78**, 111
Policy for use	23-27, 44, 46, 49, 52, 53, 109, 111, 113
Repairs	27, 43, 49, 53, **166**
Retirement	27, 43, **44**, 46, 49, 53, 54
Switchers	**23**
TP-29	**27**
X4449 East	**187**
Steps, foot	194
Stevens, W.F.	39, **40**, 43, 88, 108, 172
Stockton	**40**, 49, 55, **71**, 83, 96, 97, 163, **164**, 165-167, 191, 192, 195
Store stock, dual	158
Sunol	**50, 118**
Switcher assignment	11, 12, 23, 24, 46, 49, 52, 109, 111-113, 131, 148, 157, 174

T

Tenders, passenger	**87**, 91, 111
Tests:	
Alco	46, 49
Alco Century 415	143, 144
Alco Century 628	142
Alco 636	**144**
Alco DL 640	140, 141
Alco DL-701	139, 140
AT&SF X2667	52
Baldwin 1501	50, 51
California Zephyr with one unit	162, 163
EMD 100	52
EMD 754	37, 38
FT	79, 80
F-7	79-81
GP-20	139-141
GP-40	143-146
SD-24	138
SD-45	143, 144
SW-1	11, 12
Weyerhaeuser EMD 302-303	52
5 units	81, 82, 126, 128-131
6 units	149, 150
7 units	155
9500 hp	142
FM 1503	51
GE U25B	141
GE U30B	142, 143
GE U33B	143-146
Reno Line	49, 109
Tidewater Southern	44, 113, 199
Tobin	**185**
Tonnage and tests	44, 77-82, 124, 127, 129, 131, 138, 142, 149-151, 153, 191, 195, 197
Track, double	10, 62
Traction motor rating	39, 46, 79, 81, 129, 139, 142, 145, 202
Traction motors	12, 24, 26, 39, 46, 53, 55, 79, 81, 129, 139, 142, 152, 153, 170, 171, 178, 190
Traffic	10, 129
Traffic density	10
Training	11, 12, 21, 56, 57, 62, 63
Trains, symbol and other listings:	
AP	**93**, 144
Cal	131, 139, 145, 146, 150
CFS	46, 72, 82, 113, 127, 128, 131, 139, 151
Advance CFS	101, 151
CIX	176, 180, 183
Advance CMS	101, **145**
Expediter	128, **143**, 145, 151
FB	101, 103, 127, 130
Ford Fast	**161**
CIX	**176, 180, 183**
FMS	127
GGM	**51, 54, 72, 90**, 102, 103, 139-142, 151, 153, **156**
GRW	**162**
GWS	79, 81, 130, 131, 141, 143
NCX	81, 111, 114, 128, 141, 149, 160
PBF	130, 140-142, 151, 153
PC	127, 128, 130, 151
RT	72
SLW	130, 131
Special service	151
SWG	111, 127-129, 139, 143, 145, 146, 149, 151
TOF	**95**, 103
WPE	**101, 184**
53-54	50, 64, 80, 112, 127
61-62	14, 16, 19, 21, 52, 63, 79, 99, 127, **172**
78	79
153-154	80
181-182	19
Transition	26, 38-40, 43, 46, 177-179, 189, 190, 195
Transport, WPT	192
Trucks	48, 113, 129, 146
Turbochargers, GP20	170, 171, 174

U

Union Pacific merger	199
Union Pacific No. 50	158
Units, maximum number	157
Utilization	54, 57, 113, 114, 131, 157, 163, 167

V

Virgilia 63, **181**

W

Wendover 49, 54, 55, **67,** 83, 96, 97, **98,** 99, 100, 103, 127, **148, 155**
Wendover Hill 13, 16, 82, 129, 131, **147, 153, 195**
Western Pacific, size and nature of 199
Wheel slip 146, 153, 171, 176, 178, 179, 190, 195

Whitman, F.B. 48, 53, 83, 99, 124, 141, 149, 150, **152,** 155, 158, 163
Winnemucca 49, 54, 55, 83, 97-102, **155**
Weso 10
Wolverton, W.B. 100, 117, 118, 123, 158, **160**
Woolford, Frank 151
World War II 21, 24, 26, 27, 83, 94, 104
Wheels 186

*__Bold face__ indicates photograph or illustration.

Profile of the Western Pacific Railroad

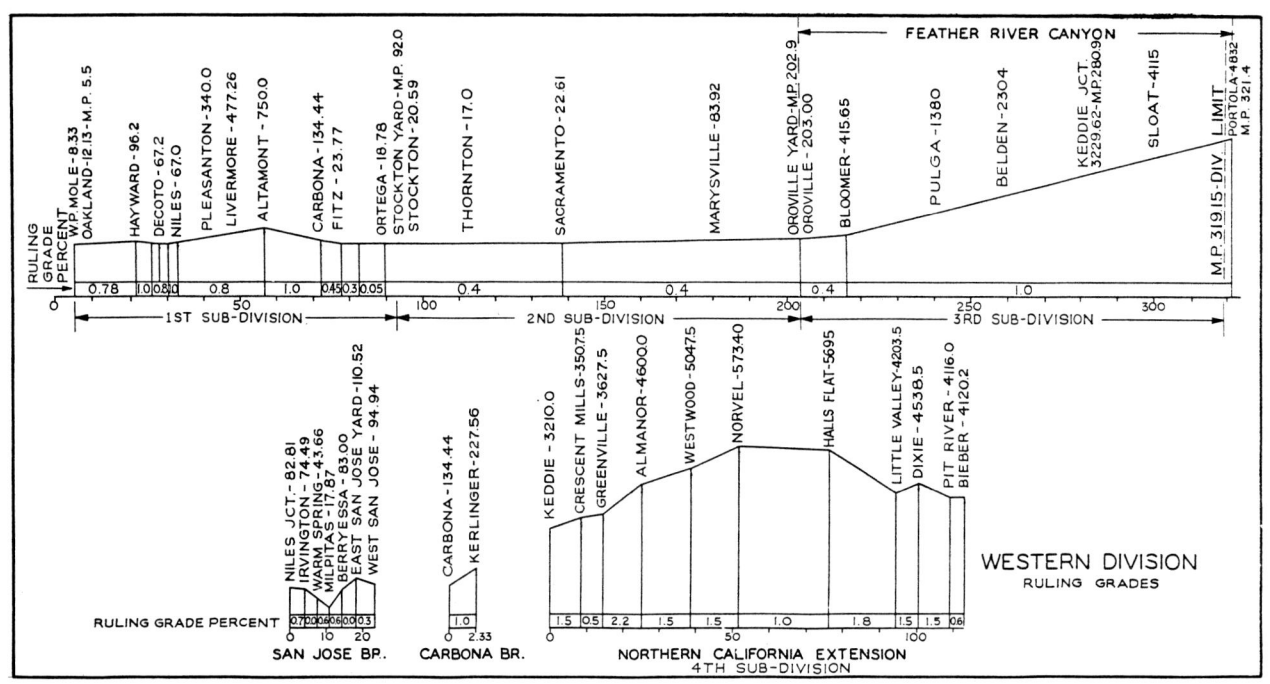

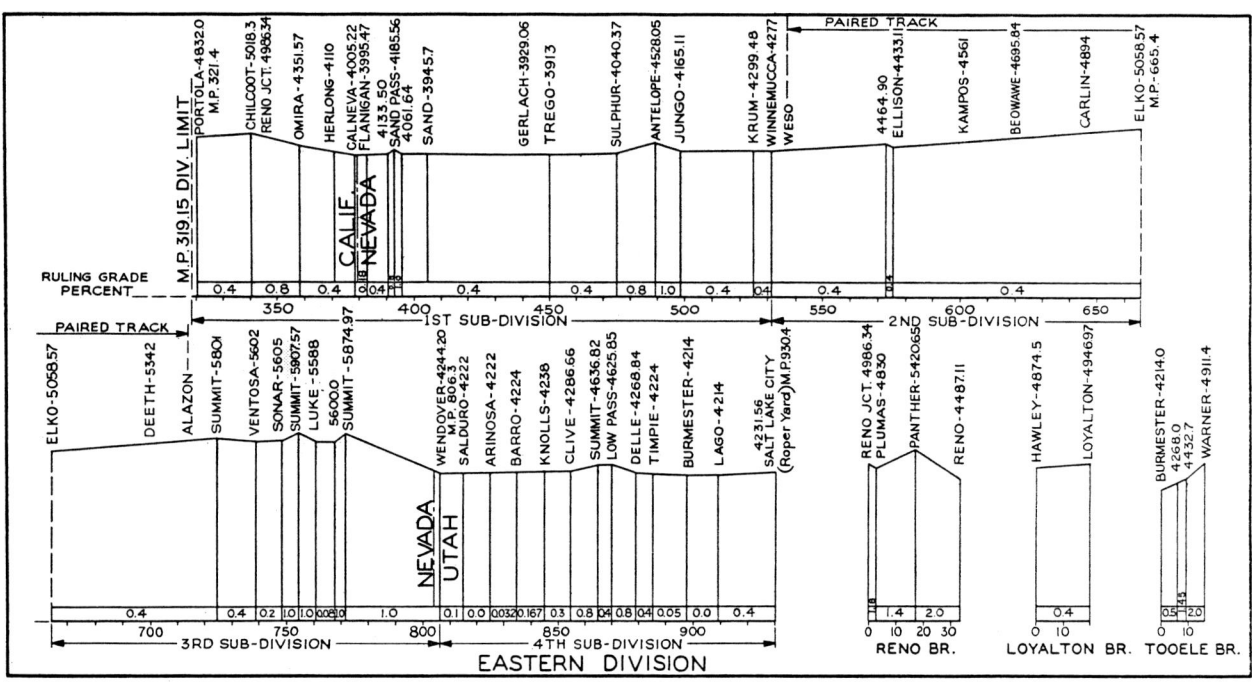